How They Made It in America

How They Made It in America

Success Stories and Strategies of Immigrant
Women: from Isabel Allende to Ivana Trump,
to Fashion Designer Josie Natori, Plus More

FIONA CITKIN, Ph.D.

ARCHWAY
PUBLISHING

Archway Publishing books may be ordered through booksellers or by contacting:

Archway Publishing
1663 Liberty Drive
Bloomington, IN 47403
www.archwaypublishing.com
1 (888) 242-5904

Because of the dynamic nature of the Internet, any web addresses or links contained in this book may have changed since publication and may no longer be valid. The views expressed in this work are solely those of the author and do not necessarily reflect the views of the publisher, and the publisher hereby disclaims any responsibility for them.

Any people depicted in stock imagery provided by Getty Images are models, and such images are being used for illustrative purposes only. Certain stock imagery © Getty Images.

This book is a work of non-fiction. Unless otherwise noted, the author and the publisher make no explicit guarantees as to the accuracy of the information contained in this book and in some cases, names of people and places have been altered to protect their privacy.

ISBN: 978-1-4808-7183-0 (sc)
ISBN: 978-1-4808-7182-3 (hc)
ISBN: 978-1-4808-7184-7 (e)

Library of Congress Control Number: 2019900453

Print information available on the last page.

Archway Publishing rev. date: 1/31/2019

Acknowledgments

First and foremost, I am deeply grateful to my book subjects, the prominent American immigrant women whose experiences inspired me, and who kept surprising me with their revelations in the extensive questionnaires and interviews. They came from all over the world - and from all walks of life - graciously sharing their success know-how and describing the often-confusing terrain in which they started their new lives in America. Each woman has shared her own success story, her ups and downs, along with practical advice, and valuable lessons to remember—all with the shared goal to be helpful "for women who will come after us."

My gratitude goes to my early reader, Dr. George Simons, for his generous heart, support, and honesty, and for being there whenever I needed advice.

I am grateful to Carlos E. Cortés for mentoring me, mostly by example.

My appreciation goes to Brenda Copeland, my exceptional editor, for her style, scrupulousness, and her scissors.

And finally, this book would not be possible without my closest consultants: my husband Alex and daughter Helen. Thank you, my love.

To my late mother Raisa,
an unwilling immigrant who just followed her children;
to my daughter Helen, who really made it in America;
and to my grandkids Anna, Margot, and William,
who were born in the USA and have the world at their feet
to get everything they may deserve.

Contents

Foreword xiii
Introduction xv
Prologue xvii

PART 1. THE ACHIEVERS

1. Isabel Allende from Chile
    A Feminist and Spiritual Force 6
2. Verónica Montes from Mexico
    The Integrated Educator 16
3. Weili Dai from China
    The Team Worker in Tech 25
4. Alfa Demmellash from Ethiopia
    The Social Entrepreneur 34
5. Irmgard Lafrentz from Germany
    The Global Matchmaker 43
6. Ani Palacios Mc Bride from Peru
    The Accidental Immigrant 54
7. Raegan Moya-Jones from Australia
    The Mom on a Mission 62
8. Josie Natori from the Philippines
    The Proud Leader 71
9. Elena Gorokhova from Russia
    The Breakthrough Author 81
10. Maya Strelar-Migotti from Croatia
    The Global Crusader 91
11. Rohini Anand from India
    The Interculturalist Leader 100

12. Ying McGuire from China
   The Global Leader 111
13. Ivana Trump From The Czech Republic
   The Intelligent Outlier 123
14. Sophie Vandebroek from Belgium
   The Life-Work Rainmaker 132
15. Rosa R. de la Cruz from Cuba
   The Philanthropic Collector 142
16. Hilda Ochoa Brillembourg from Venezuela
   The Financier in the Pursuit of Alpha 153
17. Deborah Levine from Bermuda
   The Entrepreneur of Spirit 164
18. Edwina Sandys from England
   The Intuitive Artist 174

PART 2. SEVEN SUCCESS VALUES

Introduction 185
1. Character Building 189
   Breaking the Mold 189
   Staying Strong and Positive 191
   Safeguarding the Self 193
   Breaking the Glass Ceiling 195
2. The American Mindset 198
   Realizing the American Dream 199
   Adapting to Mainstream Culture 200
   Overcoming Identity Issues 203
   Maximizing Cultural Heritage 204
   Being Generous for a Good Reason 206
3. Emotional Intelligence 209
   Achieving a Strong Intercultural Marriage 210
   Knowing How to Be Happy 212
   Fostering Work-Life Balance 213
4. Communication Skills and Creativity 216

  Overcoming the Language Barrier.. 216
  Adapting Communication Styles.. 219
  Nurturing Creativity and Innovation 220
5. Strategic Thinking.. 224
  Developing Adaptability.. 224
  Launching a Successful Company 226
  Sustaining a Successful Business 227
  Becoming an Intrapreneur 229
  Getting Used to Risk... 230
6. Inclusive Leadership 231
  Becoming an Inclusive Leader... 231
  Becoming a Modern Feminist Leader 234
7. Perseverance.. 239
  Building a Strong Emotional Base.................................... 239
  Embracing Culture to Prevent Setbacks 240
  Counteracting Setbacks 242

PART 3. THE ACHIEVER'S HANDBOOK

Success Takeaways 247
  1. *Start by Mapping Out Your Opportunities*.................... 248
  2. *Be Open-Minded and Creative* 249
  3. *Tap into Your Passion*.. 250
  4. *Turn Your Biggest Differences Into Your Greatest Assets*...251
  5. *Find Others With Shared Values* 252
  6. *Define Your Options*.. 253
  7. *Expand Your Leadership Opportunities* 254

Self-Assessment & The American Success Scale 255
Advice from the Heart 259
Epilogue... 267
Afterword 269
Notes.. 271
About the Author 287

Foreword

At a time when The American Dream seems to be broken and immigrants are a target of abuse, *How They Made It in America* reminds us that It was immigrants who shaped The American Dream, making it believable and attainable, and they are still at it. The women described in this book, entrepreneurs, artists and corporate high fliers, may serve as visible models of this success, but they are far from being alone. Rather, the book serves to acknowledge and encourage those unsung and those well on their way. The author, an immigrant herself, brings sensitive awareness to the details and nuances of the stories this volume contains.

The book has three parts. First, the stories, the results of the author's first-hand biographical intimacy with the personalities and achievements of 18 women "who made it." Then, an exploration of the values that drove them to action and success, and finally, derived from the first two parts, advice on how to follow in their footsteps but with your own direction, stride and pace, encouraged by their examples and know-how.

The stories in Part 1 offer many insights into the process of acculturation that tell not just what happened, but why and how crossing over from one culture to another is wrestled with and integrated into one's identity. There are insights into overcoming obstacles such as language learning and racism, as well as examples of confronting boundaries on personal and female identity that come from the discourse of one's native culture. Success does not lie in the repudiation of one's past, but by openness to the synergy offered by using one's existing cultural resources in adapting to a new cultural setting. In many of the stories, work-life balance, the often-hard-won integration of feminism and motherhood, is an essential theme of fulfillment and career success.

While the biographical pages of *How They Made It in America* could be a textbook in making cultural transitions, in Part 2 the author goes on to explicitly highlight for readers seven dynamics of success, quite specific to the US-American context, where individual self-development, leading to a staunch character, are prerequisites. Thus, this tome (yes, it is substantial) becomes a vade mecum on acculturation to the US environment, illustrated and reinforced with further short narratives related to the women whose stories are found in Part 1. There is good reason for men to explore these pages as seeing them from women's perspectives is likely to bring clarity to what are often unexamined male assumptions about success.

Part 3 of Fiona Citkin's work focuses on practical advice for readers, again seven brief pieces of insight and encouragement articulating the import and pointing to the pathway implicit what has been explored in earlier pages. To conclude this part, the author offers a simple self-assessment scale, an instrument which measures not only one's progress on the path to success but elicits the confidence and courage that one needs to recognize, accept, and enjoy that progress.

Not everyone needs to be lush, famous and internationally acclaimed, but each of us can better marshal our resources, both within ourselves and in our environment, to live a rich and satisfying life of benefit to self and others in the cultural context in which we find ourselves. Realization of The American Dream does not have to be measured in dollars and headlines, but the abundance found in a good life and solid reputation may live in a variety of ways in our hearts, homes and workplaces.

Dr. George F. Simons, creator of Diversophy®

Introduction

" . . . for many of us it's not just about the destination, but the very journey that takes us there." In those targeted words, Fiona Citkin frames her approach to the idea of success, the focus of her new book, *How They Made It in America: Seven Success Values and the Immigrant Women Who Cultivated Them.*"

To make her case, Citkin examines the lives of eighteen immigrant women, whom she refers to as The Achievers. From their unique and illustrative experiences, stories enriched by revealing personal interviews, Citkin deftly teases out numerous provocative insights. But rather than stopping there, she also treats those mini-biographies as a composite source of collective wisdom from which she extracts guidance and inspiration for others, immigrants and U.S.-born alike.

Citkin presents her challenge in the book's PROLOGUE: in order for immigrants to achieve, they "must learn how to crack the *immigration success code* - a set of complex and mostly unspoken cultural and socio-economic rules." The keys to that success project are two: the ability to adapt to U.S. culture; and the capacity for both personal and professional self-reinvention.

Citkin speaks from experience, a personal odyssey that she gracefully shares. A child of the Ukrainian intelligentsia and former English Department chair at Uzhgorod National University, Citkin came to the United States on a Fulbright grant and stayed when her husband obtained a job in New York City. Moving from academia to private business, she worked for a number of organizations before forming her own intercultural consulting firm. Citkin quickly developed a love for the United States as well as an appreciation of the opportunities it offered, while also recognizing the special challenges faced by immigrants, particularly immigrant women.

This autobiographical section reverberated with me not as an immigrant (I was born in Oakland, California), but as the grandson of three immigrants (from Mexico, Austria, and Citkin's Ukraine, although my meagerly-educated grandfather came from the working class). I was raised with stories of my family's immigrant dreams, immigrant struggles, and immigrant successes. Citkin's book afforded me new frames for reconsidering my family's story.

By examining the lives of women from around the world –-Latin America, Africa, Asia, Europe, Australia, and Bermuda –- Citkin provides multiple group and individual cultural perspectives on success, an idea that can be illusive, even confounding. Moreover, by focusing on the experiences of women, she explores the influence of the intersectionality of socio-cultural categories. In this way she succeeds in illuminating the unique challenges and opportunities that arise when gender intersects with immigrant ethnicity.

Today we live in an era in which immigration as a historical phenomenon and immigrants both as individuals and as a collective have become a source of heated public conflict and societal polarization. We can all benefit from the fact that Fiona Citkin has shed new light on the specialness of the immigrant experience and the many contributions that immigrants, particularly immigrant women, have made to our nation.

Carlos E. Cortés
Professor Emeritus of History
University of California, Riverside
Author, *Rose Hill: An Intermarriage before Its Time*
Editor, *Multicultural America: A Multimedia Encyclopedia*

Prologue

Writing this book has been a labor of love. It was a privilege to interview the professional women featured here, to learn from a diverse group of achievers who have had the courage to cross cultures, countries, and oceans in the hope of a better life in America. The individuals in this book are a special subset of American women, namely, immigrant women leaders with complex and fascinating stories who—although prominent within their own unique social and professional circles—have never before been viewed as a group. It's my hope that this book will act as an icebreaker, that it will break through the frozen waters of public inattention and bring recognition to the vast contributions made by these women, encouraging us to admit that we as a society are richer for their presence.

I'm probably better positioned than most to appreciate the cross-cultural experiences of the eighteen prominent immigrants profiled here. I understand these women and their aspirations because, like them, I also came to America from another country and culture. I understand their challenges, and their enthusiasm too. It's important, as a newcomer, to integrate into American culture. And it's a daunting task.

My roots in the Ukrainian intelligentsia have been a source of great resilience for me. I know what it's like to have my old life reduced to ashes, and to start fresh in a foreign land. Indeed, I've had to reinvent myself more than once. My professional experience includes two doctorate degrees and a career in academia: visiting professorships at several major European universities; full professor and chair of the English Department at Uzhgorod National University, Ukraine. These were my busy-happy-youthful years. I was doing work I loved, contributing to the country I loved. And yet, over time I started to feel like a stranger in my own land and increasingly comfortable during my assignments abroad. Professionally and politically it was a complicated and emotionally charged time. In the early 1990s, just when I was coming into my own, Ukrainian and Russian intellectuals like myself were faced with a painful choice: remain stuck in a corrupt society steeped in widespread collaborationism with the KGB and government bureaucracy—or emigrate.

I knew what life was like in established democracies. I had stayed with an English family during my teacher-study semester at the University of Edinburgh in Scotland. I had been a research fellow at the University of Vienna and the International Information Centre for Terminology (Infoterm) in Austria. After the publication of my book *Terminology and Translation*, I was a frequent conference participant and plenary speaker all over Europe. I was well aware of the quality of life in the West—and the dim prospects of life in Ukraine.

My husband and I had the means to support ourselves and our sixteen-year-old daughter Helen, but we wanted her to grow up in a country where she could fulfil her potential through her own efforts—not because of bribery, conformism, or her parents' connections. Emigration was in the air, and we pounced on the opportunity with nothing more than a vague idea of what we'd have to go through. When my Fulbright grant to America materialized, I went to my friend and our university president, Volodimir Slivka, to bid him farewell. He didn't mince words: "You need to use your brains and stay in the States. I'm sitting higher than you, so I can see farther. You won't like how things are going to develop here. I do wish you well, there."

It was our last conversation. Some ten years later I learned that he had been stabbed to death, allegedly by his political rival. The case never went to court.

Conducting my Fulbright research at Kent State University in

Ohio, among colleagues who knew me through European conferences, I began to establish myself in American academic circles. When my husband received an attractive job offer from a New York company, I gave up my research post to move to the East Coast, where I knew no one and academic positions were harder to find. Eager to try something new in my new country, I secured positions as a public relations manager at a global computer company, followed by a director's position at Berlitz Language Center, and then, as regional director of a similar company headquartered in Canada. When I felt that I had learned enough about business to start my own company, I set up Expert MS Inc., an intercultural consulting firm. Moving from the academic to the corporate world, I had to retrain myself and reframe my experience. That meant not only appreciating the complex issues faced by corporate clients with a diverse employee base but using my multicultural background to help them.

Today I feel deeply rooted in America, but not so much that I have forgotten where I came from. It feels good to be internationally recognized for having reinvented myself in a new country and culture, and to help others through my work. My own struggles as an immigrant in America have helped me understand what skills people need to develop in order to succeed in the U.S.—and the special set of challenges faced by immigrant women.[1]

THE REALITY THAT IS AMERICA

Any attempt to chart the personal goals of immigrants must be placed in the proper context of the reality that is America. Americans historically associate success with individual freedom, pursuit of abundance, novelty, and personal happiness—all of which converge to make the American Dream.[2] The American Dream has undergone many changes throughout the years, as various populations have sought refuge and a new way of life in the U.S. And yet, it has remained fundamentally the same. It is this dream—and the opportunities it offers for fulfilment—that holds our diverse nation together.

According to the Center for American Progress[3], the immigrant population in the United States grew considerably over the past fifty years. There were only 9.7 million immigrants back in 1960, while in 2011, there were 40.4 million foreign-born people residing in the United States. The foreign-born share of the U.S. population has more than quadrupled since the 1960s. In 2011, immigrants made up 13% of the total U S population, or one in every eight residents.

Ours is a country in which immigrants, as well as native-born Americans, seek to realize their full potential in a culture that emphasizes personal freedom. But immigration to the U.S., and the acculturation it requires, has never been easy. All immigrants struggle. It may not mean struggling for their daily bread (although this is certainly the case for many), but rather the challenge to fit into American society. In order to achieve, immigrants must learn how to crack the *immigration success code*—a set of complex and mostly unspoken cultural and socio-economic rules. Then, and only then, can they forge their own American Dream.

GOALS OF THIS BOOK

HOW THEY MADE IT IN AMERICA started out as an inter-cultural research project featuring prominent immigrant women adapting to America. After the initial idea was conceived and re-search commenced, I became increasingly excited by my subjects, who kept surprising me with their revelations. It came to me that, had I met them earlier, I might have been able to devise a shortcut to my own success. And so, it is my hope that, by drawing atten-tion to the lives of these extraordinary women, scores of other immigrants—as well as many native-born—will benefit from their accumulated know-how.

Part One of this book explores the individual experiences of these prominent women, using their own words to illuminate not just their practices, but the specific qualities they needed to draw on in order to reach their goals. Part Two captures their collective wisdom and lays bare the Seven Success Values they all share. Part Three presents an Achiever's Handbook with specific advice—tips and tactics to instruct, as well as inspire.

The authentic stories of prominent multicultural women have much to offer a new generation of success-seekers in America. Indeed, our subjects understand the necessity of spreading the word about overcoming seemingly unsurmountable hurdles. About 60% percent of them have authored their own books, and some have been subjects of the books by others. But their combined body of knowledge has never before been described, analyzed, and presented as a springboard for American achievers-to-be—until now.

PART ONE

The Achievers

THE ACHIEVERS

There can be no doubt that immigrant women have made their mark on this country's progress. And as the prominent achievers who are profiled here make clear, first generation women immigrants come from many different countries, bringing with them a variety of languages and customs. They may vary in age as well as ethnicity, social status, educational background, and profession, but they all came to America in pursuit of something more, whether it be freedom, stability, opportunity, or education. Some came as adults, and some came as children, brought here by their families who often lived in close-knit ethnic communities. And yet, while they may have diverse backgrounds, lifestyles, and beliefs, they share one common trait: the ability to adapt to the unique American culture, and to reinvent themselves in their personal and professional lives. All of the women profiled here have demonstrated tremendous resourcefulness and grit. And they have achieved success at the highest level in the most competitive country in the world.

Exploring the nature of success through the eyes of these achievers provides us with a unique opportunity to learn from those who have learned to survive and thrive, even under extremely unfavorable circumstances.

- What principles motivate them?
- How did they approach their goals?
- What did they do and how did they do it?
- What vital secrets can they share to help us achieve more in our own lives?

Female achievers know that they have to create their own success, on their own terms. This can be doubly hard for immigrants who first have to understand cultural obstacles before they can attempt to dismantle them. So, when considering the accomplishments of immigrant women who have had to surmount cultural and language barriers—that's in addition to the ever-present glass ceiling—we may find it helpful to recall Booker T. Washington's[4] words: "Success is to be measured not so much by the position that one has reached in life as by the obstacles which he has overcome."

The women who comprise this book are a creative lot. They have distinguished themselves in the arts, education, and literature; in tech, in business, and in teaching; as businesswomen, philanthropists, and entrepreneurs. Some are avowed feminists, and some decry the label. Many came with husbands, while some met their partners here—for better or worse, as is always the case.

As research shows, being an immigrant endows people with an additional cultural perspective, stimulating creativity on the way to success. Some of the women in our study have achieved tremendous renown in writing and the visual arts. Some are dedicated teachers who are educating a new generation of achievers. A number of them have attained leadership positions in their corporate jobs—inspiring colleagues, creating breakthroughs with products and processes, and contributing greatly to the culture and bottom lines of their companies. Yet others have started their own businesses. We know there are over one million foreign-born women business owners in the U.S. (1,018,743 to be exact), according to data released in 2012 from the *Economic Census's Survey*[5] of Business Owners. This million-plus figure tells us that approximately 13% of all women-owned firms are held by women born outside the U.S. "These numbers indicate that there is a quiet revolution of immigrant women's business ownership that is organically growing, but is going relatively unnoticed in the culture at large," says

Susan C. Pearce, co-author of the book, *Immigration and Women: Understanding the American Experience*[6].

Whether entrepreneurs, executives, educators, artists, or writers, the progressive-thinking, highly educated immigrant women achievers in this book chose their demanding jobs and busy lifestyles in order to realize their true potential—the reason that motivates many. And they chose the United States because there is something about America and American identity that captivates people. Everyone is different, of course, but the women I've interviewed made clear their fascination with their adopted country, and it's a fascination that takes many forms: appreciation for its law-based system; respect for its lack of class-rigidity; gratitude for economic opportunities and the potential for upward mobility; the freedom to be oneself; and of course, the ability to work hard and be rewarded for one's achievement.

We can learn much from watching how these women modified their lives so that their new American identity could take root. And through our best efforts and creativity, we can put this accumulated knowledge to good use in our own lives—and the lives of those around us.

Isabel Allende *from Chile*

A Feminist and Spiritual Force

Isabel Allende Llona is the daughter of a Chilean diplomat and a descendant of a "robust Basque sailor who disembarked on the coast of Chile with his head swimming with plans for greatness."[7] She tells people this because she wants them to understand her heritage as part of, in her own words, "a breed of impetuous women and men with sentimental hearts and strong arms for hard work."[8]

Isabel, master of "magical realism"

A free spirit and a feminist, Isabel authored her first novel, *The House of the Spirits*, at age forty. The best-selling book became a blockbuster movie, propelling her to international acclaim. Now the author of a dozen novels and a collection of short fiction, three memoirs, as well as plays and a trilogy of children's novels, Isabel Allende has had her books translated into more than thirty-five languages and has sold more than 65 million copies across four continents. Isabel Allende's success can be attributed to hard work, and to the way in which she was able to adapt to life first in Venezuela, and then the US, essentially marrying two cultures within her extended family.

A DOUBLE LIFE

Isabel was only three when her father disappeared, forcing her mother to leave the family's posting in Peru and return to Santiago, Chile, where she raised her three children in her parents' home. The former diplomat's wife found a job in a bank, but her salary was little more than pin money, so she rounded up her income by making hats. Returning to Chile, Isabel's mother had to cope with more than the poverty of her reduced circumstances; she had to endure the gossip and snubs of people who had once been her friends. This affected young Isabel greatly. Still, she took solace in her grandmother's interest in the spiritual world, as well as in the stories she told and the extensive library she owned. Her grandfather, whom she revered, instilled in her a strict philosophy: life is strife and hard work; discomfort is healthy, as is simple food.

Years later, summing up her personal experiences, Isabel spoke about the lessons learned: "I don't want to be like my mother, I will be like my grandfather—independent, healthy, and strong. I will not allow anyone to order me around . . . I want to be like my grandfather, and protect my mother."[9] And this is exactly what she did.

> Like many women of her generation, Isabel Allende thought that feminism was concerned solely with assuming a man's duties in a man's world—on an equal footing. It would be years before she thought to subject her household role to feminist analysis.

Isabel was only five when she first realized the disadvantages of her gender—after being corrected to sit up straight and keep her knees together, like a lady. (The push that many girls get). Years later, she would protest against the social establishment of her traditionalist country, with its all-pervading macho culture that positioned women in a subservient role. On her own she may have lacked the power to turn the tide, but when she became a journalist she was able to express her mute rage and frustration as a woman in a male-dominated culture.

When Isabel married at twenty, she started leading a double life. In private, a traditional wife and mother. In public, a TV personality, dramatist, and journalist for a feminist magazine. Despite becoming a feminist in her formative years, it seems that Isabel had internalized the time-honored formulas for domestic bliss.

> Every morning I served my husband his breakfast in bed, every evening I was waiting in full battle dress with his martini, olive between my teeth, and every night I laid out the suit and shirt he would be wearing the next day. I shined his shoes, cut his hair and fingernails, and bought his clothes to save him the bother of trying them on, just as I did with my children. This was not only stupidity on my part; it was misdirected energy and excessive love.[10]

Isabel held a full-time job and never thought of staying home to take care of the house and kids like her mother and grandmother did. Still, she did not question her duties as a wife and mother, or subject her household role to feminist analysis. Like many women at the time, Isabel believed that feminism had more to do with assuming men's duties in the world on an equal footing. Gloria Steinem put it as follows: "Women are not going to be equal outside the home until men are equal in it."[11] But this never occurred to Isabel or her husband.

And yet, it was during this time that Isabel's feminism found expression and action. For example, she had a column in an elegant magazine that promoted the feminist ideas of its director, Delia Vergara. Once, Isabel interviewed a prominent professional woman about her infidelities and discovered that this woman had the same motivations for adultery as men: opportunity, boredom, curiosity, flirtation, and challenge. In the rigid and moralistic environment of Chile of the early seventies, these revelations exploded like a bomb: How can the rights and motivation of women possibly equate to those of men?

THE IMPACT OF ARRIVAL

Everything changed in 1973. After a military coup, President Salvador Allende's violent death, and the overthrow of Chile's co-alition government, there came a curfew, outbursts of violence, and severe repression, refined to perfection. Like everybody else in Chile, Isabel had to censor her letters, be careful of what she said in public, and use caution over the telephone. The veteran journalist who had made a career out of speaking her mind had to stay tight-lipped and virtually silent. Initially, Isabel did not think the Pinochet regime would endure, but when she realized it was too dangerous to stay in Chile, the family fled.

"My roots were chopped off," she says of the move to Venezuela. "The impact of arrival was that of having fallen onto another planet."[12] Like many immigrant refugees, the family had no social standing and no money. Worse, because they were political refugees who had escaped Pinochet's dictatorship, some locals thought they were Communists. They may have spoken the same language as the local folks, but they were still outcasts. This savvy, well-known journalist had once interviewed Nobel Prize winner Pablo Neruda. But in Venezuela, nothing counted as merit for an outsider.

Isabel had to start from scratch, as most immigrants do, and she counts among her most bitter memories the fact that she "slumped to the anonymity and daily humiliation of a person looking for work."[13] Isabel learned the hard way. She saw that many talented immigrants who could not re-validate their professional pedigrees/li-censes ended up selling insurance door-to-door—if they were lucky. Isabel used all her audacity and good connections to finally start freelancing for *El Nacional* in Caracas.

It took many years, but Isabel Allende eventually broke free of the burdens imposed on her by Chilean society. Eventually, her sensuality ceased to be a defect that to be hidden for the sake of gentility, and was accepted as a basic ingredient of her temperament and, later, her writing.

Although Chile and Venezuela are both Latin American countries, their cultures are very different. Deep underlying forces of history shape both country's cultural dynamics. Isabel learned by experience that Venezuela's culture is happier and more easy-going, while in her native Chile the culture is overall more conservative and reserved. It took Isabel almost thirteen years to learn the rules of Venezuelan society, but, as she remembers, "when I finally succeeded, I felt free of the back-bowing burdens I had carried in my own country. I lost the fear of appearing ridiculous, of social sanctions, of 'coming down' in the world, as my grandfather referred to poverty, and my own hot blood. Sensuality ceased to be a defect that had to be hidden for the sake of gentility, and was accepted as a basic ingredient of my temperament and, later, my writing.[14]

A SPIRITUAL FORCE

It was some eight years after fleeing Chile that Isabel received a phone call with the news that her ninety-nine-year-old grandfather was near death. She couldn't be with him because of restrictions under the Pinochet regime, so Isabel sat down to write a letter to her grandfather, to keep him alive, at least in spirit.[15] The letter evolved into *The House of the Spirits* (1982), a manuscript she wrote without effort, she says, "as if I had a lighted flame inside me."[16]

Rejected by various Latin American publishers, *The House of the Spirits* was published in Spain and soon translated into a score of languages. It was a critical as well as a popular success, with reviewers comparing Isabel to Gabriel García Márquez, the father of magical realism.

Sensuality, passion, love—all the basic ingredients of Isabel's temperament found their way into her work. A *powerful storyteller* who transports readers to a complex world of dreams and longings, Isabel writes with a vivid humanity that engages all the reader's attention and sympathy. She writes about the love-making of powerful men and naive women, worn-out married couples, and restless rebels in such a way as to invoke readers' own desires. Much of her work is noted for its feminist point of view and for its dramatic qualities of romance and struggle. Men and women alike are attracted to the way in which she intertwines feminism and femininity.

Isabel believes that *a spiritual force* can overcome a world saturated with evil—a core belief of many men and women. Perhaps that's part of the reason her first novel still holds such great appeal. So it was that the book that arose directly out of the limitations of Isabel Allende's exile became a worldwide bestseller, propelling her into the ranks of famous international writers, and saved her from despising herself as just another bourgeois woman collaborating with the rules of a macho society.

REINVENTION—AGAIN

It was a *round* this time that Isabel and her husband grew farther apart, ultimately divorcing. This was the end of twenty-nine years of love and twenty-five years of marriage—respectfully, with no slamming doors. Isabel was forty-four. But life would take an unpredictable turn in San Jose, California when, on a lecture tour, Isabel met William Gordon, a lawyer and admirer of her work. Indeed, they were brought together by literature.

In her memoirs, Isabel relays that at their first meeting she felt a certain curiosity about the aristocratic-looking lawyer of Irish descent "who spoke Spanish like a Mexican "bandido," and had a tattoo on his left hand."[17] He was also handsome and athletic, with spontaneous laughter. Isabel sensed some blend of refinement and roughness, strength of character, and an intimate gentleness which impressed her. "Our mutual attraction was evident,"

11

confesses Isabel, who says that "the undeniable alchemy of our first meeting . . . is still the essence of our union."[18]

Marrying William Gordon: an expert in human relationships, Isabel worked hard on her bicultural marriage to make it a success.

In *Paula*[19] and *The Sum of Our Days*[20], Isabel speaks of her life-changing happiness in this late love. "To me," she said, "Willie represented a new destiny in another language and a different country; it was like being born again. I could invent a fresh version of myself only for him."[21] But it wasn't always easy. When summing up the personal adjustments of her marriage, Isabel noted: "When we met, we had very little in common: we came from very different backgrounds and we had to invent a language—Spanglish—in order to understand each other. Past, culture, and customs separated us, as well as the inevitable problems of children in a family artificially glued together."[22] Isabel understood that she and her new husband would meet profound challenges and that, as an intercultural couple, they would need to be cautious as they approached their cultural differences. But they persevered. "The two of us are bound together by our ideas, a similar way of looking at the world, camaraderie, loyalty, humor," she says. Adding, "I like sleeping with him."[23]

LIVING IN TWO WORLDS

Isabel's original culture, Chile, is almost the opposite of American culture. America is democratic society that values liberty and freedom, while Chile is a multi-layered society built on class and class-consciousness. It's birth that determines status in Chile. Only through sustained effort over several generations can a family rise: money, fame, or talent alone are insufficient.

"Chileans are sober, circumspect, and formal, and suffer an acute fear of attracting attention, which to them is synonymous with looking ridiculous. For that very reason, I have been an embarrassment for the family,"[24] recollects Isabel.

This is what she says about biculturalism and living in the two worlds: "I am an *eternal transplant*, as the poet Pablo Neruda used to say. My roots would have dried up by now had they not been nourished by the rich magma of the past, which in my case has an indefinite component of imagination. Perhaps, it isn't only in my case."[25]

Isabel found that "Being a workaholic in Venezuela—which is a hedonistic society—felt like being an alien there. But the U.S. has a work ethic that I fit in, and I do not feel like an alien here."[26]

Isabel is methodical. She works Monday through Saturday, 9:00 A.M. to 7:00 P.M. She starts work each year on January 8, a tradition she began in 1981 with the letter she wrote to her dying grandfather. Her routine, as described in her memoirs, includes trying to be silent for several hours, cleansing her mind of confusion; lighting candles to summon the muses and guardian spirits; placing flowers on a desk to intimidate tedium; putting the complete works of

Pablo Neruda, her literary hero, beneath the computer with the hope they will inspire her by osmosis; preparing her mind and soul to receive the first sentence in a trance. Isabel maintains that her subject somehow chooses her, while her work consists of providing enough time, solitude, and discipline for the book to write itself. It was only after her third novel that she dared to say for the first time, "I am a writer."[27]

> "I am an *eternal transplant*, as the poet Pablo Neruda used to say. My roots would have dried up by now had they not been nourished by the rich magma of the past, which in my case has an indefinite component of imagination. Perhaps, it isn't only in my case."

Isabel's books have enjoyed commercial success as well as critical acclaim. Still, she has had her detractors. She admitted to the Argentine newspaper El Clarín that she is not always appreciated in Chile, and that Chilean intellectuals "detest" her.

> The fact that people think that when you sell a lot of books you are not a serious writer is a great insult to the readership. I get a little angry when people try to say such a thing. There was a review of my last book in one American paper by a professor of Latin American studies and he attacked me personally for the sole reason that I sold a lot of books. That is unforgivable.[28]

But jealous critics couldn't derail worldwide success; recognition and awards kept mounting. In September 1996, she was honored at the Hispanic Heritage Awards for her contributions to the Hispanic American community. She received nominations for the Quality Paperback Book Club New Voice Award (for her debut novel *The House of the Spirits)*, the Los Angeles Times Book Prize (for *Of Love and Shadows)*, and her third novel, *Eva Luna,* was voted one of the Year's Best Books by *Library Journal.* Isabel has won numerous prizes and distinctions, including France's Grand Prix d'Evasion; the Gabriela Mistral Prize in Chile; the Italian Bancarella Prize; and the Chevalier des Artes et des Lettres distinction in France. She was inducted into the American Academy of Arts and Letters, received Chile's National Literature Prize in 2010, and was awarded the Presidential Medal of Freedom in 2015, the highest civilian honor in the United States[29]. Perhaps most notable among Isabel's many international awards is the prestigious 1998 Dorothy and Lillian Gish Prize for excellence in the arts, granted to writers "who have contributed to the beauty of the world."[30] This speaks volumes about her literary achievements.

Isabel speaks about her "four minutes of fame" when the movie version of her first novel, *The House of the Spirits*, was celebrated at the Cannes festival and she stood on stage alongside Meryl Streep, Antonio Banderas, Vanessa Redgrave, and Winona Ryder. She felt a similar emotion when she carried the Olympic flag in Turin, Italy, in 2006. "It took only four minutes for me to be catapulted into fame,"[31] she says.

But it was, perhaps, on her first visit back to Chile, sixteen years after the military coup, that she felt most humbled. A crowd gathered to greet her in the airport, calling her name, but Isabel thought they had confused her with her cousin Isabel, Salvador Allende's daughter. Only after people stepped forward with books to be signed did Isabel realize it was all for her. "I was so weak in the knees, I had to lean on Willie, as we passed through the customs and saw my parents,"[32] she remembers. Fleeing the country and coming back years later, after so many ups and downs, Isabel saw her life as one of contrasts. Indeed, she has seen much, emigrating miserably and returning heroically—and absorbing true humility on the way.

Verónica Montes *from Mexico*

The Integrated Educator

Verónica came a long way to her first Commencement

Verónica Montes started from scratch. The daughter of a divorced immigrant mother who, working as a seamstress, brought her four children to America in search of a better life, Verónica's personal stamina and goal-oriented improvement of self and others led her to become an Andrew W. Mellon Postdoctoral Teaching Fellow, and later, an Assistant Professor in the Department of Sociology at prestigious Bryn Mawr College. Successful at teaching, Verónica spent her first sabbatical year as a visiting scholar at a research institute in Mexico while publishing her new articles in the British "Gender, Place, and Culture" journal and in Peruvian "Apuntes."

Completing a Master's and Ph.D. program in sociology is a great achievement for any immigrant, but the advanced language skills and cultural penetration necessary make the challenge that much greater for someone who is not a native English speaker. This is perhaps the reason why she feels a particular satisfaction and fulfillment every time she lectures: being able to express her thoughts in another language has required so many years of effort and hard-work. But sociology was Verónica's dream, something she felt she knew instinctively, and intimately. The road was hard, but now, some twenty-five years later, Verónica finally feels at home in the United States.

WORKING CLASS ORIGINS

Verónica is proud of her working-class origins. Born in Mexico City to peasant parents who had relocated from a southern Mexican state to launch their own small-sized clothing business, Verónica had a deep-seated love of knowledge, despite her parent's lack of education. (Elementary school for her father. Third grade for her mother.) It was the seventies, and the Montes family was typical of the patriarchal domestic unit where the mother was in charge of everything at home while also working in the family business. Verónica was sixteen when her parents divorced and her mother, Maria, found herself the sole supporter of her four children. Then came the mid-1980s, and Mexico experienced a profound economic crisis that lead to an exodus of its citizens, most of whom migrated to the US— Verónica's mother among them. As was the case with tens of thousands of women from Mexico, Maria moved alone to the US, leaving her children behind. It would be several years before the family would be reunited, and a new chapter opened for Verónica.

AMERICAN BEGINNINGS

Veronica got her green card in 1990 and became a citizen in 1995. But when she crossed the Tijuana/San Isidro Mexican border at age eighteen, she was an undocumented woman of color with little to show in her luggage but a high school diploma and a bag full of mixed feelings. She had no idea what lay ahead.

Verónica's first job in the U.S. was baby-sitting, after which she landed a part-time job as a salad-bar server in a fast-food restaurant.

Her monthly earnings were $400, but the experience would turn out to be invaluable. The restaurant was only a block away from UCLA, and while Verónica served hundreds of students on their way to campus, she also fed her own dreams. "One day I will also go to college,"[33] she declared.

Having watched many immigrants struggle, including her own mother who scrimped to put food on the table for her four children, Verónica knew that higher education was the only way out—or up, as it were. College requires money, of course, so she looked for full-time work. Getting the right job took time—over a year—but eventually she found a position as a waitress that gave her the flexibility she needed to attend classes at a city college.

Despite her own lack of education, Verónica's mother implanted in her daughter the American dream of higher education. "She is my main source of inspiration. I don't remember seeing her complaining about what she needed to do in order to take care of us. She was always so responsible and hard-work[ing]. She was [the one] who from my childhood instilled [in me] the desire to go to college. That was her main dream; she wanted to see her children with a college education."[34]

Thus, it was the unwavering support of her family and Verónica's own determination that supplied her with the motivation and strength to press on. The first step was to take an English as a second language class at Santa Monica College, and it was there that she met her husband-to-be, Diego H. Pedreros, an immigrant from Columbia. The two have been bonded by education for more than two decades.

> Despite her own lack of education, Verónica's mother implanted in her daughter the American dream of getting a higher education. Thus it was the unwavering support of her family and Verónica's own determination that supplied her with the motivation and strength to pursue further education.

By mutual agreement, Diego went to college while Verónica supported the family. Diego helped his wife learn how to make her own way in college when, after his graduation, it was her turn to make her dream come true. Upon graduation, Verónica was accepted to graduate school at UC San Diego in the International Relations program. But she declined the offer because, after eleven years of marriage, she was ready to become a mother. The birth of her daughter Amara in 2002 gave Verónica the strength and inspiration to further pursue her goals. So it was that in 2005, after having been a full-time mother for over three years, Verónica started her doctoral studies in Sociology at the UC Santa Barbara. Diego's and Veronica's union is a case in point showing how a "marriage of true minds" can help a couple achieve their personal and professional goals.

CULTURAL INTEGRATION

Verónica understood that success in the U.S. meant cultural integration, nevertheless she found it hard to adjust to American culture. There is a saying in Spanish "ni de aqui ni de alla," meaning "neither here nor there," which is commonly applied to Mexicans living in the United States. It implies that people belong neither to the U.S. nor to Mexico. Not so for Verónica, whose advanced sociology degrees brought her to the point in her life where she's confident that she's "from here *and* from there." It may have taken her twenty-five years, but today she says that "Mexico complements my life, as it is my inner-energy source. However, I realized that my life is already settled here in the U.S."[35]

> The most significant differences between Mexican and mainstream American culture have to do with family and community. Family is central to Mexican life, where people rely on community for almost every kind of support: economic, emotional, social, etc., In the U.S. such reliance can signal weakness.[36]

Completing a Master's and Ph.D. program in sociology is a great achievement for any immigrant, but the advanced language skills and cultural penetration necessary make the challenge that much greater for someone who is not a native English speaker. However, sociology was Verónica's dream, something she felt she knew instinctively, and intimately. So it was that she was able to apply an insider's perspective to the examination of migration from Latin America to the U.S., providing valuable insights to the integration processes. Notably, she knows first-hand that the most significant differences between Mexican and mainstream American culture have to do with family and community. Family is central to Mexican life, where people rely on community for almost every kind of support: economic, emotional, social, etc., In the U.S. such reliance can signal weakness.[37]

That said, Verónica realizes that she has modified her behavior in the process of integration. Since moving to the U.S., she has learned to shake off many of the taboos of Mexican culture. She has become more assertive, has adjusted to a more stressful lifestyle, and has even put more pressure on herself to achieve her goals. Most importantly, perhaps, she now feels free to express her opinions: a huge leap forward for a girl from a culture where women are supposed to know their proper place—behind the men. These behavioral changes are normal. Immigrants need to be aware of them and accept them, accelerating the process as much as possible because they are part and parcel of becoming an American.

"I consider myself a leader, at least in my family, with regard to pursuing higher education," says Verónica. "I was the first in my family to get a college diploma and recently a Ph.D. degree. Having arrived in the U.S. at the age of eighteen, without knowing a single word of English and without proper documents to legally reside in the U.S., I believe that I sow the seeds of pursuing the higher education, particularly among women in my family."[38]

ADAPTING AND REINVENTING SELF

"I re-invented myself by adapting to a new culture[39]," said Verónica. And rather than fight against assimilation, she consciously embraced both American and Mexican influences. Open-minded by nature as well as upbringing, Verónica quickly realized the many advantages to accepting both cultures and languages.

Professionally, Verónica argues for full integration: "as immigrants, we develop particular social skills which allow us to be more flexible and prone to changes, compared to our counterparts who have never left their countries. I had to re-invent my cultural practices in a different social and cultural context, and in that sense, I have consciously selected those practices that I find more significant and relevant to me. Living in a different country brings about a series of challenges, as you suddenly lose certain cultural references by leaving your country behind. To some extent, it is like becoming an orphan and . . . needing to make your cultural framework [anew]. In order to survive, you need to re-invent your own world."[40]

"The main challenge for me was to overcome the racial prejudices toward Latina immigrants, as they are perceived as passive, submissive, dependent and uneducated,"[41] Verónica said. She described a case-in-point to illustrate her statement. When she worked as private Spanish tutor in Santa Barbara, CA, a neighbor judged Verónica by her appearance and asked how much she would charge to clean her apartment. There were plenty of incidents like that—and she associates stereotyping with racial prejudice.

Nevertheless, two things made assimilation challenges easier to overcome. First is the fact that her husband is from Colombia, so they both speak Spanish. Second is the increasing number of immigrants from Latin America. (The 2010 U.S. Census reported 53 million Latin American immigrants in the US.) Thus, her supportive husband and overall support of the family and U.S. Latino community have been the major factors to lean to. And yet, while these elements made Verónica feel like less of an alien, it was not until she completed the milestone of her Ph.D. that felt fully integrated into American culture.

ENGLISH WITH AN ACCENT

Verónica knew that living in the Hispanic community of Los Angeles wasn't doing anything to further her English language skills. And even though she took jobs that allowed her to work on her English when she first arrived in the U.S., she soon realized that she needed a more formal structure. It would be several years of learning English as a Second Language before she felt confident expressing herself in her new language.

So it was that, despite her youthful enthusiasm over her newly-adopted country, Verónica's major challenge upon arrival was her complete lack of English language skills. She was tempted to give up multiple times, but kept telling herself that she could do it, that it was just a matter of perseverance.

> In Verónica's experience, many Americans hold an unfavorable attitude toward those who speak with a foreign accent, particularly if they are people of color.

Research has proved that, while students can successfully learn a new language after puberty, their accents will stay forever because the vocal cords have stiffened. That's not news to the many immigrants whose occupation involves professional speaking and who feel insecure about their accents, Verónica included. Asked if speaking English with a Mexican accent hindered her chances, she answered candidly: "Yes, it does." America prefers an English-only language policy that conveys an unfavorable attitude toward those with a foreign accent, particularly people of color. "For many years, I felt that my accent was a shortcoming in my professional development as college professor, as I thought my students would evaluate my teaching performance based on my accent. Yet, to my surprise, students have never – at least so far – evaluated me negatively based on my accent."[42]

TRANSNATIONALISM

Verónica tends to see successful cultural adaption as the incorporation of the best American traits into her own Mexican culture, thereby enriching her world. But, like many other immigrants, she dislikes the word "Americanization." Verónica much prefers the concept of "transnationalism," which is commonly used in the studies of international migration. Transnationalism involves the movement of social, economic, cultural, and emotional practices between two specific geographical locations, and which mark people's daily practices. In her mind, Verónica is constantly moving back and forth between Mexico and the US, for that's the way she experiences culture.

She encourages her daughter to be transnational as well. "I try to take my daughter to Mexico or to Colombia, where my husband is from, to make sure she gets the culture flavor of our [original home] countries. I am very conscious about the great opportunities that my daughter has by having a triple cultural identity: Mexican, Colombian, and American. That means that she not only speaks Spanish without the traditional American accent, but is also very culture-sensitive to others."[43]

GRASSROOTS FEMINISM

Verónica Montes is a grassroots feminist who believes that the "family first" principle of her culture doesn't contradict any feminist principle. Indeed, while the Latino culture may be known for its machismo and subservient treatment of women, this is not the case in Verónica's family. In fact, in our first conversation she told me how she managed her substantial workload in parallel with her studies: with the full support and active help of her husband, believes that feminism, like charity, starts at home.

Case in point: Verónica cites her mother as her biggest role model. An independent woman who travelled alone to the US, making a life here despite a low level of education, she inspired all of her children to go to college. And it was while earning her doctorate that Verónica researched the household economic strategies of two transnational Mexican communities and examined the role women play in the development and diversification of household economic strategies.

Verónica believes that feminism, like charity, starts at home.

A unique study with manifold implications[44], this research influenced the development of Verónica's own feminist views, as she was able to demonstrate the vital role women play in the Mexican family and community—and their significance contradicts current stereotyping. Analyzing immigrants' livelihood strategies and tactics, as well as women's role in their community's development, has fostered Verónica believe in solidarity among women—and has made her a leader.

Weili Dai *from China*

The Team Worker in Tech

Little Troublemaker. That's the affectionate nickname Weili Dai's family gave the girl with excessive energy and an inquisitive intellect. The youngest of three children, Weili was encouraged by her parents to engage in sports, where she became a skilled basketball player, actually competing semi-pro from the ages of nine to fourteen. Years later she's still proud of her Michael Jordan layup. Weili credits her involvement in sports for her unflagging energy, self-discipline, and results-driven outlook, saying that it gave her the "self-confidence and a good foundation"[45] to be able to work 24/7.

> Weili believes that basketball enhances the team spirit, important in work and life

Weili is a team player who considers her philosophy of *be fair and care* to be one of her greatest assets. And it's all thanks to her parents. Growing up in a supportive family environment with a lot of love and encouragement, Weili believed that her opportunities were limitless. Her family gave her the best head-start any child could dream of, arming her with the confidence, positive attitude, and self-discipline that have powered her life and career. Today, the former president of Marvell Technology Group remains one of the most successful[46] American women entrepreneurs and is the only female co-founder of a major semiconductor company.[47]

A modern maven and mother herself, Weili advocates for more women to be involved in science and technology, and to engage in team sports, which she believes provide an invaluable resource for thriving through teamwork and relationship building. A driving force[48] in the push to expand access to technology in the developing world, as well as opportunities between the United States and China, Weili took a short break from the intense life of running Marvell, preparing for her quick comeback as an entrepreneur. And guess what? Today she is up and running again, as Co-Founder, President, and Vice Chairwoman of FLC Global.

FROM SHANGHAI TO SAN FRANCISCO

Weili grew up in Shanghai and immigrated with her family to the U.S. when she was in high school. She found the transition from one big city to another—Shanghai to San Francisco—fairly easy, but the language barrier proved to be a huge obstacle. The girl who loved to talk to people worked hard to overcome this great challenge by carrying a pocket Chinese-English dictionary with her everywhere.

A lifelong lover of math and physics, Weili was happy to win a place to study computer science at the UC Berkeley. It was there that she met Sehat Sutardja, the man who would become her husband. With her background in software and Sehat's in chip design, the husband and wife complemented each other intellectually, a good foundation for building a mutual understanding. It was a marriage of the nerds.

> Newcomer Weili Dai overcame her language obstacles by carrying a pocket Chinese-English dictionary with her everywhere.

Weili recalls that Sehat, who was studying electrical engineering, was always coming up with new ideas and designs. She enjoyed hearing about his plans, and one day told him: "This sounds wonderful and, some day, when you're ready, we will start a high-tech company." An internship at the famed Bell Labs in New Jersey clinched things for her. She was hooked on the high-tech environment.

HANDS-ON GEEKS

Weili and her husband were becoming increasingly attracted to the freedom inherent in owning their own company. In 1995, together with Sehat's brother Pantas, the young couple embarked in earnest on launching a technology company. But what to call it? The founders wanted a company name that would reflect what they considered to be their "great purpose" for making technology: creating affordable products that can change the lives of "regular people." And so it was that sitting around a kitchen table they came up with Marvell, a nod to the word "marvelous."

It was tough going in the beginning. Potential customers were wary of dealing with a small start-up and required a lot of convincing. Marvell had to demonstrate that not only did they have the requisite product knowledge, but market savvy as well. Weili remembers how she landed their first business customer, Seagate from Minneapolis. "People always thought of me as a maven," she says. Nevertheless, it took "a couple of years to fully engage that first customer. In 1995 we delivered the product, for this is a long design cycle. I courted them, with business meetings, etc. but finally got a contract. The first victory, the happy memories![49]

Initial funding for the venture came from friends and family. To save money, the founders used second-hand furniture and old computers brought in from home. Weili would sometimes cook Shanghai stir-fries for the engineers. It wasn't long before their cautious approach paid off, with the business becoming profitable after just three years. Never mind the humble beginnings: after five years in business Marvell went public.

> As the face of her young company, Weili had to demonstrate that she and her partners had market savvy as well as the requisite product knowledge.

The no frills, hands-on geek approach helped a husband and wife establish a solid foundation for their company and position Marvell to innovate further. Now, with operations and research and development centers spread across the globe, Marvell is one of the world's biggest designers of silicon chips, powering digital storage products, mobile devices, and increasingly, smart TVs. "Today, if you look at all the disk drives, most of silicon chips are made by us. We have a seventy percent market share," Weili proudly said.[50] Indeed, Marvell now employs about 7,000 worldwide, with annual revenues in excess of U.S. $3 billion.[51]

AMERICANIZED, WITH ASIAN TRADITIONS

Weili recognizes that she really belongs to two worlds, the United States and China: "I'm Americanized, but we upheld Asian tradition too," she says, noting that her upbringing encouraged her to respect "family values, creativity, and educational environment."[52]

The challenges of adaptation were, to a great extent, cushioned by the self-confidence fostered by her loving family. That's not to say that she hasn't faced her fair share of hurdles, many of which were caused by her own naiveté. Speaking of her arrival in the US, Weili says: "I used to see only the positive side in everything, only the blue skies; I could be easily fooled... so there were incidents when people took advantage of me."[53]

Some of her challenges came from the cultural differences between her two countries. Weili was surprised to see that her American neighbors didn't know each other and they lived in relative isolation. And she was shocked to see how children graduate from high school and leave the family home at age eighteen. In China, it's quite the contrary. Chinese families are multi-generational, says Weili. "You never 'graduate' from your family."[54]

HER OWN AMERICAN DREAM

"There is a very simple way to describe the American Dream," says Weili. "It means freedom for people with passion, commitment, determination." Elaborating, she acknowledged that the American Dream requires a foundation, which for her is education. "I'm always so respectful of the teachers, professors. I think of this as a worldwide issue. I brought it up during my meeting with President Obama, saying that they [professors] should be better rewarded and recognized. The country and the families need to pay more attention to the education system; we all have responsibility to address it from different angles. My husband and I, we like to help education, so we're constantly thinking of how we can help the university, our alma mater, and the grad students. I remember the many hours my professors spent communicating with and teaching me and others, and I want to show my gratitude.[55]"

> "There is a very simple way to describe the American Dream: it means freedom for people with passion, commitment, determination."

Weili acknowledges the profound influence of tech leaders who inhabit the fifty-mile radius around Silicon Valley. "There's a big concentration of mavens here because the best schools in our nation—UC Berkeley and Stanford University—plus top high-tech companies, research centers and manufacturing industry, are all here. And don't forget the venture capitalists." Weili understands that it's the people of Silicon Valley who make all the difference. She refers to the ethnic mix as "the United Nations," and is proud of Marvell's diverse employee base, that includes "all possible backgrounds." [56]

TEAMWORK

Weili has retained the love of teamwork she developed from her days playing basketball, as well as the collectivist values she was taught in China. So, while others at the company may have viewed her as a boss, she regarded herself as a caretaker and worked in a cubicle alongside everyone else, not in an executive office.

Weili also encouraged her employees to invite their families to visit the company at work, to feel "like we're all family." At the head office, they'll find a 6,000-gallon fish tank, a coffee shop, volleyball, courts, and an exercise facility. There's a basketball court too, of course, with a giant "M" painted on center court can be seen. Weili designed that court, and it's an active symbol of the teamwork that she encouraged at Marvell.

Not surprisingly, Weili never tires of talking about sports: "I love basketball. I like the teamwork," she says. "But I also like that there is a result. You shoot the ball and you make a basket. It feels like you accomplished something."[57] During a technology roundtable with President Obama, Weili joined other Silicon Valley leaders to discuss ways to make the country more entrepreneurial.

During the conversation, the president brought up basketball, one of his own hobbies, and Weili jumped at the opportunity to challenge him to a pickup game. She's still waiting for his response.

A WOMAN'S PLACE IS IN TECH

Traditionally, every Chinese individual knows his or her place in family and society, as determined by philosopher Confucius[58] whose "five relationships" establish who obeys and listens to whom. These relationship "truths" dictate that the husband is dominant over the wife, but Weili was raised in a progressive-thinking family in Shanghai and spent her formative years in San Francisco. She developed into a fusion feminist who developed her own sub-system of values and made it work for her in the United States.

Weili believes that differences between females and males can be used to complement partners in business, just as she and her husband have. At Marvell, she was the face of the organization, taking care of clients and establishing relationships. Sehat, on the other hand, was responsible for making ever-innovative products. This separation of duties worked well for the husband-and-wife duo, and established a foundation of success. Weili sticks to her long-held belief that "women are caretakers," but she doesn't feel constricted by that, because she extends its meaning beyond the traditional, to include getting business results and gluing teams together.

Weili elaborated in Lydia Dishman's article, "Innovation Agent Weili Dai, Semiconductor Pioneer," "Women have their own natural talents which are fundamentally different than men's, so I use my common sense to leverage those. For example, for thousands of years, women have been the glue of the family. The way I look at it, Marvell is my big family and then I have my two sons. The fundamental value systems are the same, just on a different scale."[59]

> Weili was raised in a progressive-thinking family in Shanghai and spent her formative years in San Francisco. She evolved into what I call a fusion feminist who developed her own sub-system of values and made it work for her in the United States.

That said, Weili is dismayed by the fact that too many capable female executives are still seen only as strong women, while their male counterparts get praises for being great leaders. Indeed, it is an issue engraved in our society, an attitude putting down great women and excluding them from leadership ranks. Really, who fully deserves to sit at the leadership table? For years, men in suits and ties got used to the idea that most leaders are coming from their ranks. The lady-leaders, strong as they may be, are something else, not belonging to the upper-end corporate table.

As upsetting as this is, Weili feels optimistic that those perceptions will continue to change with time. Today, Weili has become one of the leading advocates for increasing the number of women in engineering jobs and in corporate leadership positions. One of eleven women honored by the California Assembly with its Breaking the Glass Ceiling award (an honor that recognizes female pioneers in science, civil rights and government) Weili continues to promote women in technology, mentoring women entrepreneurs such as Julia Hu, CEO and co-founder of Lark Technologies, Inc.,[60] a mobile health company. Weili and Julia share a vision of using technology to better the lives of people around the world, and Weili is a Chairman of the Board for Lark that continues to make good progress.

While acknowledging the slow progress made by women in the technology sector and in corporate leadership positions, Weili nevertheless . . . remains positive: "I believe that there will be more women engineers,"[61] she says. As technology becomes more deeply embedded in every part of our lives, particularly in our homes where women have a better perspective on how such products could be improved. "It's not just about developing 'nerdy' technology . . . It's about relating it to the social aspects of our lives."[62] It's also about the natural talent for design that women have, and about the look and feel for fitting new technology gadgets into our lifestyles, adding to her *care and be fair* life philosophy.[63]

Indeed, Weili's vision of the "connected lifestyle" became a reality with the launch of Google's new Chromecast video adapter in 2013. [64] Marvell's gadget enables 1080p video playback, common DRM standards and everything else you'd expect from a smart TV device with very little power consumption and a low price tag, which allowed Google to debut the device for just thirty-five dollars. Low pricing is the international language that everybody loves. Equally understandable is the fact that Chromecast is really bringing mobile devices and TV together. "I call it the magic glue," Weili said with pride, pointing out that Chromecast is part of a bigger change for the semiconductor business, and companies such as Marvell are about enabling technologies that power devices for contemporary connected consumer. Chromecast was named as the Gadget of the Year in 2013 by *Time* magazine.[65]

NEXT ACT

Weili's activities didn't end with Marvell. She promoted partnership with the One Laptop per Child[66] program, sits on the board of the disaster relief organization Give2Asia,[67] and was named to the Committee of 100,[68] an organization representing the Chinese Americans. She is active in STEM initiatives that help steer young minds into technical fields. Weili serves as mentor—sharing her life experiences, lessons learned in business and her technology expertise—to numerous executives and entrepreneurs. She is also a member of the C200[69] and executive committee for TechNet.[70] Sutardja Dai Hall, at her alma mater UC Berkeley, was named for her along with her husband and her brother-in-law. Sutardja Dai Hall is home to the Center for Information Technology Research in the Interest of Society[71].

And Weili has no plans to slow down any time soon. She knows that if there's one thing exciting about technology, it's that the bar is constantly being raised. Her mission of bringing advanced technologies that power the next-generation of devices—thin, smart, affordable, and low-power consumer electronics products—make the lives of people around the world better. Weili's contributions to American well-being and culture are truly inspirational.

Alfa Demmellash *from Ethiopia*

The Social Entrepreneur

As a young girl, Alfa Melesse Demmellash lived on less than a dollar a day, against the backdrop of torture and murder. These days the Ethiopian native and social entrepreneur is living the American Dream and helping others do the same. As the co-founder and CEO of Rising Tide Capital, Alfa empowers entrepreneurs to start and grow their businesses, making it her business to help them succeed. To date, over 2,390 entrepreneurs have graduated from her Community Business Academy, forming a community of change agents and local business leaders that are transforming their neighborhoods from within.

Alfa joined her mother in Boston after years of separation. It was in part because of seeing her mother work so hard as a waitress and seamstress that she became a social entrepreneur, helping the disadvantaged people – especially women - start their own businesses.

ABUNDANT LOVE

Alfa was born in Addis Ababa amid instability and unrest, of a loving mother and a charismatic, but abusive father. Her parents married to legitimize her birth, but divorced three months later. Alfa was only two years old when her mother had to flee the country, first to Kenya and then to the US, to escape the ravages of the The Ethiopian Red Terror (Qey Shibir), a violent political campaign that left more than 1.4 million dead. A remarkable woman, Alfa's mother left her small daughter behind in the care of her parents and younger sister, on two strict conditions: that the girl be enrolled first in the Montessori School and, later, in the highly regarded Cathedral School for Girls; and that she would not be subjected to female circumcision, as was the custom. Thus, for most of her first twelve years, Alfa was raised by her aunt and grandparents in an extended family, surrounded by cousins and a myriad of people taken in by her generous and liberal-minded grandparents. Despite the chaos of the time, young Alfa wasn't aware of all the turmoil and poverty around her: she felt protected. Joy and hospitality were the family's wealth.

Alfa remembers how, each morning, family members would take turns walking her to kindergarten. She also remembers her grandmother, an amazing woman who instilled in her a sense of justice, generosity, and faith grounded in loving action. Alfa would watch her grandmother feed and clothe the poor, the sick and the maimed, sharing what little she had with abundant love.

Despite growing up amid turmoil and poverty, Alfa Demmellash felt protected. Joy and hospitality were her family's wealth.

And then the unexpected happened. Alfa's father turned up determined to take her away. The family attempted to protect the child from this abusive man, but he had primary rights as her biological father, so their efforts were in vain. Alfa's father forcibly took charge of his daughter, keeping her in his house for over a year, far away from where she was growing up. The teachers in her new Cathedral school saw evidence of the abuse she suffered—beatings and sleep deprivation—but they felt powerless to interfere. And then, as unexpectedly as he appeared, Alfa's father disappeared. After a long and tumultuous year, he drove Alfa to a far-away town and just let her go. At the age of nine, Alfa found her way back to her grandparents' home in Addis Ababa, hitchhiking with truck drivers. The experience left her scarred, but Alfa proved to be a survivor.

THE POWER OF POSITIVE ACTION

From her grandmother, who took in people in need, despite her own modest means, Alfa learned a lesson on taking positive action and bringing good to the community. And from her mother, who wait-ressed by day and sewed dresses in the evening for Ethiopian im-migrants in Boston, MA, she learned the value of hard work. Alfa's mother put in long hours, saving every cent she could to cover her daughter's clothes and school fees, and later, to pay for her airfare to the United States. After Alfa finished her 6th grade studies in Addis Ababa, she flew to the U.S. to reunite with her mother, who by that time had married her stepfather. Her mother's sacrifices and her stepfather's goodness (he was protective of her and her independent thinking), were major influences in Alfa's formative years. It was his family name, Demmellash, that Alfa took in gratitude when graduating from Harvard.

FINDING HER VOICE

The U.S. was luxurious compared with Ethiopia, and twelve-year-old Alfa was overwhelmed. What's more, her efforts to immerse herself in American culture were hindered by her rudimentary communication skills. Alfa's first friend in the U.S. was a Russian girl from a new immigrant family. The girls had been spending a lot of time together, if only because neither spoke English well enough to make other friends. Alas, this resulted in them being bullied mercilessly by some other classmates, some of whom taunted the girls being gay.

This was a jarring cultural experience for Alfa. "I did not at the time understand anything about gender diversity and was extremely concerned and uncertain about what I was doing wrong to be the source of so much attention. I was further confused since [the word] GAY in dictionary translated into something joyful but seemed to be spoken with so much spite by classmates, at recess and on the playground."[72]

Nevertheless, by the 8th grade at St. Andrew's School in Boston, Alfa had become Valedictorian of her class. Later, when attending the famed—and highly competitive—Boston Latin School, she discovered how important it is to be able to present in front of a large audience. Extremely shy, Alfa was almost paralyzed in front of a large groups. But giving up wasn't in her nature, so she signed up for public declamation classes and learned to hold her own while presenting.

After Boston Latin, Alfa was admitted to Harvard, where she attended with the help of financial aid. Interested in how laws are made and how a political, military, and economic environment like the one she faced in Ethiopia could be changed, she studied government. Alfa took a class on the political economy of Africa and learned about the Rwandan genocide—a catastrophe that happened because of the absence of any enforced rule of law. Captivated, she raised funds for a study tour to Rwanda for herself and five other sophomore students, to research the Gacaca, a traditional form of Rwandan conflict resolution that had been adopted to address the 1994 genocide.

Thus, in 2002, Alfa received a history lesson beyond anything she could discover in books. She learned first-hand how investing in women can bring benefits to a nation at large, the obvious benefits being the quick growth of female-led businesses and national GDP; the reduction of poverty; and social norms shifting to a more female-friendly direction. She also observed female entreprencurism being played out: women were running farms and managing successful coffee bean cooperatives, rebuilding Rwanda's economy. It was research and curiosity that brought her there, but surviving her own childhood in Ethiopia helped her empathize with these local women. The Rwanda trip channeled her train of thought in the direction she would follow for life.

> Alfa's poverty-stricken childhood helped her understand the challenges that faced the female entrepreneurs of Rwanda.

Reflection after her study tour led Alfa to realize that laws meant nothing if people were economically poor and fearful, because such people have no voice in how they are governed. It was then that she focused her studies on development work, talking to a wide range of practitioners in the field. Alfa understood that it was easier to make a real difference by starting with a small effort, so she began thinking about how to best make a practical contribution. Alfa graduated cum laude from Harvard University in 2003.

OPEN HEARTED INTEGRATION

Not until she attended college did Alfa start to feel fully at home in America. Naturally intelligent, she couldn't help but see that cultural integration is the way to go. "I definitely consider myself a global citizen residing in America," she said. "Part of what makes America particularly unique is that it is *more a platform rather than a cultural hegemon* [italic, FC]. Daily global influences, including those being imported by immigrants in America, ultimately shape what it means to be an American."[73]

Alfa has come to appreciate a lot of things in the U.S., including a level of openness in conversation and a ready willingness where people feel able to admit what they don't know—more so than in most other cultures. Her own experience of the integration process convinced Alfa that a traditional dichotomy used to characterize integration is too superficial to describe the reality of today.

RELATIONSHIPS—PERSONAL AND PROFESSIONAL

Alfa gets philosophical when talking about the importance of relationships in both her personal and professional life. "My husband's parents really put it best for their son, [saying] that the purpose of life is to learn how to love well. I don't know how many people will relate to that, but if someone told me the purpose of life, I would be one to listen carefully. It is what you might call the 64-million-dollar question. When my best friend, now my husband, told me that was what they taught him all his life, I knew I had found the right person. If someone begins [his/her] every day with the question of "what does it mean to love well today?"[74] This very question demands a relationship.

Turning her attention to business, she applied the *loving well* principle here as well, saying that "Most often, people who are far away—as well as those who are near us—just require our attention and our time. ... So, go out and make some connections, and whatever you do, please do not limit your potential friends to just those who share your circumstances. Make a point to talk to the deli owner, the banker, the restaurant hostess, and anyone working within your city hall, government agency, or those in your industry. Remember – you don't have to have the answers—just the right questions! Organizations like mine exist to help people ask the right questions in order to get the answers that lead to personal and business success."

SOCIAL ENTREPRENEURSHIP

Company co-founders Alfa Demmellash and Alex Forrester met when they were freshmen at Harvard University. By his senior year, Alex knew that Alfa was the smartest woman he had ever met. For her part, Alfa felt she had found her soul mate. The young couple married and—wanting to be near New York because of its many philanthropic institutions—set their sights on Jersey City.

Once in New Jersey, Alfa and Alex soon realized that deep

poverty and economic injustice were widespread in the U.S. So, in 2004, they recruited help from colleagues and friends to found *Rising Tide Capital*[75] . The goal: to offer people a way out of poverty. A daunting task, but one that the young Harvard graduates were unafraid to take on.

The couple call themselves *social entrepreneurs*, an innovative concept in business leadership that highlights the enterprise's goal of alleviating social problems and effecting change. Learning that access to finance—small and micro-business loans—was not the bottleneck problem they feared was an invaluable lesson. It led Alfa and Alex to focus on training aspiring entrepreneurs in *How to Think About Business*, that is, how to structure business plans, access markets, develop their confidence, and maintain early success.

The original plan was to create a micro-lending organization that would help people get loans. But it soon became clear that the issue was larger than that: How do you give people money if they have little idea of how to use it, or pay it back? Training was needed. That's why Alfa and Alex started a Community Business Academy[76] to support individuals with a hands-on approach to the management side of their businesses. An intensive training course coupled with year-round coaching and mentoring, this initiative took New Jersey by storm and solidified social entrepreneurship as a leadership trend.

Today, *Rising Tide Capital* has gone from aiding 30 clients per year to more than 600. The days of working from their one-bedroom apartment in Jersey City and meetings in clients' kitchens are long gone. Alfa and Alex now run an intensive business academy[77] taught in English and Spanish in Jersey City, Newark, the City of Orange Township, and Union City. Classes are held in church basements, local schools and universities, and in spaces provided by other nonprofit partnering organizations. Graduates of the Community Business Academy participate in year-round Business Acceleration

Services, which provide coaching, consulting, and access to capital they need to meet their business goals.

Alfa's efforts have not gone unnoticed. In 2008, she addressed the United Nations Global Summit on Women to talk about the connection between the entrepreneurial spirit and the economic empowerment of women.

Alfa at the time she was recognized as a CNN Hero

Saluted as a CNN Hero, Alfa was invited to the White House[78] where President Obama honored her along with other creative community organizers.

COMING INTO HER OWN

Alfa is now thinking about how to expand *Rising Tide Capital* to encompass Ethiopia and Rwanda. She's working to create a licensing operation that will equip local organizations to emulate Rising Tide's practices—the programs, the ways to measure outcome and demonstrate return on investment—and adapt them to their local context. Alfa's dream is to reach 100 of the neediest communities, to identify and support 1,000 entrepreneurs in each of those communities, and help empower 100,000 entrepreneurs who will rebuild their communities and make an enormous difference.

Alfa believes that her cultural heritage helped her to become an achiever in the US. As she says, "Coming from a country with 3,000 years of autonomous history and known as the birthplace of humanity—the only country in Africa not to be colonized by Europeans—gave me a level of cultural confidence that underscored my independence. Even the challenges of my cultural heritage (e.g., Ethiopia being highlighted as one of the poorest nations in the world or often portrayed in the media as a foster child for starvation and the third world misery) were fuel to me to work hard and exceed my own expectations. I have not been negatively impacted [by them]."[79]

Irmgard Lafrentz *from Germany*

The Global Matchmaker

Few public relations professionals have succeeded in the international world of high-tech like Irmgard Lafrentz. With a large and loyal client base that included scrappy start-ups and established industry leaders alike, her company—Globalpress Connection helped clients engage with key media from around the world. Irmgard's business model delivers huge cost and time savings to clients wanting to increase their brand exposure. She brought together high-tech executives, leaders from the analyst community, and editors from top-tier media to share news and discuss emerging technologies and business issues in a way that benefits all parties. This revolutionary turnkey service engaged approximately 70% of electronics companies each year, hosted some 20,000 editors, and generated more than 10,000 articles. And now the German farm-girl who built her American business on professionalism and a "no detail is too small" perfectionism is known as The Global Matchmaker.

> Irmgard, a recognized "global matchmaker" connecting high-tech companies and media

HUMBLE BEGINNINGS

Irmgard grew up in post-war Germany, near Munich, in a family that believed in integrity and honesty—not to mention tough love. Educated to high school level—university was out of the question for this family of modest means—she was expected to contribute to the household finances from a very young age. As an apprentice in a legal office, Irmgard handed her small salary over to her mother. The result was a frugal mindset typical among Germans of her generation. Irmgard worked hard and progressed from apprentice to paralegal, but with the move came the realization that her true ambition lay in communications, and not the legal profession. So, she found a position in the advertising department of *Die Zeit*, a national newspaper based in Hamburg. Later, working as an au pair in England, she developed a curiosity for the larger world. Trips to Africa, the U.S., and throughout Europe contributed to her global awareness and cultural sensitivity, all the while feeding her curiosity.

Irmgard moved back to Munich after her travels, working her way up to a managerial position in international marketing at a leading optical manufacturer, Optical Works Rodenstock. She had managed an advertising and public relations department for seven years, without an official title as such—very typical for Germany in the 70s.

While at Rodenstock, Irmgard was sent to New York on a two-month internship. She was fascinated by the buzz of the city, and especially impressed by the way in which the American team worked together. "Old and young employees collaborated, and no one dominated—so different from the executive meetings I attended in Germany. It was also the first time I was referred to as having a 'career' by other women." Prior to this, Irmgard had considered her work in Munich to be a job and not a career, but all that changed in New York when she says, thanks to a language shift, "I realized that I very well had a career in Munich, just didn't know it."[80]

SOMETHING NEW

Back in Germany, Irmgard met an American with whom she maintained a long-distance relationship. This led to several trips to the U.S., which in turn led to marriage. Relocating to the U.S. was an easy decision, Irmgard says: "At the time, we considered living in Germany but my husband's limited German and his high expertise in laser technology made it unrealistic. And at thirty-three I was ready for something new."[81]

> Today, Irmgard's idea of a computer-associated PR services would be called "having a vision." At the time, however, she considered it just "common sense to see what was obvious."[82]

It took Irmgard about six months to get her first job in the US, that of a part time bookstore clerk with a salary of $5 an hour. But she wanted to find her way back to public relations—known as marketing communications in the U.S.—so she kept her eyes open: "Arriving in the Silicon Valley in 1984, I quickly saw my opportunity. At my Munich employer Rodenstock, we had just begun to computerize, and it was clear to me that the computers from the Silicon Valley would be needed in many German companies. The idea of a computer-associated PR services was born right then." Irmgard goes on to say that now, her idea would be called "having a vision," but she considers it just "common sense to see what was obvious."[83]

The first few years of setting up her own business were far from easy. Indeed, they were a session in hell. "I offered a service solution no one even knew they needed. Everything was focused on the U.S. market, and I was kind of a crazy person who said "hey—there is Europe out there" and got the response 'Europe—where is that?'" Irmgard recalls. It took a long while to establish the value proposition of something so new and unique."[84] But finally, her ideas were accepted, and her persistence rewarded.

HER BIGGEST CHALLENGE

When a young woman with a family, starts a ground-breaking business, we want to know how much the demands of that family can be a limiting factor for her. Having no extended family in the States to help out was an easily foreseeable predicament for Irmgard as a busy-busy businesswoman.

Irmgard is a formidable woman, however, when her husband announced that he was gay several years into the marriage, she faced her most difficult challenge of all: single-handedly raising a ten-year-old son while running a business. Irmgard's focus was rearing her son, Daniel, to be an upstanding and healthy young man, and also keeping her career afloat. "The constant time pressure was unbearable," she says. But Irmgard's love for Daniel, coupled with a primitive survival instinct, moved her forward. In time, she did more than survive. She thrived. "What helped was that my service was in demand at the time, but the constant guilt [for] not doing my best as a mother and a business owner was terrible."

Irmgard looks back at that time as one of her worst. "[T]he realization that my Prince Charming was gay and my marriage was basically a lie—it put me into deep depression in the mid-90s. But I didn't know anything about depression," Irmgard says. She tried to move on with her life, but moving on takes time. Immediately after her divorce, she lost focus and was on the verge of losing everything she had worked so hard for. "I didn't pay attention to the business but focused on Daniel and pretended everything was fine. With $10k left in the credit line, I hired a high-profile business consultant who kicked my ass and refocused my responsibility as a business woman. Fear made me snap out and be accountable again."[85]

After this setback, Irmgard went full speed ahead. She watched over the needs of an increasing number of clients and added novel items to the roster of her agency's services, culminating in a series of global events that grew in prestige and value.

AMERICA'S LARGEST ETHNIC GROUP

Irmgard chose to remain in the U.S. after her divorce; nevertheless, she felt it was important to preserve what she believed to be the essentials of German culture and pass these down to her son. So, she exposed him to the German language and to the rich world of German traditions, especially at Christmas. The two loved attending parties, drinking *Glühwein* and *Advenskafee* in the Advent season, eating *Lebkuchen*—Christmas cookies and pastries—and of course, singing, which unites people in the holiday spirit.

Born and bred in Europe, Irmgard never misses a chance to connect to her original culture: "When I am in Germany, I go to museums, stroll around historical town areas, admire the 1000-year-old churches and buildings—and realize that I am lucky to be living in the "new world" of America."[86] But this natural nostalgia is unlikely to ever make her feel truly German again.

> Anti-German sentiment was extreme after the two world wars, and that made many German-Americans hunker down, anglicize their names, and stop speaking German at home in a bid to hide or downplay their origins.

A brief look at the history of German immigrants in America[87] shows that they have assimilated so profoundly as to be barely identified as an ethnic group. *The Economist* labelled[88] them "the silent majority" because, according to the Census Bureau, they outnumber any other ethnic group. (Forty-six million people of German descent compared to thirty-three million of Irish, and twenty-five million of English). Yet, despite their numbers, German-Americans are barely visible. Everybody knows that Mario Cuomo is Italian-American and that the Kennedys come from Irish stock. But nobody mentions John Boehner's origin—or Rand Paul's. This comes as no surprise.

German-Americans, and businesses originating in Germany, tend to downplay their roots for historical reasons. The first

Germans migrated to America in 1607, founding big cities in Pennsylvania, around Milwaukee and elsewhere. These immigrants gave us the taste of pretzels, sauerkraut, and hot dogs. They introduced the first kindergartens and spread progressive ideas. After the failure of the 1848 German revolution, which prompted a great number of disillusioned Germans to decamp to the US, the next large waves of immigrants came during WWI and WWII. But anti-German[89] sentiment was extreme during this time, and that made many German-Americans hunker down, anglicize their names, and stop speaking German at home in a bid to hide or downplay their origins.

The German-Americans of today are quietly successful: they have assimilated and progressed without any political help tailored to their ethnic group; their median household income is eighteen percent above the national norm; they are more likely to have college degrees than other Americans, and less likely to be unemployed. However, German-American identity does not appear to be as prevalent as that of other cultural groups. For example, when the new prime minister of India visited America, Indian-Americans went wild with cheer. But when Chancellor Merkel visited, German-Americans hardly noticed. It's not just a matter of temperament; it's the depth of assimilation.

But what may be true of a group can sometimes stand in stark contrast to what individual immigrants feel. That's certainly the case with Irmgard: after thirty years of living in the US she still feels like an outsider. Despite being integrated, she's not clear where she belongs. "I feel more American, but as I get older, I long for more belonging somewhere. I am rooted neither here nor in Germany.[90]" These are the identity issues that are hard to resolve. In fact, Irmgard questions whether it's possible to become totally integrated. "I am not sure if this is an emotional or intellectual issue," she says, "I feel like a person with two passports but no home."

A RIGOROUS REINVENTION

Coming to the U.S. as an accomplished individual at age thirty-three, Irmgard went through a rigorous reinvention. The biggest shift came with the transition from employee with a steady paycheck to entrepreneur with financial insecurities. Financial security is a large part of the German psyche, and to this effect Irmgard observed that Americans are much more entrepreneurial. Indeed, she uses the phrases "risk-averse" and "security-obsessed" to describe Germans, noting that "most Americans are risk takers, and in the US, where everything is financially driven, debt is part of life and considered normal."[91] If all this is true, then Irmgard has certainly proven herself to be different from many of her countrymen. She always wanted to have her own business, it just took the opportunity that America provided. Now over sixty, she's still willing to take risks and try new and exciting things.

Irmgard feels that a number of her traditional values have changed since moving to the U.S. Compassion being one example. "I learned to be compassionate here in the US," she says. "I contribute financially and actively to several organizations now. In Germany, this is taken care of by the government through higher taxes. In the beginning, I resented my ex-husband for donating so much money and time. Now I do it myself because I realized the system's different here."[92]

Her attitudes toward money have also changed. "Germans are traditionally very frugal, and split a dinner bill exactly by consumption. I did that here in the beginning, but now I generously split the bill by people and don't care if someone had a second glass of wine and I pay a little extra. I am more generous now."[93]

Irmgard feels there's a social identity that unites all immigrants regardless of their country of origin. "I believe immigrants are more open on personal issues, sharing their hardships, pain and suffering," she says.

It's not just the country that has influenced her, of course. Irmgard's America-born son, with his liberal thinking and can-do-anything attitude, has made a terrific impact on the way she leads her life. Irmgard says she is more liberal now, and is becoming a better communicator. Still, certain original values and traditions remain no matter how long an immigrant lives in the U.S., and for Irmgard, these invariables are her work ethic, preference of Christmas Eve to Christmas Day celebrations, and, of course, food.

Irmgard feels there's a social identity that unites all immigrants regardless of their country of origin. In fact, she socializes a lot with immigrants from France, Mexico, Germany, and Sweden. "I believe immigrants are more open on personal issues, sharing their hardships, pain and suffering. Most American people are guarded [protecting their privacy], and everything is "fine." In fact, the rather guarded nature of Americans has posed a big cultural challenge for Irmgard. "I had a hard time understanding that Americans rarely say what they really mean. The language was a big obstacle for me—interpreting the subtleties. I was so direct in the beginning. I don't know how I really became a success. Now—I learned [American ways] and apply this less-direct way of communication too."[94] So, it seems that, in terms of everyday challenges, culture comes first and language comes second.

NATURAL LEADERSHIP

Irmgard built her business on three sturdy pillars: personal strength; an inclination toward risk taking; and a willingness to modify her business behavior. Still, while she's looked up to by colleagues and clients alike, she acknowledges that the word "leader" is so loaded that she's not sure if it should be applied to her or not. Consider:

> I had no experience in leadership when I started. Just what I learned from my managers in Germany. Maybe I am a natural leader, who can build trust, deliver on a promise and go

an extra mile."[95] Natural leadership often shows in your new ideas, confidence, as well as in how you help others.

Of course, I don't think I am so unique, she says. I did not have any fear of failure then, totally believed in the value of my ideas and service, and helped make many small companies (like Cisco in 1989) a success—until they didn't need me anymore. I have helped launch hundreds of companies, some are huge now and some went bust, while many were acquired by other companies. For a woman to make it now should be easier because the opportunities are bigger than in 1984. Education, access to funding, research is much more available now.[96]

Irmgard is concerned more with a vision of leadership than with leading people. Her dream team of five women needed practical guidance on how to deal with European clients in general, and how to communicate across the cultures in particular—and help with day-to-day issues, coupled with the leadership from the front on the idea side.

FAILURE IS AN OPTION

The most successful entrepreneurs demonstrate a quality of grit, not to mention the ability to stay in play. That's certainly true of Irmgard. As a tough, never-give-up type, she developed her own way of counteracting setbacks: going through three or four weeks of worry and despair which, in her experience, paves the way for something positive to happen. From there she continues with life—and business—as usual. "I think most immigrant women tend [to move] upward because they want to stay here and don't return to their country of origin when something happens, like spouse' death, divorce, etc. After my divorce, I worked even harder because I did not want to go back to Germany. I had achieved a lot in the ten years here."[97]

Facing a set-back? Analyze. Act. And then move on.

When talking of failures, Irmgard isn't afraid to get specific. "I know my business very well," she says, "so I know why a failure happens. Just recently I had a major setback and had to cancel one of my projects. Re-entering the market I had left six years ago, underestimating the competition, and an industry that doesn't value PR have been the reasons [of that setback]. Very painful, high dollar loss—but once I decided to cancel, it was liberating. I had to reimburse $45K to clients who had committed, which was utterly painful. But the next project had been already lined-up.[98] So for coping with failure, Irmgard's method it to analyze, act, and then move on.

VISION AND COMMONSENSE

Irmgard Lafrentz has come a long way: from a farm in Northern Germany, to au pair, to office worker, to communications manager in a major company, to owning her own company. It may have been her marriage that brought her to the U.S., but it was her dream of entrepreneurship, mixed with financial and emotional security, that kept her here.

Smart at identifying opportunity, Irmgard formulated a vision to bridge Silicon Valley with European and Asian media. Her global PR agency has withstood thirty years of ups and downs, including three recessions, and is a leader in global tech PR. And yet, while Irmgard may have integrated linguistically and culturally, she never lost her accent or her incredibly direct communication style. Today, this former farm-girl is a happy and accomplished American whose curiosity and creativity never rest.

Indeed, when her business slowed down due to unseen number of mergers and acquisitions in her client base, she had the vision to close the company and prepared for "life after GlobalPress Connection." Now financially independent – and always a quick thinker – she decided to do something totally new and adventurous—and moved to the highlands of Ecuador. Today Irmgard lives in a beautiful city of Cuenca, volunteers, and helps with fundraising to support a shelter for abused women and children.

Continuing as a global matchmaker, Irmgard managed to connect a local Rotary Club of Cuenca, Equador, with her own club in Cupertino, California. And now there is Global Grant application pending through Rotary International that may generate $50,000 a year to be used for women/children trauma healing, growing healthy foods.

I am curious to see where the next adventure will take her, because women like Irmgard are the world's movers and shakers - wherever life takes them.

Ani Palacios Mc Bride *from Peru*

The Accidental Immigrant

Ani feels good about being a cultural ambassador

It's a familiar story: a woman follows her husband to the U.S. while putting her own ambitions on hold. That's what Ani Palacios Mc Bride did. Upon moving to the U.S., this journalist and mass media communications professional made sacrifices for her husband's work and her family's well-being. When it came time to restart her own career, she did so from scratch, using her personal experience to understand the wider phenomena of immigration.

Ani based her career on helping newcomers successfully acculturate to the U.S. without losing themselves in the process. She founded her own publishing and editing business, including a news aggregator and original content website outlet in English, Spanish, and Portuguese—Contacto Latino. And now the author of many articles and several popular books about what it takes to be a success in a new world has become a successful entrepreneur, Latino culture ambassador, and role model in her own right.

FIRST STEPS

Born into a prominent family in Lima, Perú, Ani was well educated, receiving a B.A. in journalism from Universidad de Piura, followed by a B.A. in mass media communications from Universidad de Lima. She married in her mid-twenties and worked as a creative writer and producer in the top advertising agencies in Lima. When opportunity for her husband to earn his M.S. struck, the young family ventured to the United States, arriving with their first baby, Mariana, in 1988.

> Ani and her husband, Felix, had goals typical of many immigrants: financial stability and a creative environment that would enable professional growth.

The family's American beginnings were modest. Ani and her husband, Felix, came on a student visa, with plans for Felix to earn his M.S. degree before heading back to Peru. They figured it would take two years. But terrorism and a bad economy made returning to their homeland untenable, so when Felix received an offer he couldn't refuse—more than one, in fact: a scholarship for a Ph.D. and a dream job—the family decided to remain in the U.S. It wasn't an easy decision. Pregnant with her second child, Ani wanted to return to Peru and her extended family. But she knew that staying in the U.S. was in the family's best interest, so they became, as Ani put it, "accidental immigrants."[99]

THE OPPORTUNITY OF BEING HERE

The couple's goals were typical of many immigrants: financial stability and a creative environment that would enable professional growth. Although it was practical for the family to stay in the U.S., those first few years were rough for Ani. Better career opportunities for her husband did nothing to make her feel comfortable. And yet, as much as she was basically alone in a foreign country, with no extended family to lean upon (very important in her culture), Ani remembers this time as exciting: "It was liberating to know most of it was up to me."[100]

Ani learned first-hand that emigration is not for the faint-hearted. She saw many immigrants leave. Indeed, after a series of job-related humiliations, there were times when she herself was tempted to pack up and return home. It was pride that kept her here, the pride of a woman from a well-established Peruvian family the members of which not only could help themselves but often helped those less fortunate too, materially and spiritually. She would never admit her defeat in America and reach out to the family for help—she even stopped communicating with them because they considered her and her children too Americanized. But challenges were real: "It's hard to be treated like you are a second-class, token Hispanic, or some novelty. It's hard to work harder than the rest . . . constantly proving yourself. It's heart-wrenching to give it all up for the opportunity of being here."[101]

But stay she did.

The challenges Ani faced as a female immigrant have been mostly cultural, not gender-based, such as replacing her entire social network and trying to understand how to advance professionally. Not only did she find it hard to follow the societal rules of her new country, but the boredom and loneliness of being a stay-at-home mom exacerbated her integration challenges, as did the fact that most of her friends were Latinos. When asked what helped, Ani got very specific: "Family values. Laugh about it until the pain is gone. Rely on friends. Know who your friends are."[102]

"Nobody is ever ready for the emotional toll of immigrating. It changes you and many come out of it stronger."[103]

Like many immigrants, Ani found language to be a substantial hurdle. In fact, she spoke and wrote such limited English upon arrival in the U.S. that she thought she'd never return to her original profession in communications. But her first job as a cashier actually helped improve her English language skills—and leave that job fast. Today, she has a "near-native" proficiency in American English, even though she admits that she's still "working on it."

"People say they 'love' my accent, but sometimes you can tell they love it . . . but just not as an employee." In other words, Ani understands that certain people who find a foreign accent charming will never hire a person who has one. "I know that people equal accent with not being able to do the job. The only way I can cope with it is by showing I can do the same or better [job] than people without an accent."[104]

As time went by, Ani made her way through the immigration jungle into a clear-cut space of her own: "The first thing I did was to start writing about the immigration experience. That was in 1992, when nobody was talking about what it was like to be an immigrant, and there were few resources available. My entire career was built on the fact that I'm an immigrant and want to help others not go through what I went through."[105] Reflecting on her immigration experiences and expressing her learnings on paper were good for her—and, later, for others. "The U.S. is really the country of opportunities, even today," she says. Even so, she acknowledges that "nobody is ever ready for the emotional toll of immigrating. It changes you and many come out of it stronger."[106]

THE AMERICAN MENTALITY

Ani must have done an excellent job adapting to American culture to become the successful entrepreneur that she is. However, when asked if she considers herself an American, she doesn't hesitate: "Definitely [I am] living in a double world, just like the title of my book."[107]

She admits that her cultural make-up has changed in the US, and maintains that "immigrants end up being hybrids with two hearts; two countries they love; two languages; and two cultures."[108] It's important to Ani to retain her original values, especially in the areas of language, food, family and holiday traditions, and of course, respect to elders. That's why she's naturally inclined towards preserving her original cultural identity and not fully immersing herself in the melting pot of American culture.

Still, Ani has worked hard to overcome cultural hurdles, one of which was the typical Latino scarcity mentality. The Latino scarcity mentality comes from a lack of many things, primarily a lack of opportunity in their native countries. Its opposite, abundance mentality, is not something that's acquired, but something that's tuned into. Of course, there are many people in the U.S. who do not enjoy abundance or an abundance mentality; nevertheless, this is certainly a rich nation with a great deal of material wealth, which makes it easier for an abundance mentality to dominate. "Realizing and learning to keep an [American] abundance mentality was hard," says Ani. But finally, she made it—partly because she came to appreciate Americans. She likes them for being a can-do people, organized, positive thinkers who believe that "everything is possible if you work hard enough."[109] She likes them for their directness and straightforwardness, because they "do what they say they are going to do." Over time, Ani's own scarcity mentality faded away, as did the "negativity towards anything government."

Ani quickly learned the differences between her original culture and American culture. As she did, it struck her that "Americans are fast to call themselves friends, and even faster not to behave as friends."[110] Disappointed in some of her American friendships, she's not the first to notice this; in fact, many intercultural trainers and consultants instruct on exactly this point, to mitigate culture shock. For example, they'll advise newcomers that "Come round anytime" may not be the invitation it seems, and that dropping into an American household without a pre-arranged date may result in something other than a warm welcome. This is not to say that Americans aren't friendly, only that their friendliness comes with its own set of rules.

Ani thinks of Americans as can-do people—organized, positive thinkers who believe that "everything is possible if you work hard enough."[111]

Smart as she is, Ani is also well aware of having modified her cultural make-up in the adaptation process. Today, she is glad that all her children—two of them born and raised in the US—share the same American mentality. Ani says she would like them to preserve some original cultural traits and be cultural hybrids like her. "I'd like them to preserve what they value [of Peruvian descent] and mix in with what they value out of the U.S. culture. Being a child of an immigrant is a great opportunity to be more, to have more, to give back more."[112]

A DOUBLE WORLD

Ani identifies "the emotional pressure cooker of being an immigrant"[113] as one of her greatest challenges. Especially frustrating were language and cultural issues, which she says were "enough to make anyone break into pieces. But not immigrant women." Ani is proud of belonging to this tougher breed. She knows that immigrants "take the challenge and get it done (almost) without complaining." And she's made it her business to help them.

One of Ani's earliest initiatives was founding Centro Esperanza Latina in Columbus, Ohio. The Center for Latin Hope, as it is known in English, is a bilingual organization dedicated to individual, family, and community development. It offers clinical services, prevention programs, family activities, educational programs, and assistance to workers—services that help the newly arrived immigrant families in the acculturation process.

Ani is proud of belonging to a tough breed of immigrant women. She knows that they take the challenge and get things done.

Ani has also worked with the Ohio Civil Rights Commission and the Ohio Commission on Latino/Hispanic affairs in projects serving the Latino communities to better understand their rights and available resources. She founded Contacto Latino[114], where she is editor and creative director. A trilingual portal that brings news and information to Latinos worldwide, Contacto Latino is also a news aggregator that provides original content, as well as stories from sources around the world, averaging around 600 stories a day. And in 2010 she wrote the book *Living in a Double World.* An immigrant writing for an immigrant audience, she provides readers with inspiration and advice on how to navigate the immigrant experience.

A CULTURAL AMBASSADOR

A woman who has built her career on her own immigrant experience, Ani Palacios Mc Bride is a cultural ambassador and role model for immigrant women. One of the first communicators to write about and for immigrants, she explores multiple immigrant-related topics in her work. Yes, life for this girl from a wealthy Peruvian family changed completely when she arrived in the U.S., but with determination and resilience she proved that she could make it on her own, without the help of her family's last name.

Ani's leadership lies in showing Latinos and other immigrants how to integrate into American culture and establish themselves professionally—and she leads by example. This *double cultural ambassador* [115] represents Latinos and the Latino-market in the U.S. explaining that they should be marketed to with different strategies; and on the other hand, becoming a recognized U.S. guide for all Latinos who want to successfully adapt and succeed in the US.

Ani gives a lot of credit to her husband for helping her stay the course. It was Felix who drove her to be ambitious, and to seek success in her new country. Today, both are enjoying fulfilling careers, and together they have the satisfaction of watching their children come into their own. Nowadays, Ani happily lives in Columbus, Ohio, with her husband, Félix, daughters Camila and Mariana and son Diego. As to *when* she felt fully integrated into her new culture, she answers that it was some ten years into her emigration when, visiting her home country, she found herself missing the U.S.A.

Raegan Moya-Jones *from Australia*

The Mom on a Mission

Raegan Moya-Jones didn't look like a CEO when she walked into a Manhattan club for our interview. Still, it was easy to see why she's so convincing in her executive role—despite the skinny jeans and ponytail. With her piercing blue eyes, confident posture, and contained passion, this mother of four projects resolve and inspires trust.

Her main business idea occurred to Raegan because she was an Australian. But only in the US she discovered her calling to be a Mom on a Mission.

Raegan learned early in her career that necessity really is the mother of invention. After the birth of her first child, the Aussie transplant went looking for a muslin wrap in which to swaddle her first baby. These durable wraps are very popular in Australia, but Raegan couldn't find what she was looking for in New York, or anywhere in the country for that matter. So, having identified a gap in the newborn market, she made it work for her—and in 2006 the *Economist* employee turned baby industry entrepreneur launched the children's brand aden + anais[116]. Raegan spent several years living and breathing muslin and perfecting its quality, which is why her company's muslin is as soft as it is, and why it doesn't shrink or pill. Today aden + anais has annual revenue of over $100 million and ninety-four full time employees. The brand is carried [117]at 10,000 stores in 68 countries and counts Prince George and Blue Ivy among its famous customers.

BLUE-COLLAR BEGINNINGS

Born and raised in Sydney, Australia into a blue-collar family, Raegan credits her parents with instilling in her a sturdy optimism and strong worth ethic, not to mention no-nonsense family values. This firm foundation proved to be invaluable, spurring her on to a postgraduate degree in business administration and management and a career in sales and marketing.

Raegan had been working in Australia for a while when her then-boyfriend was offered a position in the U.S. by his Australian company. "He asked me if I wanted to move to New York for two years and I jumped at the chance, even though it meant leaving my own career and studies," remembers Raegan. It wasn't easy to pack her bags and leave everything she knew behind, but she did so, and, long story short, she and boyfriend Markos (now her husband) landed in New York in 1997.

THE BUDDING ENTREPRENEUR

Raegan started her American career in sales at The Institute for International Research. A year later she was offered a position at *The Economist*. This new job presented an invigorating environment, nevertheless there was a definite downside: the assumption by some high-brow colleagues that she, a young woman with young children, had limited upward mobility. Many didn't hesitate to tell this to her face. It was extremely humiliating, but Raegan had to swallow it because she loved the general intellectual environment. In fact, only one of her bosses treated her fairly. Condescension to women is a familiar attitude in the traditional corporate world, unlike the world of entrepreneurship. Says Raegan: "Corporate America is still very much a male-dominated arena and I have on a number of occasions been discriminated against in my career in the USA: sometimes blatantly, and other times inadvertently."[118]

Raegan kept at it, working full-time at *The Economist* for over ten years[119] while moonlighting as a budding entrepreneur for the last three. "I have always been competitive," notes Raegan, "I most definitely was born with an entrepreneurial spirit, and after reading many books written by famous entrepreneurs, I recognized a lot of traits in myself that they talk about—especially in childhood."[120] Raegan's entrepreneurial essence is written all over her: vision, confidence, attention to innovative details, and most of all—respect to colleagues she works with. How could they not notice that?

But growing a company from scratch was tough: more stress, longer hours, feeling guilty about the family she felt she wasn't taking proper care of. And then there were the managers at *The Economist* who continually underappreciated her, telling her she needed to be content with her existing role because she had no entrepreneurial ability, that she had better give up her budding business and get back down to earth. "It was never an option to me to not keep on going, even though most of the people closest to me were asking me to stop given the toll they could see it was taking on me."[121]

> Growing a company from scratch was tough: stress, long hours, feeling guilty about the family she felt she wasn't taking proper care of. But Raegan's grit kept her focused.

She worked full-time during the day and, after putting her three daughters to bed at 9pm, built her own business at night. At one point, she hadn't had time to wash her hair for ten days. After finally looking into the mirror at 4am, she fell to the floor in tears of exhaustion. "Have I bitten off more than I can chew?"[122] she asked.

The rules of the start-up game were tough. Raegan was both lucky and cursed to be an insomniac. Staying up at night was no hard task for her. But living on three to four hours of sleep, night after night, put her on an emotional roller coaster. Only Raegan's grit kept her focused.

Raegan managed her setbacks one way or the other, and the rewards followed. She recalls one of her most joyful moments during this stressful period: "It was probably the first time I saw someone I didn't know walking down the street with one of our blankets. Now, I still get a buzz out of it." And she gets tremendous joy when she receives the wonderful letters and emails from moms who love her product. "I am also humbled and honored to hear from moms who have sick babies with heart diseases and canccr, who use the blankets as security during treatment and take the time to write me to tell me how much the blankets meant to them and their babies during this horrible time; it is incredibly rewarding to know that you are having a positive impact in other people's lives. I truly am incredibly grateful to get letters and emails from these women, especially given what they have gone through.[123]

OLDER AND WISER
Coming from English-speaking Australia and continuing in the same profession, Raegan didn't have to reinvent herself. In fact, she says she feels like exactly the same person she was when she left her home, perhaps just a bit older and wiser. She notes that Americans are rather fond of Australians, and believes that her accent has even helped her sales career. "Of course, I had to be aware of certain cultural differences and 'curb' my Aussie-ness a bit when I first arrived, but it was nothing too drastic. Australians tend to be much more direct than Americans, which can get you in trouble if people are not used to you."[124] She continued: "Americans tend to talk around things. Australians just want to get straight to the point."

In time, Raegan came to identify with her American counterparts, specifically New Yorkers. "They get labeled as rude and dismissive," she observed. "But I find New Yorkers really friendly and helpful for the most part. I think the misconception comes from the fact that we New Yorkers are just 'busy,' so it is often perceived as rudeness."[125]

> "My children will be culturally richer for having parents from Australia and Chile. Life and work are all becoming more global, this is nothing but a good thing for me personally and for my children."

Raegan still thinks of herself as "an Australian before an American." Sure, her family happily embraces both the American Thanksgiving holiday and the country's diversity, but she continues to hold onto her traditional values to the extent that Australia Day is celebrated at the New York aden + anais office every year.

"Australia formed me, and Australian is what I am in my heart; I am forever 'connected' by default."[126] She would like her children to preserve the traditions of both Australia and Chile (her husband's) cultures. She makes sure to get the girls home to Australia at least once every two years, and Marcos has also taken them to Chile. "My children," said Raegan, "will be culturally richer for having parents from Australia and Chile. Life and work are all becoming more global, this is nothing but a good thing for me personally and for my children."[127]

THE TENACITY GENE

The enviable tenacity with which she managed her setbacks may cause some to suspect that Raegan carries a tenacity gene. It may well be, as she comes from a lengthy line of people who settled Australia centuries ago and relied on the same tenacity and grit that any pioneer does. According to some cultural anthropologists, that cultural DNA, or a bio-psycho-social-spiritual code that underlies every aspect of our lifestyle and culture and holds it together, is transferable. It's metaphorically similar to our unique biological DNA, although not as clearly defined. Every form of cultural expression is a manifestation of American cultural DNA: our values, sense of identity, work ethic, norms and forms of government, language, arts, and more. This is what immigrants need to make their own as they integrate. In Raegan's case, the tenacity gene, if such exists, has been enhanced by her own immigrant-entrepreneur experiences.

Raegan considers herself to be one of the tough, never-give-up type people. She launched her startup on a combination of personal optimism, professional persistence, and commitment to the product. It's her belief that if economic success is slow in coming, the best course of action is to work that much harder. "This goes back to the entrepreneurial spirit of never giving up no matter what. It most definitely worked for me. I went to market with aden + anais in 2006, at the beginning of the worst recession since the great depression. I had no access to capital and was constantly being told 'No'. If I had not persevered through extremely tough economic times I would not be where I am today.[128] Raegan's success came from perseverance and optimism, not to mention a lot of hard work and a willingness to take risks.

FAMILY AND FEMINISM

A woman with a strong maternal instinct, Raegan grew her business out of her dedication as a mother and her belief in traditional ways of baby care. And she knows that being a woman has helped her in business. She remembers the time when, meeting with a company that wanted to buy aden + anais, the reps happened to mention a "super comfortable" breast pump they had been launching. It struck Raegan that they didn't know what they were talking about. She knew that if any of those men had actually put a breast pump on their own nipple they would *know* there's no such thing as a "comfortable breast pump." The point: many businesses can benefit from being led by women and mothers, because women are the built-in test market for the products they consume.

> Raegan sees no contradiction in being a devoted mother and a feminist.

Raegan always wanted a big family. She has four daughters with husband Markos, and considers the fact that she's raising "respectful, unbiased, globally-minded children"[129] to be her proudest achievement. And yet she sees no contradiction in being a devoted mother and feminist.

Raegan and her family on the terrace of her Brooklyn home; from left: Arin, Raegan, Amelie, Lourdes, husband Markos, Anais

It was the limitations on the advancement of women in America that triggered Raegan's feminist worldview—as she didn't experience any such limitations in Australia. Since coming to the U.S. she has faced down critics who considered her decision to start a family a limiting factor in her career, and has received condescending "advice" that insulted her intelligence and questioned her drive. These naysayers couldn't kill Raegan's spirit, and she doesn't hesitate in labeling this criticism for what it was: sexism.

But Raegan's not naïve. She acknowledges that her work-life balance comes with a compromise.

> I feel that if I didn't have a career I would obviously have more time to dedicate to my family and if I didn't have four daughters I would have more time to dedicate to my career. In spite of that, I do the best I can and feel that neither "suffers" for the other; I just know I could give more if I only had one or the other. Women can have it all, but there is a huge amount of compromise on both sides that goes along with that.[130]

But family always comes first.

> My family is everything to me; it's not an option not to keep that intact. Lots of hard work is what it's all about. If you stop working at a job you get fired, if you stop working on a marriage, you get divorced. A strong relationship with your spouse makes for a strong family unit. It is extremely important to me to keep that intact for the sake of my four daughters.

A WORTHY ROLE MODEL

Raegan Moya-Jones created a very big "something from nothing," and turned an idea into a global retail brand. Being a creative immigrant helped her to identify the gap in the market. Being a savvy salesperson helped her to roll out product distribution. Her vision and general sophistication helped Raegan to propel aden + anais to global brands stardom, creating a new category in the juvenile products industry in the U.S., which in turn, has led to the company creating a number of job opportunities. Her tenacity-and-creativity genes were activated in competitive American environment, strengthening America's own cultural DNA.

Interestingly, it's not an unusual that "passion founders" like Raegan - the very people who are sought for the most authentic ideas and innovations - find themselves at odds with an investor's more profit-focused initiatives. And this is exactly what happened with Raegan in 2018. As the biggest individual investor, she remains on the company board and works with a global law firm, to determine whether she can continue to participate in the direction of the company.

And yet, while Raegan is proud to call herself a self-made person, she never fails to mention those who helped her. "I would not have the success I am today if it were not for other peoples' "help," both large and small. Their support and guidance and their hard work building this business with me has in no small part contributed to my personal success."[131] Raegan Moya-Jones represents a younger generation of immigrant women leaders who are idea-driven, tenacious, feminist, and successful—a worthy role-model for many.

Josie Natori *from the Philippines*

The Proud Leader

Successful global brands don't happen overnight. They take time, talent, creativity—and a lot of entrepreneurial spirit. Fortunately for Josie Natori, she had plenty of each as she moved from an inexperienced island girl, to New York college student, to Merrill Lynch vice-president and, ultimately, to founder of The Natori Company.

> Josie made being a woman an asset instead of a liability—that's the key lesson from her.

A role model who feels a moral obligation to mentor and help other immigrant women, Josie was appointed during the Clinton administration to serve as commissioner on the White House Conference on Small Business; she now sits on the board of the Asian Cultural Council and is active in many diverse organizations. Josie is a woman of intense drive who has always taken a "no boundaries" approach to life. Her success bears that out. Josie Natori[132] crossed continents, surmounted countless obstacles, navigated varying careers, and finally, created the global brand that bears her name.

THE MATRIARCHAL PHILIPPINES

The eldest of six children, Josie was born in the Philippines and grew up in a close-knit family with parents who spared nothing to raise their children well. In Josie's case, that included music lessons. Young Josie was a gifted pianist—so gifted, in fact, that she performed solo with the Manila Philharmonic Orchestra at the age of nine. And yet, despite being born with an ear for music and an eye for art, she was hesitant to make a career as a concert pianist. Proficiency on the piano came a little too easily for her and she wanted to be challenged. She wanted a career in business.

Josie was torn, no doubt about that, and during her years at an all-girls Catholic high school she vacillated between wanting to become a concert pianist and going into business. It was advice from her grandmother that swayed her: "Don't put yourself in a position where you have to depend on anyone," she said. [133] Strong words from a strong woman, and not at all surprising considering the matriarchal society of the Philippines.

CULTURE SHOCK . . . AND THEN ACCEPTANCE

Josie was just seventeen when she moved to Westchester, New York to attend Manhattanville College. What a culture shock that was. The cold winters, the food, even the American sense of humor felt alien to the young girl. Josie was homesick, but she didn't let this didn't stop her from pursuing an education. She graduated with honors with a degree in economics, and the awareness that her dreams were beginning to take shape.

Josie stayed to live and work in the U.S. after she graduated. She liked the American way of life and, like so many young women, the "special energy" of New York City. Not only did she appreciate the anonymity the city offered— "in the Philippines, you sneeze and everybody knows about it"—she recognized a quality of acceptance, a "great tolerance to others being different, or even controversial." [134] So it was that in the big city Josie found she could feel more accepted, included, and independent—free to be the person she wanted to be.

Josie went to work at Merrill Lynch, and quickly rose through the ranks to become the first female vice president in investment banking.

Josie was accepted by merit in the Merrill Lynch upper management team where a woman was a rarity, at that time.

It was while working on Wall Street that she met her future husband, Ken Natori. The couple married in 1972. "I married a Japanese-American, but my marriage was not a factor helping me to integrate, as I was sold on America, and acclimated before Ken came into my life," Josie explains. "I am too advanced and bold in my free spirit to have married an Asian-born Asian. This is why I married a Japanese-American born in the US: he still had the Asian values but grew up here and was more assimilated in the US—so he accepted a strong woman as his wife."[135]

CULTURAL HERITAGE

Josie was very clear on those aspects of her native culture that helped her succeed in the U.S,[136] number one being the westernization of Philippine society and language. Because English is taught in all Philippine schools, Josie didn't struggle with a language barrier. Moreover, with English as her first language and Tagalog her second, she never really thought about her accent at all. The Philippine entrepreneurial spirit with its attendant self-help attitude also aided her, as did the matriarchal tradition that gave rise to her free spirit. Josie always felt equal to men. She was never shy about her ideas or expressing herself, nor was she apologetic about anything, especially about being an Asian woman. "My Asian heritage is an asset to me and that's all that counts."

Josie was exempt from many typical immigrant challenges. Because she had no pre-conceived ideas about Americans, she wasn't disappointed or beset by feelings about what they should or shouldn't be. And in terms of either *going with the flow* or choosing to *swim upstream,* she admits that she "went with the flow—everywhere," while also acknowledging that it helped to have well-to-do parents who had her back. "When I was not too happy at Merrill Lynch, I just left," she said.

> The Philippine matriarchal tradition gave rise to Josie's free spirit. Never shy about her ideas or expressing herself, she always felt equal to men.

Immigrants often have identity issues and the feeling of living in two worlds. This wasn't the case for Josie. "I consider myself Asian-American but am closer to the Philippine culture. The Philippines— that's where my soul is, where my roots are. I feel it strongly."

Hard-working, busy-busy, and always focused on immediate goals, Josie never took the time to even think about the possibility of being discriminated against, either as an immigrant or as a woman:

I never had an issue with being a woman. . . I never doubted I could do whatever I wanted. Gender was never an issue in my career. I got promoted on merit. At Merrill Lynch, I used to say that I counted as two [for diversity's sake]—being a woman plus being an Asian. I made being a woman an asset instead of a liability, and was surprised that they make such a big deal out of this issue in this country."

READY FOR A CHANGE

Climbing the corporate ladder wasn't enough for Josie. Five years after the rising Wall Street star had married (and just one year after giving birth to her son Kenneth), her corporate job was beginning to bore her. She was ready for a change. "I also had a very strong desire to build something myself," she remembers. Together with her husband, Ken, Josie brainstormed a number of entrepreneurial ventures, from opening a car wash to running a McDonald's franchise. But none of these ideas inspired her enough. Only later would she realize that, subconsciously, she had wanted to do something that would tap the resources of her native Philippines.

> Climbing the corporate ladder wasn't enough for Josie Natori. She had the desire to start something for herself.

It was just by chance that she ended up becoming a high-end women's sleepwear designer. The story goes that, trying to find her own way in what seemed to be pitch dark of the business world, almost on a whim, Josie brought a Philippine-embroidered blouse to a buyer at Bloomingdale's—and was encouraged to turn it into a sleep shirt. She took the buyer's advice immediately because it spoke to her heart: bringing the beauty of her native land—its colors and styles and workmanship—and sharing it with America. Her mind was made-up. Her heart and her business were beating in unison ever since. Josie worked hard to develop the ways of applying the idea, and finally found her niche. At the time, lingerie was either lewd or old-fashioned, so Josie formed the mode to fill the space between and create an upscale market that didn't previously exist.

Josie didn't want to be financially bound to other people—and she didn't want the associated risks of outside partners—so she ran her company solo. She invested her own savings and, with help from her parents who financed a factory in the Philippines, mastered her new role. "It's easy to take for granted the amount of work that goes into [making] the clothes you see in stores," she says. "There are so many elements—from the design concept to production—that all need to work in order to make something happen."[137] Josie quit her Wall Street job when the lingerie business took off and has never looked back. Today, The Natori Company has nearly 400 employees and distributes its products through high-end department stories such as Saks, Neiman Marcus, Bergdorf Goodman, Nordstrom, and Macy's.

THE SECRETS OF HER SUCCESS[138]

Josie and her husband honed the production process down to a very efficient system. Designs based on her concepts are formulated at the Natori design center, with Josie personally approving each one before it is sewn into sample. Once the garment gets the ok, the samples are used in her showroom to solicit orders, which are then processed in the company's factory in the Philippines.

Quality comes first, which is why her business mantra is *beautiful, unique, and price-efficient.* It's also why Josie manufactures in the Philippines, as she finds the craftsmanship, quality and handling to be superior there.

Starting with an Asian aesthetic based on a hand-embroidered Filipino blouse, Josie was able to build a distinct brand of lingerie, melding the visual appeals of both East and West. In other words, she produced a fresh product concept. Up until that point, it was common to treat lingerie as simply women's sleepwear. But Josie saw it as fashion. She took risks, to the extent that she based her first collection in orange. With no preconceived notions or dogmas to adhere to, she started with her own good taste, envisioning her customer as a sophisticated woman who buys lingerie as a gift to herself. As Josie put it, Natori is "where life meets art."[139]

> Starting with an Asian aesthetic based on a hand-embroidered Filipino blouse, Josie was able to build a distinct brand of lingerie, melding the visual appeals of both East and West. In other words, she produced a fresh product concept.

Josie treats her products as an evolving business concept—a "moveable feast." When she sensed that she had hit on a highly marketable concept, she expanded it to other product lines. More than three decades after inception, Josie's business grew to include ready-to-wear, accessories, home textiles, bath, rugs, and fragrance. The Natori Company has grown into a lifestyle brand, using an expanded business concept to move forward in an extremely competitive field. This proved to be a good idea: in 2011, the company generated $150 million in retail sales. Today the Natori brand has offices in New York, Manila and Paris, and is sold in forty countries[140]. And it's poised to grow further.

SETBACKS AND SUCCESS

Success is rarely easy. "I had no idea what kind of business I got into when I started my company. The customer is different today; and the internet is a game changer,"[141] Josie said about the constantly evolving rules of business and retail. The new era brings about new kinds of challenges and pitfalls. She remembers the 1983 crisis in the Philippines most vividly:

> One big setback was when old Senator Aquino was assassinated—the chaos occurred in the whole country of the Philippines, and we had to cancel orders for the season which happened to be Christmas: millions were lost because we could not deliver the goods we had promised. Customers

understood the situation though; they were forgiving because that order cancellation was not our fault.[142]

Josie does her best to take setbacks philosophically. And she doesn't take things personally. "Well, ups and downs happen in every business and I accept it as a given: it comes with the territory. I learn from my setbacks; I am positive in general, because, as my father used to say, 'Something good comes out of everything; it's a cycle of life.'"[143]

Well aware that competition is fierce in both manufacturing and in fashion, Josie follows the advice of her father who recently passed away: "I made a choice to be independent, to build my own business, and I take all consequences, good and [not so good]. At the beginning, doing business was easier—then it slowed down, so I had to reinvent the product[144]." Josie has learned to keep in step with the times. That's the essence of her continued success.

GENDER EQUALITY

Interestingly, Josie, a woman of well-deserved fame in the world of female garments and accessories, does not feel a strong attachment to feminist ideas: "I never understood feminism, but in some countries it's necessary, they have to do it to get noticed."[145] Expounding further, she said, "In the Philippines there's a strong matriarchal society—one of the few matriarchal societies in the world. Because of 300 years of Spanish rule, we are more westernized. Then American influence became very strong, and we are much Americanized. Women are more equal and less subdued [146]in the Philippines than they are in other Asian countries."

> A role model by virtue of her achievements, Josie exemplifies d the notion that it's not necessary to be a pronounced feminist to be a role model for other women.

So, according to Josie, because gender equality, the key goal of feminism, already exists in the Philippines, there's nothing to struggle for.

But there's always a personal struggle to wage. Josie has consciously molded herself after strong women leaders such as Margaret Thatcher, Marisa Meyer, and Meg Whitman—women who themselves have decried feminism and exemplify the notion that it's not necessary to be a pronounced feminist to be a role model for other women. Exactly the line chosen by Josie, who herself became a role model by virtue of her achievements.

Josie believes there's a lot left to be done: "I think women made a great progress, but they have way to go. I pity the poor women of Afghanistan; we need to help [them] and also lift other women around the world[147]." Recognizing that many women's issues still wait to be resolved, Josie stands ready to help.

A MORAL OBLIGATION

Josie's leadership qualities are apparent in the way in which she leads her company, and in her expressed desire to help guide others. She feels a "moral obligation" to inspire those who are trying to find their way in life. And she's found ways to effectively lead on several fronts.

"I am trying to be a role model, to the best of my ability," she said. "I feel it is my responsibility to mentor and help. Whatever I can give back, I do when the opportunity arises. We, the immigrant women, need to help each other."[148]

Asians comprise the largest group of immigrants to the U.S., according to the 2010 U.S. census[149], and Josie's efforts to support them didn't go unnoticed. She was the first Asian member on the Board of the Statue of Liberty-Ellis Island Foundation, helping to modernize this important site. She's been recognized by both the U.S. and Philippine authorities, and honored for her achievements with the Galleon award, presented by Corazon Aquino, then President of the Republic of the Philippines. During the Clinton administration, she was appointed to serve as a commissioner on the White House Conference on Small Business—the first such appointment of an Asian woman.

"I love my work, but success in fashion is not enough"[150] confesses Josie. Giving back by sharing her know-how is one way she lives up to her values. Today, Josie sits on the boards of the Asian Cultural Council and the Orchestra of St. Luke's. She also serves on the Fashion and Design Council of the Philippines, helping to get funding, especially for Asian-American artists. She is also an active member of the Committee of 200—a group of female CEOs who provide mentoring and scholarships to other women.

NO BOUNDARIES

A woman of diverse talents and a keen mind, Josie Natori could probably have been successful in any field she chose. It just happened that she revolutionized the lingerie industry with an evolving business concept and a stylized translation of the sophisticated handiwork of traditional Filipino dressing, sometimes addressed as a West-East mix of culture and design.

Josie is an exemplary role-model for all would-be achievers: she came to the U.S. to get the best education possible, and started her own business fairly quickly after that. Today, she is an internationally successful businesswoman who gives back to the community, while taking care to nourish her own talent as a musician. The result: the young girl who played solo with the Manila Symphony Orchestra at age nine turned into the woman who played Carnegie Hall concert at fifty.

Elena Gorokhova *from Russia*

The Breakthrough Author

Elena Gorokhova knows how powerful stories can be. In her 2010 memoir about growing up in Soviet Russia, she made a name for herself by publicly unpacking her suitcase of memories and laying bare her emotional, sexual, and spiritual maturation. Praised for being the "Russian Equivalent of

Elena, deep in thought

Angela's Ashes,"[51] *A Mountain of Crumbs* was followed-up five years later by Elena's second memoir, *Russian Tattoo*, which carved out for the author a respectable place in the American literary landscape.

Elena's work offers a breadth of revelations illuminating the inner make-up of immigrants, the perpetual challenges they face, and ways in which to overcome them. Her story is in some respects typical of many young immigrant women who marry Americans eager to get away from the controlling clutches of their motherlands or their mothers—or both. They marry, take care of a family, and grow professionally, all the while performing a unique balancing act between two cultures. Quite apart from any professional success they may have, these women display an ability and competence in balancing cultures that is itself an achievement. That's certainly the case with Elena Gorokhova.

A PUBLIC AND PRIVATE SCANDAL

Born in Leningrad (now St. Petersburg), to a family of Russian intelligentsia, Elena Gorokhova spent her childhood in a courtyard that was a more accurate symbol for Soviet life than the ubiquitous hammer and sickle: a crumbling façade with locked doors and stinking garbage bins behind them. Elena was ten when her father died, at which point she was raised by her mother alone. Dedicated to tradition, Galina Maltseva was herself a portrait image of Motherland Russia: overbearing, protective, and difficult to leave.[152] Galina was a beacon of discipline, patriotism, as well as Russian tradition. She wanted her daughter to be the same way. Her stern mentality, that of a front-line surgeon during WWII, influenced[153] Elena to a degree she never wanted to admit. Elena's early years were quite typical for people crowded on the Soviet side of the Iron Curtain: communist ideology ruled every aspect of everyday life filled with material stagnation, deficiencies of food and basic manufacturing products—and taboos on the ideas propagated by the "rotten West." Elena could not oppose the way of life she was born into; nevertheless, at age ten she was seduced by the beauty of the English language and studied it with gusto.

> Leaving Russia, Elena left behind a society where people had to queue for hours to buy basic foods, and where she and her friends silently agreed that the communist experiment had failed.

In 1978, Elena graduated from the English Department of Leningrad University and went on to teach English to the next crop of undergraduates. Two years later, to her mother's dismay, Elena married a visiting American graduate student who had come to Leningrad for his semester abroad, and who graciously offered to help her get out of the Soviet Union. Elena felt she had little choice but to accept the marriage proposal.[154] What else could she do but jump at the chance to escape a society where people had to queue for hours to buy basic foods, and where she and her friends silently agreed that the communist experiment had failed?

The marriage caused a public scandal in her University department and a private scandal in her family kitchen.[155] Nevertheless, after six months of family turmoil, Elena left for America with a KGB-ravaged suitcase containing what used to be her life.

CARVING OUT A NEW LIFE

Life in the U.S. presented its own challenges. "I desperately needed someone to explain all this to me. . . . When I first went to the supermarket, I cried because I had no idea what was in front of me. I felt like a three-year-old,"[156] she said. Elena had expected her husband to help her carve out a new life. Robert, however, had assumed that his capable new wife could figure everything out herself. He didn't bother to provide explanations for many American lifestyle details, assuming that they could easily be figured out. But American culture is not easy to navigate for the newcomer.

Elena has since observed that Americans don't judge others—at least not openly. She observed that of Robert, who, she says, "measured movements and calculated words." Elena never had the nerve to ask him what she feared were stupid questions. She felt embarrassed to pester him about things that he assumed to be elementary. "Everything I came across in my first few weeks here—from eating a hamburger to looking for a job—was unexpected and unknown," remembers Elena. "I had no idea how to take a bus; I had never seen a multiple-choice exam; I couldn't buy a pair of shoes. I was an alien, and I felt like one."[157] Elena's gut instinct was that her ignorance, which may have seemed exotic in Russia, looked silly and annoying in the US. A liability rather than a charm.

Americans aren't quick to judge, nevertheless many don't appreciate how difficult American culture can be for the newcomer to navigate.

Luckily for Elena, others stepped up: the man at the bus stop who noticed that she was waiting too long in the Texan heat and told her to wave a hand if she wanted a bus to stop. (Russian buses stop at every stop). The students who showed her how to take a multiple-choice exam—unheard of in Russia. Her mother-in-law, who showed her the simple act of buying shoes.

Elena tried hard to comprehend what it takes to become an American. She found a minimum wage job at a sandwich shop in Austin, TX where she served customers and mopped floors. Still, the slow pace of adapting to her new American reality, not to mention a series of culture shocks and humiliations, hardened her relationship with her husband. It soon became obvious that their relationship was not working. Robert, unwilling to put more of his time and effort into the marriage, sent his young wife to New Jersey, to live with his mother, hoping against hope that time would smooth out the rough corners of their relationship. It worked out for Elena, but not as Robert may have intended, for in New Jersey she met a man who cared enough to invest his time into helping her acclimatize to American culture.

"I think my challenges were mostly cultural," Elena said, looking back through the prism of thirty-five years, adding that she lived in Texas during her first few months here. Quite apart from discovering what America is all about, the Texas melting pot of Southern and Southwestern features, with its peculiar mix of cowboy attitudes and "the bigger the better" assumptions, meant that Elena was in for a "double culture shock."[158]

As is typical of millions of immigrants, Elena's journey was filled with countless everyday mistakes, small humiliations, and an overall loss of dignity. But through perseverance and resilience, she gradually adapted to her new country. Having come from a materially-needy country to a country of abundance, Elena couldn't believe all the choices she faced. When she bought herself a new pair of sandals, for example, she didn't dare to wear them immediately, but kept them in the box. For a former "Soviet" girl, used to shortages of everything including footwear, the brand-new high-quality sandals seemed too precious to be worn in the street. Incidents such as these made Elena think of herself as utterly un-American and even doubt her future.

FINDING HER FOOTING

Elena isn't one to give up easily. She persevered, choosing to stay in her original profession as an educator, teaching English as a Second Language (ESL). To enhance her status as a teacher, she attained an E.D. in Language Education, earning a doctorate from Rutgers University. Working on her doctorate was far from easy, but the academic environment was familiar to Elena, and she loved to study, research, and find solutions. In academia, ideas, hard work, and perseverance play a huge role in student success. Elena had those qualities in full measure. The choice was right for her.

When I asked Elena if her accent affects her teaching English as a Second Language negatively, she didn't hesitate to answer. "It does not," she said. "I feel that everyone in the U.S. has an accent, either foreign or regional. I think this may be the only country where people—most of the time and at least on the coasts—are not judged by their accents."[159] It may be that non-native English speakers make the best teachers for the beginner-through-middle level courses of language acquisition because these teachers went through the same learning processes as their students and know the short-cuts. (For example, practicing conversational patterns by filling out structured substitute wording, which promotes automation of speech habits.) Elena explained that her two languages function as if she has two separate brains: "My Russian brain does the speaking with my Russian friends and sometimes with my daughter. My English brain takes over when it comes to writing. I only write in English. It is my second language, and because I came to this country as an adult, I will always speak with an accent. What I don't know is whether I write with an accent."[160]

COMPARING CULTURES

After more than thirty years in the US, Elena has made some astute observations regarding the differences between Russian and American society.[161] The disparity in material cultures was a shock. Elena never knew she could buy six different types of lettuce, that she could eat raw vegetables, or that people *sip* vodka, rather than *down* it. These external differences aside, she notes that the U.S. puts more value on the individual rather than the collective. In the U.S. each person is a separate entity in his or her own right and not just a cog in the larger machinery. Elena feels that while Russians are more outgoing, inclusive, and warm, she has learned the meaning of social courtesy and respect since coming to the U.S.—values in terribly short supply in Russia. (She's still grateful for the fellow waitress who "adopted her" in New Jersey, helping her understand the general code of taking orders and payments, coping with "strange" client orders, distinguishing the salad-dressings or the sides she never heard of, and even accepting tips.) Nevertheless, despite this courtesy and kindness, Elena finds Americans less emotional. Maybe that's why, when writing about her in-laws, she says that they "smiled reserved American smiles." Of her first husband Robert, she says that his "brain has always been the master of his heart."[162]

> Elena notes that the U.S. puts more value on the individual rather than the collective. Moreover, she has learned the meaning of social courtesy and respect since coming to the U.S., values in terribly short supply in Russia.

When continuing to articulate the differences between Russians and Americans, Elena notes that Russia is a much more intellectual country. Because the Russian people don't have many possessions, they place a greater emphasis on books, theatre, and ideas. Indeed, there was very little distraction in the Soviet Union: three television channels and few opportunities for going out. As a result, people read and had long talks with friends discussing literature, films, philosophy—not to mention the meaning of life. This emphasis on ideas helped Elena focus on important things—such as getting a Doctorate and conducting research—and helped her to become an achiever in her new country.

Cultural differences aside, Elena came to appreciate the American people. Most of all, she appreciates diversity, tolerance of different viewpoints, and democratic process in politics: "Americans are very rule-oriented. The U.S. is a country that lives by its laws, unlike today's Russia."[163] This is what she wanted, and she happily embraces it.

AN INNER DIVIDE

Over time, it became clear to Elena that despite the greater ease of life in the United States, she is ultimately unable to sever all ties with Russia, the lost land of her youth. "Russia will always remain in my blood, and visiting my country and those places where I grew up is something that charges me as a writer. I visit my hometown at least once a year, staying with a friend, visiting the courtyard where I grew up. To lose my Russian connection would be like losing my soul."[164] She believes this split is characteristic of all immigrants and that along with all those who left their countries for other shores, she belongs to neither land.

"Like a spy, I live with two identities, American and Russian—two selves perpetually crossing swords over the split inside me. My American self is freshly cheerful and shiny as a newly minted coin. My Russian self is stale and dark. . . . it broods and ponders . . . about the questions that have no clear answers. . . . The 'American me' is for Andy, his family, and our mutual friends. The 'Russian me' is my inheritance, rooted in my veins from birth. The 'Russian me' is for my mother and my sister and my daughter, my blood."[165]

Elena takes her identity seriously. Today, after thirty-five years in America, she holds that she has become as much of an outsider in Russia than she is in America, because her Russian friends now perceive her as a foreigner. "There is no bridge between the two lives," she says. "There is only a wound, the inner divide of exile."[166]

> "Like a spy, I live with two identities, American and Russian— two selves perpetually crossing swords over the split inside me. My American self is freshly cheerful and shiny as a newly minted coin. My Russian self is stale and dark."

Elena's effort to reinvent herself applied only to her worldly make-up. It hasn't changed who she is. "Moving to America failed to make me a different person … I was silly to think I was hovering on the brink of a brand-new life. I didn't yet know that Russia, like a virus, has settled in my blood and hitched a ride across the ocean."[167] Russianness is deep-seated in countless first-generation immigrants like Elena. But Elena strived for clearer demarcation. On a recent visit to St. Petersburg, enjoying again its radiant air and the arms of its open bridges across the Neva River, Elena said she finally realized that she belongs there no more. Although Elena repeatedly states, "What I don't know any more is where I belong,"[168] deep down she came to comprehend that – after more than a quarter century living on a different continent and speaking a different language – she belongs to America. But Russia's pictorial image is tattooed on her daughter's arms as permanently as it is "tattooed" on her heart. So now, on her regular yearly trips visiting the city of her youth, she knows full well that no matter how long the jet flies eastward, she'll never come home: her new home is back in America.[169] But she keeps going eastward anyway.

FAMILY MATTERS

Elena has been married to Andy, her second husband, for over thirty years. She has been blessed to find a soul mate in him, a person she wanted to grow with and become better for. "What I see reflected in Andy's eyes is a different *me*, the *me* I would like to be."[170] With Andy, she was feeling free, completely un-Russian, and their life-style has been good for both of them. Most importantly, Andy has always been the voice of reason in the family. A professional coun-selor, he helped Elena confront frustrations caused by her mother, saying, "It's really just the luck of the draw. You're dealt a hand of cards when you're born and that's the hand you play. You cannot change that. You have to learn to play the hand you've been dealt. Stop wishing for another hand."[171]

Elena's daughter was born in the US, and as any second-generation immigrant she is essentially American, not Russian. Elena said that for years she tried to control her daughter the same way that her mother had controlled her—history repeats itself—while also agonizing about detaching from her, afraid that their relationship would be a replica of the one she had with her own mother. But as her daughter grew up and became an adult, the two became friends.

Elena's mother, Galina, was big on protecting her younger daughter and taking care of her in her own way, although that was exactly what free-spirited Elena detested. Galina loved her daughter, but she always insisted that she knew best and would never show her warm side. Galina, with her sense of duty and discipline, is typical of women in many cultures, and thought her strictness was in her child's best interest.

Her mother's overbearing presence may have stifled her, but Elena also "felt guilty about shutting her out, resenting that she was always here, a constant witness to every moment of my less than perfect, tattooed life."[172] Galina joined Elena in the U.S. to help with her new born baby—as is customary for grandmothers in Russia. She never left, and for twenty-four years, until her death in 2012, they lived together. While fretting about their relationship, Elena said she never fully understood why she kept her mother at an arm's length, and that their connection had always been dramatic and traumatic.

WRITING HER LIFE

As a writer, Elena started small, occasionally publishing essays in journals and newspapers over a period of about fifteen years. These diverse publications included fictionalized pieces about her childhood and youth in Leningrad during the Brezhnev era. Her essays have appeared in the *Southern Review*, the *Virginia Quarterly Review*, the *North American Review*, *New Letters*, *Colorado Review*, the *Southampton Review*, and *The New York Times*.

> Elena never tried to write when she lived in Russia. Only when she came to the U.S. did she feel the necessity to tell her story.

"I never tried to write anything in Russian when I lived in Russia," explained Elena. "But when I came to this country, I felt the necessity and I allowed myself to write—in English. It took me a few years to learn the English rhetoric."[173] Her transformative moment as a writer came in 2004 at the Southampton Writers Conference and saw that the legendary Frank McCourt was teaching his memoir class. She submitted an application, and got accepted. That class was a new beginning of her as a budding writer.

Elena felt an urge, a necessity to express herself in writing: "I simply had to write, so I kept writing. As Chekhov said, "if you can *not write*, don't." I guess, I couldn't *not* write. I went on writing, and I was fortunate that all this writing paid off and my essays and my book saw publication."[174] Her second memoir about her American life, *Russian Tattoo*, describing her life as a Russian immigrant in the U.S. was published in January of 2015, which makes hers a fairly good track record, right? Its success shows that her best is surely yet to come.

Maya Strelar-Migotti *from Croatia*

The Global Crusader

With her global mindset, Maya Strelar-Migotti knew better than to be domineering. As VP and head of Ericsson in Silicon Valley, she had been on assignment in Australia, Spain, and Sweden, before coming to the U.S. Her American job was to integrate two newly-acquired companies into Ericsson and spur innovation—a daunting task. The Croatian native surveyed the scene and, recognizing the inclusiveness of Silicon Valley, took it even further, creating a *Women in Leadership* group to empower female team members in the male-heavy telecom sector. She refined the company's way of working not just by focusing more attention on employees, but by creating a culture of support and risk-taking, where mistakes are considered a learning opportunity and not a subject for retaliation.

Maya was a tough, never-give-up expatriate. A global crusader for her company's interests, she has always been a culturally-sensitive

Maya, an impeccably inclusive global leader, landed in America.

leader whose efforts have resulted in increased innovation and stronger business results worldwide.

THE PROMISE OF TECHNOLOGY

Maya was born in the city of Zagreb, Croatia—the former Yugoslavia—where, as a high school student, she worked one summer in a computer data center. That was all it took. Intrigued by what computers could bring to the world, she completed her MS in electrical engineering at the University of Zagreb, then joined Ericsson, where she took advantage of the opportunity to work globally.

Maya spent twelve years in software design, market product introduction, and customer support before rising to the top in managerial roles. She gained several years' experience working in Australia, Sweden, Spain, and Croatia—countries in which collectivistic culture prevails over individualistic tendencies. Maya became adept at team-building, and learned how to create a company culture that spurs innovation,[175] while boosting both productivity and the bottom line. With her responsibilities growing, she completed executive management training at New York's Columbia University in 2004 and 2005, and in 2007 received a <u>Ruter Dam</u> certificate for a leadership course. When an internal-Ericsson job opportunity in Silicon Valley presented itself in 2009, she moved to the US.

REINVENTION—AND NO GUARANTEES

Maya likes to pursue novelty, and she was curious about the world-famous creative environment in Palo Alto, CA. Still, even with her prior global relocation experiences, she knew that she would have to reinvent herself yet again in the United States. "It's like any other thing in life," she says. "You plan and God laughs!"[176] Maya was well aware that, in many ways, all she had learned before would have to be revisited as she discovered how things were done in Silicon Valley. She knew there were no guarantees: "I did reinvent myself, and culture, and the ways of working."[177]

> Maya has enough global savvy to know that cultural influence is a two-way street.

Maya had accumulated enough global savvy to know that cultural influence is a two-way street. Not only do expatriates and immigrants acquire some of the culture in their new country, by the same token, their successful integration enriches and modifies the American culture.

> My experience of the US, being here in California, is that the U.S. is a great country that is open to progress and values contribution of hard-working capable immigrants. Without immigrants, Silicon Valley would not be a success. I have been an immigrant worker in four different countries, and there is not a place that is more inclusive than Silicon Valley. I feel great here.[178]

Feeling great at the workplace—feeling included and respected—is key to productivity. Maya extended her personal influence to business-to-business best practices of Silicon Valley-at-large: "A lot of what I have done within my organization has now been copied in other companies; also, I am an advisor to a smaller company that wants to become global[179]." Maya made no secret of the particulars of her direct cultural influence in her own company, specifying that it was along the line of creating a culture of support and risk taking, and making sure that mistakes are taken as opportunities for learning, and not a subject for retaliation.

TOLERANCE AND INCLUSIVENESS

Maya's cultural background in Croatia, where different ethnicities coexisted for centuries (the war in Croatia/Balkans broke-out after she left), certainly helped her understand the different cultures of the countries in which she has lived and worked. She's taken the best practices from her prior experiences—tolerance and inclusiveness—and applied them to her new workplace, starting with the values closest to her heart: creative teamwork culture and women's issues. It was Maya's own way to integrate, and it's never failed her.

In the process of integrating into the all-American culture, Maya was still able to hold onto her core values. Nevertheless, she recognizes the major differences between her own culture and American culture. For one thing, she says, the U.S. "is more gender-traditional than Europe, especially Sweden."[180]

Maya had no language barrier in coming here, as she speaks four languages fluently. In terms of her accent, Silicon Valley at large has developed great accent tolerance, having so many predominantly Asian immigrants. And in a place where diversity is tolerated, and even encouraged——creative, innovative, and talented people thrive. So, it seemed that she came to the right place.

Interestingly, while many in the U.S. complain that our country is not as diverse and inclusive as we would wish (and some surveys[181] place America far from the top on diversity-inclusion lists), Maya believes the opposite is true, that it's actually tougher to assimilate into other countries. That notion is at the center of a lot of current U.S. immigration reform debates. Comparing her own multi-immigration experiences, Maya knows for a fact that an immigrant among the locals can sometimes be a kind of scapegoat-in-waiting—but not here where she is now.

FORGING NEW BONDS

Being successful in a new country starts with making friends, right? Maya made friends with many like-minded people, among them Weili Dai, co-founder of Marvell, and also an immigrant. This isn't unusual. Many residents of Silicon Valley recognize a kind of a social bond that unites all immigrants, regardless of what country they're from. It's the fact that they are not American that unites them. Maya's worldwide expatriate experience bears this out: "Yes there is [a bond]. And that was the case in the other countries I lived in. So, we immigrants belong to "OTHERS," and that makes us bond somehow."[182]

Having said that her core values never faded and that she held onto her cultural traditions, Maya still acknowledged that she has modified her behavior in America. She has learned to adapt to having less privacy and more stress, especially self-induced pressure to achieve goals. Maya believes that "integration is great – you create diversity of thoughts."[183] She's put that same philosophy into practice at Ericsson, where diversity of thought leads to creativity and innovation.

LIFE LESSONS

Maya always liked Americans, and her opinion of them hasn't changed since moving to the U.S. What she likes most is that Americans are "easy to talk to, approachable, and care a lot about community/church/schools—much more so than [the people in the] EU countries where everything is left to government and social management to do. Here people are pulling off so much by themselves."[184]

> Maya is straightforward when it comes to learning from setbacks: "I analyze and see what I can learn, and then I keep the learning and forget the failure."

In terms of societal norms, behaviors, and perceptions, Maya found nothing radically new in America because she had lived in a western society where the basic values and ways of living are very similar. In comparison to other cultures she lived in, characteristically American traits are[185]: being more family and community oriented, as well as being more religious, prude, law-abiding, hardworking, and open.

And yet, despite being so well prepared, Maya's start to her new career in the U.S. was far from easy, as she expected:

> It was tough to come here and integrate several different companies that my company [Ericsson] acquired in Silicon Valley. I didn't have the background in the technology and was not well received by the existing leadership. It took time to get accepted and change the culture of these companies, [for them] to become the accountable members of my global [mother] company.[186]

So, there were setbacks and heartbreaks along the way, but Maya doesn't care to remember them—she'd rather focus on the future. To this effect, she shared one of her strategies for counteracting setbacks: "What helps is that when I define my goals, I also prepare myself for the journey towards them to be very tough, and setbacks and failures are always a possibility."[187] Some call it a pre-emptive strike, including both mental preparedness and having an actionable Plan B.

There's another thing too: Maya views her setbacks as life lessons, and focuses on the learnings rather than the actual setbacks: "I analyze and see what I can learn, and then I keep the learning and forget the failure."[188] It's a survival skill that has served her well through her assignments in Melbourne, Australia, Madrid, Spain, Stockholm, Sweden—and now in Silicon Valley.

GLOBAL MINDSET

Initially appointed as vice president, Head of Development Unit IP & Broadband, in 2009, Maya supervised ten other vice presidents with more than 6,000 indirect reports, including contractors, in North America, Europe, China, and India. She managed research initiatives from five acquired companies, including *Marconi, Entrisphere, and Redback,* and evaluated new technologies and research and development areas, and more.

Highly successful in that role, in 2012 she was promoted to *Head of Ericsson Silicon Valley Site*. In this enhanced position, Maya has dramatically improved innovation at the firm. She created the role of Innovation Director and instituted a new innovation framework (*Ericsson Innova*) – which was later adopted into other parts of the company. She also created new leadership positions, and helped improve overall employee performance by emphasizing motivation, quality, and customer satisfaction. That's what Inclusive Leaders do[189].

THE INCLUSIVE LEADER

Running a successful organization within the culture that you have created, and delivering on the goals that were set for you, requires a great leader. This is especially true in America, where some executives are sure they know best about desired corporate culture and are unwilling to change their ways. It's especially rare when the change comes from an outsider who's also a woman. In America— as elsewhere—a corporate culture can only be achieved by someone who leads from the front, by example, and who appeals to innovative individuals and teams in the organization. In other words, an inclusive leader.

How did her inclusive leadership skills develop[190] in the US?

Ambition: Maya's strong career ambitions—thriving on change and technology innovation—drove her to seek success in the U.S. She relied on her previous management experience, her attention to the people's side of business, her professional connections, and her business acumen. But America demanded more of her sweat equity than other countries: more of her hard work, persistence, and perseverance; more of her street smarts; and more of her charisma.

Risk Taking: Maya's approach to inclusive leadership incorporates risk-taking, a very American trait. This is how she expressed it: "I believe that "blood, sweat and tears" is what a journey to success looks like." Her personal courage revealed her ability to take risks in order to change life and work—for the benefit of all.

Innovation: In May 2013, speaking to a gathering of entrepreneurs at TiEcon, a popular annual tech and networking fest, Maya acknowledged that her innovation initiatives were born out of her own culture shock. She was surprised by Silicon Valley's unique innovation culture, and that spurred her to develop her own culture of innovation.

EXECUTIVE FEMINISM

Maya has made it a point to promote women's equality [191] and fair treatment in the workplace.

While she has been successful in balancing her career with the obligations of her private life, especially thanks to her husband who has always shared family obligations and household work, she makes a distinction between how things are for her, and how they are for other women in her chosen field. Too few in number, overlooked for advancement, often treated unfairly—things are tough for women in engineering.

Too few in number, overlooked for advancement, often treated unfairly—Maya knows that things are tough for women in engineering.

Maya admits that her greatest challenge in the U.S. was gender-based because, in telecom engineering, her peer leaders are all men. She may have broken the glass ceiling, nevertheless, she knows from experience that "being a woman and an immigrant is tough wherever you go, and so it is in the U.S. The U.S. is still much more traditional than Europe for executives, and I have seen this in my work environment." Simply put, Maya is aware that Northern Europe is markedly ahead of the US—and the rest of the world—in providing equal rights for women. That fact was confirmed again by the expert 2014 Global Gender Gap Report[192], ranking the USA #20, behind other rich countries of Northern Europe, Belgium, Switzerland, Germany, and France, to name a few. Still, as a carrier of the flagship corporate standards for women, Maya has instilled her goals on how to combat the women's practical inequality into the culture of her new workplace.

A RESULTS-DRIVEN LEADER

Maya is a results-driven executive who has boosted the bottom line of every organization she worked for. A culture-sensitive, inclusive leader, she introduced cultural change into the companies acquired by Ericsson, thereby uniting employees around her vision and systematically spurring their innovative spirit. She made her distinctive mark as EVP at Marvell Semiconductors and Executive Board Member for ACG Silicon Valley—and her start as a CEO and Investor at 4PIA, Inc., an Artificial-Intelligence-driven predictive analytics company, promises the new contributions to American people and business.

Maya's remarkable loyalty to the companies she works at, their employees, and especially to their female employees, is to be admired.

Rohini Anand *from India*

The Interculturalist Leader

Dr. Rohini Anand is SVP Corporate Responsibility & Global Chief Diversity Officer for Sodexo, one of the world's largest multinational corporations with almost half a million employees in eighty countries. Drawing on her own diverse cultural experiences, Rohini facilitated a more inclusive culture for Sodexo, one better aligned with its business growth strategy. By raising awareness of gender equality, addressing issues of work-life balance, and developing women's careers through mentoring initiatives, Rohini helped this huge company develop a brand that has become synonymous with leadership in diversity, sustainability, and wellness.

Rohini, navigating global cultures comfortably

An inclusive leader and professional interculturalist, Rohini approaches her job as she does her life, with authenticity, resolve, and appealing optimism—highly sought-after qualities among American achievers. Her leadership formula did not mature overnight, but its results make her one of the most brilliant human resource professionals worldwide.

A SOLO VENTURE

Born and raised in Mumbai, India, Rohini was fortunate to have parents who reinforced the message[193] that she could be and do anything she wanted. They resisted their traditionally minded friends who advocated an arranged marriage for their daughter, and encouraged her to attend graduate school in the U.S. So it was that, at age twenty, with a new degree in history but lacking any well-thought-out plan, Rohini did indeed go to the U.S. (Albeit with the notion that an advanced degree might just make for a more attractive arranged marriage.)

> Rohini's journey to attend the University of Ohio marked her first time on a plane. And she did it with only $8 in her purse.

It was unusual venture for a single Indian woman to travel half-way around the world. Indeed, that flight to the U.S. was Rohini's first time on a plane—and she did it with only $8 in her purse. Rohini earned an MA in History from the University of Ohio, then attended the University of Michigan where she earned a PH.D. in Asian Studies. This willingness to take risks and jump across cultures taught Rohini to face challenges on her own, and gave her the courage to deal with events that would follow. After earning her Ph.D., Rohini decided to stay in the U.S. She liked the country and felt that her experiences here had molded her into a different, better person[194].

Now that Rohini has lived and worked here in the United States for over twenty-five years, she is able to reflect back at how her ideas about the country have evolved over time. She remembers that in India people got their ideas about the U.S. from the TV, USAID, the missionaries, and expats with their wonderful stories. Real life is different, of course, and Rohini observed early on that not every-body is well-off in the U.S. She understood that there was plenty of poverty in the U.S., and recalls that, as a graduate student, she would save money by eating Cream of Wheat three times a day so that she could afford the expensive long-distance calls to India.

FAMILY VALUES ALIGNED

Rohini met her husband, Sudeep, while still in grad school. She became acquainted with him through his cousins, whom she had known in India. "Much of the dating was long distance," she said. "Sudeep had graduated with a Ph.D. from the MIT Sloan School, and was working in Connecticut." She's proud that theirs was not an arranged marriage, that "it was clearly a case where our values were aligned."[195] The wedding took place in India in 1982, with both the bride and groom's families present, as dictated by tradition. After the wedding, the couple returned to the U.S.

There's much talk in the U.S. about family values diminishing in the 21st century, but not in Rohini's experience, where mutual respect keeps their family close, no matter the physical distance. Indeed, for Rohini, one of the keys to success has been the shared values and support of her family. Having such a demanding job, she acknowledges much to those close to her, especially her husband, who backs her up unequivocally.

This work-life balance is Rohini's "moveable challenge." which is extremely hard to maintain since it's exacerbated by business travel that can take up to seventy percent of her time. "I'm not a whiner; let's move on and get better at what we do—that's my attitude to setbacks." Easier said than done, perhaps, but Rohini certainly serves as a role model who maintains a work-life balance as a successful woman leader.

SELF-DISCOVERY

For more than ten years, Rohini and her family had one foot in the U.S. and one in India. They even bought electric gadgets suited for two kinds of voltage, reflecting how rooted they were in both countries. That wasn't the case initially, however.

We both wanted to go back to India; and in 1989 we actually did move there—with the intention of staying for good. After staying in India for three years (my husband had a good job there while I was staying home with my small children), we realized that it was not for us. To a great extent, it was about our mindsets that became too American for us to live [and be happy] in India—so we went back, became U.S. citizens . . . because the U.S. felt like home."[196]

Coming from a middle-class family, the lifestyle that Rohini led in the U.S. wasn't dramatically different from the one she led in India, except for one crucial point: "It's in the U.S. that I realized who I am and made some important self-discoveries—really focused on career ... I came into my own in the US."[197]

One of the toughest challenges that Rohini had to face was the perception of herself as a minority. In India, she was exposed to diverse backgrounds, yet the whole environment was homogenous. She may have been surrounded by individuals with many variations in socio-economic class, religion, etc., but all of them were Indian. Immigrating to the U.S. was a truly transformational experience. It was the first time she was identified as a minority and the first time she identified herself as such. This experience prompted the question: "If this can be so impactful for me, what must it be like for those growing up in the U.S.—those who really have the minority identity shaped for them at a very early age?"[198] What is it like for African Americans, "who are a minority in their own country."

Reinvention is hard. It requires changes in life philosophy, values, and even life strategies. And it doesn't happen overnight.

Finding herself in this new role—that of a minority—was a transformative experience for Rohini. And it wasn't all positive.

There was the episode in Canada, for which I was not prepared. When being a student, I went to Vancouver, Canada,

and got my first big culture shock. There is [an] Indian population that settled there a while ago, and they were perceived
negatively by some others—and that negative attitude was
transferred on me. [It was humiliating.] I did not see myself
less than anybody. Why should I feel less than anybody else?
Those local people knew nothing of the other Indian people;
they wouldn't recognize one Indian from another—which was
the reason for the negative stereotyping.[199]

It was her minority experiences—positive and negative—that
brought her to the work she does today. It took courage to recognize and accept minority status, and from there build her life on
this new premise. Reinvention is hard. It requires changes in life
philosophy, values, and even life strategies. And it doesn't happen
overnight. However, Rohini Anand's personal drive impelled her to
do more than reinvent herself, but to discover her true self under
American skies.

AMERICAN VALUES

The notion of belonging had been the theme of my conversation
with Rohini: "This is home; the U.S. is home, not India. I'm comfortable with my culture mix and can navigate cultures comfortably. I
love the sense of the extended Indian community and an associated
support structure. If my family were here, it could change the whole
dynamic for me."[200] One reason: like so many American women,
Rohini realized that "A big part of my identity is my work." Indeed,
this is one of the major reasons that Rohini identifies herself as an
American.

In her usual clear-thinking way, Rohini brilliantly summarized
her family's decision to live and work in the United States:

It was not for the financial reasons that we returned to the US,
not at all. The reason was that American values became more
attractive; our values changed while we were here in America,
and we wanted our daughters to grow up with these important

values as well. The American education system for children was also playing a key role in our decision-making. Most importantly, it was the work satisfaction; I realized that I changed tremendously in America, what I valued had changed – and what I valued most was the possibility to make an impact for what I did, in the workplace.[201]

Indeed, her analytical prowess and willingness to integrate—for her own as well as for her family's sake—have proved to be the main drivers in the long integration process.

ACROSS CULTURES

As a professional interculturalist, Rohini loves comparing her native Indian culture with mainstream American culture. This is what she had to say about her experience: "The Indian culture is community and family-oriented. Everyone's decision is influenced by community and family (and *"who* will say *what* if I do this?)*"* Community and family are extremely important.

"In the US," she continued, "culture has more sense of individualism, along with a single-minded hard work focus and one can find positive and negative outcomes [of that]."[202] To her mind, the common traits of these cultures—such as career ambition, competitiveness, and can-do approach—are evident at first sight and very compatible. These qualities make it easier for Indians to adapt to American culture, even if things are more laid-back in India.

ETHNIC HERITAGE

Ethnic heritage often helps people find ways to adapt and put down roots in a new country. Rohini's experience bears this out. First, her family's focus on academic achievement helped her to choose and then navigate the right career path, Likewise, while Rohini and her husband never pressured their own daughters to be academic achievers, the girls still made it to the Ivy League. Evidently, it's the general spirit of the family, the family orientation that matters.

Nothing stimulates kids to aspire to bigger and better things than the example set by their own parents. If you're looking for a foolproof methodology to influence your children: do it yourself, do it well, and they will follow. There is nothing like leading by example.

Rohini identified the enablers from her culture as: emphasis on academic achievement as a base; drive (the notion that she could be anything she wanted to be); a high level of empathy for people of different backgrounds; her own immigrant experience; the ability to build relationships; and flexibility.

If Rohini's cultural heritage helped her stay on course, being bicultural certainly enhanced her position in a global company. In fact, her dual cultural perspective may have been one of her greatest assets with her company's French clients. Rohini knew only too well how the French and Americans differ in their approach to decision-making, so she helped "build the bridge of understanding critical for business." It didn't hurt that she was hired by the French boss five years before transitioning into her global role. Interestingly, Rohini connects with the French but doesn't speak fluent French. "They trust me," she said. "It became clear to me when I came into a global role that I have a clear cultural advantage.

Obviously, it was Rohini's dual cultural perspective that let her see and accommodate the French perspective on the one hand— and her cultural sensitivity and subsequent trustworthiness that attracted the French counterparts on the other.

> Being bicultural enhanced Rohini's position in a global company. In fact, her dual cultural perspective may have been one of her greatest assets.

Language can shape our perspective, but Rohini said that language was never a problem for her. Because the official languages of the Union Government of the Republic of India are Hindi and English, she learned at an early age how to switch from one language to another. A huge boon to living and working abroad.

Accents can sometimes bring problems to newcomers, especially if the new language is acquired after puberty, as multiple linguistic studies attest. Still, Rohini wasn't concerned. "I have no issue with my accent, and feel comfortable; never knew of a negative reaction to my accent; of course, you don't know what you don't know . . . and who thought what,"[203] she said. It certainly helped that she studied at the University of Michigan which has many international students, or that she lived and worked in cosmopolitan areas, namely Washington D.C., New York, and Maryland. These places are populated by of immigrants of all stripes and cultures, so having an accent is no big deal.

NOURISHING HER SOUL

Rohini's career and family have given her much happiness and satisfaction. "[I]t was choppy at the beginning, with going to India and stepping back staying at home with children, then picking up upon return to the US," she acknowledged. Nevertheless, she faced her challenges undeterred, and prevented them evolving into setbacks. And now she has the accomplishment of a strong career and a loving family, with life-work issues tightly interwoven.

What really matters to Rohini is her community work of all kinds:

> I work with Asian women who are victims of domestic violence. It keeps me connected with the Asian community. In a more ad hoc way -- particularly when my kids were in the public-school system in the Montgomery County -- I worked with ESL students on their basic language skills. This fits - because English was not my first language; Hindi was. There also is a men's shelter where my husband and I cook once a month. It's been an eye-opener [for me] to see the kind of people [who come] there, particularly in this economy. And it's important because I hate to cook. That's the only time I cook.[204]

Nourishing her soul and connecting with the people who really need help has been sustaining Rohini and feeding her inspiration for Diversity and Inclusion work. What's more, she has passed this connection down to her daughters.

> I feel proud that they are such accomplished global citizens, and have a tremendous sense of giving back to the community; they both want to make the world a better place. With our daughters, leading from the front works best—this may be a conversation at our dinner table; to me, they are so accomplished, so caring about society—and we need this in our next generation.

ACCUMULATED CHALLENGES

It is not easy to be a woman in this world; being an immigrant woman compounds the pressure. Rohini is well are of this:

"I bring many skills to the table and want to be perceived for what I am, not be pigeon-holed/categorized as an Indian immigrant woman good for the diversity role. Typecasting as such is frustratingly limiting—and does [no] good for anybody. I've been fortunate with my three bosses, who advocated for me—which opened many doors." But there is another side to this coin, she admits, and wonders if she would have had the opportunity to work in her position if she hadn't been a woman and an immigrant, however sharp and well-prepared for the job. "If I were not an immigrant and a woman, would my potential unleash in a different way?"[205] she asks.

> Early in my career, I toggled between the corporate world, government agencies and education. ... I knew I wanted to go internal. I saw this as tremendous opportunity to make a difference. What closed the deal with Sodexo was my interview with the CEO, Michel Landel. His level of commitment, his vision, his leadership, his clarity on what he wanted to see happen was absolutely unparalleled. ... Michel's big deal has

been diversity. He instituted a scorecard for executive compensation (tied to diversity) against the resistance of his entire executive team.[206]

The company certainly needed her badly. In 2006, Sodexo settled an $80 million class action discrimination lawsuit brought by African-American employees. It was at that time that they hired Rohini as the company's diversity officer. Under her diversity stewardship, Sodexo has received widespread recognition for leadership and equal opportunity. Indeed, it was the only company ranked No. 1 and 2 for five consecutive years on the Diversity Inc. business index of Top Companies for Diversity and Inclusion. Perhaps most significantly, Sodexo won the prestigious Catalyst award in 2012. The company's remarkable culture change has been featured as a Harvard Business School case study[207]. These are the continuing corporate achievements that Rohini helped to make happen.

A UNIQUE PERSPECTIVE
Rohini believes there's nothing women can't do as well as, or better than, men. Moreover, she believes that women add a unique perspective that can enhance a company, making decisions more meaningful and outcomes more innovative. It was certainly the case at Sodexo, where she's been working since 2002.

Today, she wants to work on developing the "influencing skills" of her fellow female employees, helping them become stronger, more confident, and more strategic in their thinking. She also wants to help make female talent more visible globally through sponsorship, consistently helping women to be promoted to top positions in her own company, as well as supporting women's organizations like Global Summit of Women. She knows full well that when it comes to equally promoting women, we as a country have so much work to do: "Now we're behind other countries. There's a huge responsibility for men: we need to move the cycle. Sodexo's goal is to move women-in-top-management from 23% today to 25% by 2015."[208] She did deliver on that promise.

Despite her youth when first coming to America, Rohini has been able to look beyond her personal culture shock that included multiple "un-pleasantries" associated with being a minority in a large foreign country. This capability to understand and sympathize – along with a strategic focus on changing things to the better for all stakeholders of the huge organization - have served her well, and she made it in America as only a truly inclusive leader could.

Ying McGuire *from China*

The Global Leader

Ying McGuire is an innovative global leader who possesses a unique blend of skills and experience. She has built a career in sales, marketing, procurement, operations, and diversity, and earned the respect of colleagues world-wide.

It took courage and stamina, but Ying who started as a pretty shy girl from China grew into a recognized leader in a male-dominated industry. VP of International Operations and Business Development for Technology Integration Group, this energetic woman serves on an advisory board of International Trade Center (United Nation and WTO joint agency); on the board of the Greater Austin Asian Chamber of Commerce; and other organizations like US Investment Advisory Council, promoting international cooperation and social well-being. Quite an array of accomplishments for the timid but ambitious Chinese immigrant with "toddler English."

> Ying, a sophisticated businesswoman, fits the circle of global business leaders as a glove.

REBELLION

Ying McGuire witnessed the Chinese Cultural Revolution in her early childhood. It was a confusing time for her generation, and Ying's rebellious nature pushed her to reach new goals. Her family led a modest living—drawing drinking water from wells, cooking out of coal heated stoves, and watching every Yuan—until they eventually became textile entrepreneurs. Ying helped with the family business and took to heart her parents' high regard for education,[209] graduating from Nankai University, ranked fourth in China.

After graduation, Ying found a privileged (by Chinese standards) job promoting Chinese Tourism to the North American market for a State-Owned Enterprise. But the realities around her were dismal. "In those days, we could not even migrate freely within China. Getting a visa to travel outside of China for a young woman was nearly impossible. Three generations often cramped in a two-bedroom apartment. Our means of transportation was bicycles. You can imagine that my early dream of having a house, a car, and traveling around the world was a far-fetched luxury, to be sure,"[210] remembers Ying.

And then came Tiananmen Square.

The Tiananmen Square Massacre of June 3rd – 4th 1989, and the subsequent months of intimidation, deception, and violence dashed popular hopes for political reform. Shocked by the bloodshed and the blatant violation of democratic principles, the young men and women of China struggled to balance personal agendas. Those who could emigrate, did. Ying was among them. She packed her life in one suitcase and arrived at Los Angeles with $1,000 in her purse. Her family was unaware of Ying's move, until she called them from Phoenix, Arizona.

"Where's Phoenix?" they asked.

And Ying answered, "It is in the United States."

A STEP IN THE WRONG DIRECTION

Ying's progress in the U.S. was painfully slow and her first steps seemed to take her in the wrong direction. Her Chinese credentials didn't count. Her classes for a Master's degree in tourism bored her to death, and she was supporting herself by working for a mean boss at a Chinese-Korean restaurant where she earned less than $10 an hour, including tips. [211] "That was the period of time when I had the lowest self-esteem," she said. "I thought my American dream . . . had died." Nevertheless, she pushed forward and ever complained, even though she "was in a state of despair" for that entire first year.

> Ying's progress in the U.S. was painfully slow and her self-esteem was low. But she pushed forward and never complained.

Ying thought she had found a silver lining when she married an American man of Irish descent. The marriage gave her some sense of stability, and helped her adapt to life in the U.S. She postponed her graduate studies to start a family and became a full-time mother and "desperate housewife"— taking several years off to look after her children. Ying was devoted to her family, but that couldn't protect her from a measure of unhappiness.

> I sobbed when family members and dear friends' lives were taken in extreme circumstances; I was disgusted when people you helped turned their back to you for their personal gain; I worried when my children were injured in sports . . . One of the worst times [I] was to go through [was a] divorce and a fierce child custody battle—all the while trying to prove myself in Corporate America in early 2000's. I grew up in a traditional and conservative family. Divorce was not in our vocabulary. I had to act against my belief in the pursuit of happiness and growth. I overcame it. . . . I received a tremendous amount of support from my family and friends during that period of time. [212]

Ying found help and compassion not just from her near and dear in China, but from her American colleagues and friends who offered a helping hand when she needed it most. Their combined kindness helped Ying to truly appreciate America:

> After I lived there for a few years, had the opportunity to pursue further education, traveled in several continents, and gave birth to my two children, I realized there was no better place in the world to call home. Ample space and opportunities, respect for privacy and individual rights, warm and compassionate people with appropriate etiquette, advanced technology, affordable living, fair competition, high service standards, appreciation for diversity, and more - make America a great place to live.[213]

COMMUNICATING BEYOND LANGUAGE

Initially, Ying was able to speak, read and write only limited English. And because she was taught British and not American English (it's British English that is taught all over the world, China included), she was at an even greater disadvantage. "A toddler's English was superior to mine," she said. "I could not understand American slang and had a tough time comprehending American humor."[214] But she persevered, taking a part time job as a reservation sales agent for an airline. This forced her to speak without worrying about mistakes, and resulted in accelerated learning.

Ying's accent and the initial deficiency in English limited her ability to communicate effectively at work—an issue common to all immigrants. She compensated with passion and personality. What's more, she had the ability to connect with people from diverse backgrounds, and that encouraged people to look beyond her accent. Charming, eloquent, earnest, and insightful, Ying found a way to communicate despite her language and accent barriers.

> Ying's poor language skills limited her opportunities. But she possessed the ability to connect with people from diverse

backgrounds, which encouraged people to look beyond her accent.

It took her years, but today Ying has few language impediments. "One morning," she remembers, "when I woke up and realized I had a dream in English instead of Chinese, I knew I had crossed a major language hurdle and hit a significant milestone." And more: "A few years ago at the World Export Forum, I shared the podium with high-ranking ministers from various English-speaking countries. I received accolades for a strong impactful speech from this same group. It was then that I truly realized my accent was not a limitation but just a unique signature[215]." Her commitment to continuously improve her English is exemplary.

CHALLENGES ABOUND

Success in America comes with considerable stress. Challenges abound, and life can be particularly tough for single immigrant mothers, many of whom are stigmatized. So how did Ying deal with setbacks? "I do not swallow my tears," she said. "I grieve about it, talk it through with my family, mentors or trusted advisors, think about positive aspects of setbacks, remember the lessons learned, and move on. ... [Often], failures lead to opportunities and lay a good foundation for success."[216]

It took her quite a while to develop this philosophical attitude. She used to be more of a softie, but America has made her tougher, more committed, and better able to rally people around her to stay on track. Of course, there were life-altering moments.

> When my children grew a bit older, I became involved in the local Asian community in Phoenix. I was the director of the Arizona Cultural Summer Camp [for] one year. At the camp opening ceremony, when I stepped off the podium after my first public speech in both Chinese and English, a prominent business and community leader came up and said: "Ying, I think you are very talented and you need to expand beyond

your housewife role, have a career, and maximize your potential. You will be a corporate vice president one day.

His words struck my consciousness and hit home. Apparently, he saw something I did not see about myself at the time. I began to think about ways of transitioning to [become] a professional and a leader. A few months later, I picked up a GMAT training book, studied for one month, took the GMAT test, and applied for the MBA program at the Thunderbird School of Global Management, the leading graduate school for international management. Prior to graduation, I was offered four jobs including two opportunities with Dell Inc. in Austin, Texas.[217]

Thus, the unexpected encouragement became a wild card affecting her priorities and turned out to be life-altering. Ying's newly inspired confidence led her to overcome what looked like a desperate housewife's dead-end.

MAKING THE TRANSITION

While the vast majority of immigrants have to reinvent themselves in the USA, some need to make a greater effort than others. It all depends on occupation, education, and culture. Ying had to reinvent herself big-time on all counts: she was involved with the tourism and textile industries in China but transitioned to high tech in the U.S.; she had a BA from China but had to complete an MBA to qualify for good jobs in America; and to top it all off, she came from a culture remarkably different from mainstream U.S. culture.

Coming from a top-down, teacher-centered education system, Ying had to make the transition to an educational approach that emphasizes analytical skills, individual opinion, critical thinking, and personal choices. And she had to become more assertive.

That's why she had to start reinventing herself almost immediately: learning a new language while adapting to a different culture, lifestyle, and a new way of learning. Ying spent most of her youth in top-down guru-teacher-centered education, a system that emphasizes memorization. For her, as for many Asian students, it was hard to make the transition to an educational approach that emphasizes analytical skills, individual opinion, critical thinking, and personal choices. Essentially, Ying had to change her ways from conservative and reserved to vocal and assertive. Easier said than done, but she did become a confident public speaker, leading by word and voice, along with leading from the front, by example. This "new" Ying was increasingly more poised to conquer corporate America.

FROM CULTURE SHOCK TO CULTURAL INTEGRATION

Ying experienced severe culture shock when she immigrated to the U.S. It was more than just the unfamiliar customs, clothes, conversation, and food. That she expected. What she didn't expect was to feel like an alien in her own skin. Ying had grown up within a hierarchical structure of business, academia, and social life. In China, children are expected to obey their elders at all times, and students are expected to show deference to their professors. That's the time-and-culture honored rule. In contrast, American culture encourages greater fluidity between groups of employees and superiors, children and adults. Ying was often shocked by the manners of her fellow students. "I almost fell off my chair when I came across a fellow student at Thunderbird [University] who verbally challenged our professor with a lollipop in his hand during a class, and made the professor turn red and lose face."[218] From Ying's perspective, that student got away with murder.

Raised to value group cooperation, Ying had difficulty with a culture that places a high premium on individualism and self-reliance. According to the Chinese high-context culture which prescribes humility and extreme modesty, you should never praise anybody directly as it may cause embarrassment, nor should you accept even a well-deserved gift or compliment right away. "When my neighbor told me I was the smartest kid on the street," remembers Ying, "I had to contradict him, instead of saying 'Thank you.'"

Ying was raised to be both humble and indirect. Self-promotion is unthinkable in China. Likewise, direct conflict or—God forbid—confrontation is highly discouraged. Harmony and harmonious relationships are the treasured cultural values, and showing respect is more important than telling the truth. Compare that to American culture that rewards people who speak their minds openly and challenge others.

Still, despite the differences, Ying found many advantages in her native culture.

> Strong work ethics, discipline, and the relentless pursuit of excellence helped me overcome obstacles and make progress over the years. I watched my father work around the clock voluntarily for many years in China. He never complained about his work load. His satisfaction came from the amount of impact he made on people around him. ... Although he was retired from his school job for many decades, people still remember him as a selfless leader. Two years ago, I returned to my elementary school in a little town of China to speak at its 100-year anniversary celebration. The audience raised the roof with their warm applause and they shouted: 'That is Mr. Shen's daughter! Like father, like daughter! We are proud of you!'[219]

Certain limitations of her cultural heritage delayed her success in America, and Ying is well aware of that:

> Humility is a well-regarded virtue in the Chinese culture. In my early years in corporate America, I downplayed my achievements while my American colleagues confidently and frequently talked about their achievements, contributions, and results. The management team perceived me as someone in a supporting role, not a driver. My cultural behavior impacted

my career in my earlier years and delayed my promotion in large corporations.[220]

But Ying made an enormous effort to "Americanize" enough to overcome her culture-bred humility and stand in line with her co-workers. She's broken free from the bonds of humility and is now very vocal about her achievements and contributions.

NATIVE CULTURE: AN ASSET AND A LIABILITY

A well-known—but not universally accepted—belief holds that while immigrants are influenced by the mainstream culture they struggle to fit into, they also influence it from their end. Ying has some thought on how her cultural make-up and results-oriented perseverance influenced her American-born friends:

> I believe my fellow Asian immigrants brought new skills, unique perspectives and ways of thinking, and of course, outstanding food to this country. We demonstrated our family values, strong work ethics, and our ability to conquer the unknowns and succeed with limited resources. We are rugged, hungry, and would do whatever it takes to seize the opportunities this great nation has to offer. That mentality and behavior greatly impacted the American culture and helped Americans to compete with their ruthless counterparts in emerging economies.[221]

On a personal level, a fairly self-analytical Ying knows that her basic strengths—work ethics, education, and pursuit of excellence—are in her cultural DNA. She also knows that these good-for-business values are contagious: "People around me were impacted in a positive way." Indeed, Ying's personal influence goes far beyond the work place, and here's why.

Taking prominent leadership positions in the local communities, becoming the president of the Greater China Club at the Thunderbird School of Global Management, and serving on the board chair of the Texas Asian Chamber of Commerce in mid-2000 in Austin Texas, Ying developed a rapport with people from diverse social-economic backgrounds while also rallying them toward common goals. She led teams of volunteers to organize cultural and commerce events, and to build collaboration among diverse constituents. Through these events, participating native-born Americans expanded their understanding of the rich Asian culture and heritage, and by the same token, obtained access to business opportunities in Asian countries—a worthy goal all round.

Here's one example of such community cultural education. Ying likes to celebrate major Chinese holidays. To share the spirit of Chinese lunar New Year with the locals, she led a team of volunteers of the Texas Asian Chamber of Commerce in organizing the annual Lunar New Year Gala. It became a well-attended event in Austin, held with participation of business and political leaders in the community. So, growing mutual cultural understanding and getting stronger because of it are doing well in Austin, TX.

BECOMING AMERICAN

After interviewing fifty immigrant women leaders as well as countless other immigrants, I maintain that it's necessary to integrate to be a success, both professionally and personally. In my opinion, being Americanized equals being well-integrated and successful. That's all there is to it.

As far as Ying is concerned,

> Becoming an American is beyond passing the citizenship exam; taking a citizenship oath; singing the National Anthem; getting a US passport; going to a happy hour with co-workers; watching a football or baseball game; or eating a hot dog, or apple pie; and driving a Chevy. Becoming an American means being free and unafraid to express your whole identity, explore your full potential, and capture opportunities while obeying laws and defending the United States Constitution. Becoming

an American means you should go vote and exercise your rights whenever you can; travel freely to explore the world; embrace diversity and treat people as equals. Becoming an American means you need to get involved and make impact in the community you work and live.[222]

Ying considers herself very Americanized and for good reason. She is an independent and creative thinker who speaks her mind. She volunteers a lot of her time and resources for the well-being of the community, and makes a point of connecting with people from diverse socio-economic backgrounds. To top it all off, said Ying, "My friends, family, and business associates in both the U.S. and China told me that I have Americanized: the way I dress; the confidence I developed; the individual opinions I express on important matters; the directness in my communication; sense of humor; and more. I think I adapted and feel well suited in this society."[223]

That said, she is candid when talking about discrimination. "During the first five years of my life in U.S., once in a while, I felt I was discriminated against as an immigrant by culturally-insensitive people who typically did not have higher education and had never traveled outside of the U.S. Today, I surround myself with well-travelled, open minded and progressive individuals. Discrimination is no longer an issue in my life." So, after she realized that discrimination is a fact of life, she put it in perspective, and found her own way out—to pick the company of progressive-minded individuals. End of story.

LEADERSHIP
I asked Ying what makes her a leader:[224]

- I can translate my vision into goals, objectives, actions, and milestones. I can inspire and mobilize a group of people to support my vision and help me carry out actions.

- People often say that I am inspirational in words and actions, and my passion and energy are contagious.

- I care about my team members but use my accumulated knowledge, instinct, and insights to challenge them to think harder and stretch themselves to reach for more. I keep our people on their toes and do not allow them to get too comfortable for too long. I believe when you feel uncomfortable, you are learning and making progress.

- I am a candid communicator and also open and willing to receive feedback and act on good feedback and ideas.

CROSSING CONTINENTS, CROSSING CULTURES

It's rare that someone achieves success in several different professions in one lifespan, especially someone who has overcome the challenges of crossing cultures and continents. That's what makes Ying McGuire so exceptional. Optimistic, casually elegant and business-focused, she contributed to America's well-being and culture while skillfully navigating the many obstacles of her new country.

Ying McGuire reinvented herself as an outspoken, confident, calculated risk-taker, leading her colleagues from the front. She possesses the stamina necessary to combine a demanding leadership job with being an involved parent active in her community. She started her American career from scratch, rising to the top of her game in a global high-tech company, in a heavily male-dominated industry. And she did it all while embracing America on her terms.

Ivana Trump *From The Czech Republic*

The Intelligent Outlier

In the spotlight for over thirty years, Ivana Trump is a household name. In fact, in 1989 her name actually did become a U.S. registered trademark. Ivana was a press magnet even before her much-publicized divorce from husband Donald, but American mass media, with its love of the rich and famous, created an image of her as a foreign-born trophy wife, the beauty who formed the perfect background to her real estate mogul husband. While it may seem that Ivana made it in America the old-fashioned way—by marrying a millionaire—her continued success was the product of intelligence and tenacity, not to mention a strong work ethic and sturdy values.

Ivana, a businesswoman in her own right

A SOLID BEGINNING

Born in Czechoslovakia (now Czech Republic), Ivana Marie Zelníčková was the only daughter of her middle-class parents. Her father was an excellent sportsman who nurtured her skiing talent at a very young age. Says Ivana: "At the age of six, I joined the ski circuit and won the first downhill race I competed in . . . I skied competitively through high school and continued competing after I graduated."[225] Her specialties were downhill and giant slalom.

> Ivana Trump's father put her to work on the assembly line in a shoe factory, so she could see what her life would be like without intellectual achievement.

Her lifetime interest in sports has given Ivana a firm grip on discipline and an understanding of the value of teamwork, not to mention the most essential of all talents: the ability to count on her own strength and survive. In school, however, Ivana was a poor student—until her father put her to work on the assembly line in a shoe factory so she could see what her life would be like without intellectual achievement. He proved his point. Ivana got her act together and applied her smarts to schoolwork, especially math.

Life in post-war Czechoslovakia was tough, as it was everywhere under Communist rule. Ivana became adept at maneuvering through the cross-currents of daily living and politics. As a child, she tended to be quiet and controlled, even reticent; a necessary survival skill under the Soviet Big Brother. Such was the backdrop for Ivana's coming of age. It was around this time that she caught the attention of one of the best skiers in Czechoslovakia, George Syrovatka, a student in Prague. They fell in love, and Ivana became a student too, earning her Master's Degree in Physical Education and Languages from Charles University

THE PROMISED LAND
When George moved to Montreal, he invited her to follow. Easier said than done. Ivana had to marry and obtain a foreign passport[226] so that Communist authorities would not consider her a defector. Otherwise, she wouldn't be able to visit her family. Canny Ivana immigrated to Montreal, then dissolved the marriage.

Montreal was a gateway to the Promised Land, the perfect

stepping stone between the Old and the New World, with a large enclave of minorities and an international milieu. Ivana worked as a model in Montreal for five years. Audrey Morris, the agency owner, was impressed not only with Ivana's natural beauty but also with her poise, grooming, quick-study ability, and strong work ethic.

Remembers Ivana:

> I began modeling for Audrey Morris, a top modeling agency in Montreal at the time. In the summer of 1976, my agency sent several models to New York to promote the Olympic Games held in Montreal. A night on the town led us models to an overcrowded, trendy restaurant where we were immediately seated at a special table; compliments of a man named Donald Trump.[227]

The Canadian models were very pretty, and Donald had certainly met many slim blondes with bright red lipstick. But he was captivated by the young Czech. Norma King notes in her book *Ivana*, that it was "her interesting international background, and a kind of built-in sophistication that gave her an obvious edge over many untraveled and unworldly people."[228]

Ivana was a beautiful outlier: she seemed to possess some natural advantage through her birthright, upbringing, and life story. Indeed, many people noted that Ivana's value-add has always been her presence and international flare. Additionally, her accent made her unique too, this "international bouillabaisse" of words, phrases, and sounds that charm as well as mystify and confound the average gourmet conversationalist.

Fascinated, Donald Trump started calling Ivana, travelling to Montreal from New York, inviting her to meet his family—and finally committing to her, because, as Norma King put it, "he was searching for character and attitude as well as intelligence, in the woman he would share his life with." Not to mention that "she was a mirror image of him"[229] in a number of ways: solid middle-class values, bold chic, persistence, pragmatism, and adaptability." At that time, the name Trump conveyed no magic or controversy. Donald was just a rich developer, the son of another rich developer. But he had a vision for his entire career. He proposed marriage on the ski slopes of Aspen, Colorado. Raised to desire a husband, family, and children, Ivana accepted.

INTO AMERICA ON A WHITE HORSE

Ivana married Donald Trump in an extravagant society wedding. "We were married in 1979 and after a year of marriage, Donald Jr. was born. Over the next five years, I gave birth to two more children, Ivanka and Eric,"[230] recounts Ivana. But stay-at-home parenting didn't last long. Their married life was typically in overdrive; Donald constantly wanted to show off his wife, while she was eager to learn about and fit into American culture. They became leading figures in New York high society and business during the 1980s. And then Donald called Ivana in to help in his business.

> Ivana had an unmistakable taste for all things rich, and her design skills had the Midas touch. And yet, despite the ostentatiousness of her design choices, people felt uplifted by the kind of comfort and luxury that she represented.

Since Ivana was skilled at decorating their Central Park apartment, Donald put her in charge of interior design at the Trump organization. He recognized that his wife had an abundance of natural talent and, practical as he was, put this talent to work.[231] Some people perceived Ivana as just a titular head of these projects, and assumed that she was in place to ensure family representation in the different ventures. Nothing could be further from the truth. Donald Trump is a pragmatic businessman who would never entrust anyone with such a crucial role unless he was 100% percent sure of her abilities—even his wife.

Ivana set to work on several massive projects.

> While married to Donald, I became the VP of Interior Design for the Trump organization. I was responsible for all of the interior design of Trump's real estate; The Grand Hyatt Hotel, Trump Tower, Trump Plaza Hotel and Casino in Atlantic City where I supervised construction, interior designed and eventually managed the project. I was CEO and President of Trump's Castle Hotel and Casino for 5 years and then the CEO and President of the Plaza Hotel, NY.[232]

Ivana took her job seriously, creating bold and beautiful interiors that wowed the public. She had an unmistakable taste for all things rich, and her design esthetic echoed the Midas touch. Despite the ostentatiousness of her design choices, Ivana won over public opinion. People felt uplifted by the kind of comfort and luxury that she advocated. Donald recognized the value of Ivana's instinct, and spared no expense to make her ideas come to life.

She played several major roles in the Trump organization. As Vice President of Interior Design, she spearheaded the signature design of Trump Tower. Afterwards, she served as CEO and President of Trump Castle Hotel and Casino. Managing the Casino was like running a small city—with over 4,000 employees with a payroll of $1.2 million per week. Ivana learned on the go how to manage projects and people. "My biggest challenge," she said, "was to motivate."[233]

With many competitive casinos nearby, there was little margin for error. Ivana signed every check and every receipt, re-trained and re-groomed personnel, redesigned interior and uniforms—all while coming down from New York to New Jersey several times a week. "I am not tough, but I am strong. You can't be a pussycat,"[234] said Ivana. As a result, the Casino went up in the ranks and became the third among ten rivals.

In the late 1980s, Ivana decided to leave their Atlantic City casino. She'd planned to devote more time to her family—but Donald empowered her to oversee the restoration of the landmark Plaza Hotel, and she became its CEO and President. Under her leadership, the Plaza was recognized as the "The Best Luxury Hotel in the USA" and she was named Hotelier of the Year in 1990[235]. Ivana's work at the Plaza would be the zenith of her work within the Trump Organization.

A TRADITIONAL WIFE,
A TRADITIONAL WORK ETHIC

Ivana has stated that she is not a feminist, even though she might do things that fit the definition: "I am a very traditional European wife . . . I like it that way. I have to have a strong man, not someone I can just ride over. This is my upbringing."[236]

When Barbara Walters came to interview Ivana, she noticed the framed one-dollar check on the wall of her office, Ivana's "official" salary for one year. The salary was a joke, of course, but in Walters' report, it evolved into a phrase attributed to Donald Trump: "I give her a dollar a year and all the clothes she can buy."[237] The same joke was repeated when Ivana was appointed President at Plaza Hotel. "Donald got a beating from all feminists around the country," Ivana said. Nevertheless, she took it with a grain of salt—until, that is, Donald's divorce attorney brought it up as evidence of her professional incompetence.

Ivana, who was raised in a hard-working, middle-class family, says of her work ethic: "I really don't do anything much different than I used to in Czechoslovakia. You know, there, everybody works. And it's the upbringing, you know. I never knew anything different from working. ... I can't sit at home and look up at the ceiling."

Ivana credits her hard-working, middle-class family with her work ethic.

Norma King described how the tire on Ivana's car blew out on her way to meet a friend in Connecticut. Instead of calling for help, Ivana rolled up her sleeves, retrieved the tire iron, wrench, and changed it herself—all in the interest of time. Says Ivana, "My father always raised me like a boy . . . so changing the tire is one of the things that you just do . . . Everything that has engines, I am good at."[238] Useful skills and positive attitude for an engineer to pass on to his daughter.

Creativity, intelligence, and diligence are all part of Ivana's make-up. Not to mention always giving 100%. She's been endowed with an enormous amount of energy, and she needed it to manage her large work load and take care of her family and herself. It took a toll, however. Towards the end of 1990 she was exhausted. And Donald was looking around.

Rumors circulated that Donald was having an affair with a former Georgia beauty queen. Ivana had her suspicions, but she put up a brave front for her family's sake. Nevertheless, the couple drifted apart. Alas, the private became public when, on a Christmas vacation in Aspen, Colorado, Marla Maples confronted Ivana on the ski slopes. Their altercation was reported in the press as a celebrity cat fight. "My marriage and troubles were printed on the covers and front pages of publications elsewhere," remembers Ivana. The Trumps separated. In 1991, Ivana, feeling deeply wounded and fed up with lies, filed for divorce, seeking more than had been set out in her prenuptial agreement. Donald fought back in court, protesting Ivana's claims that she had contributed to the Trump organization. The facts, however, spoke against him.

The divorce battle was a holiday gift for the media, fueling extensive pieces in the gossip columns. Ivana emerged with a substantial settlement. Sealed by the courts, the settlement was estimated at $20 million, plus the $14 million family estate in Connecticut, a $5 million housing allowance, $350,000 annual alimony, all her jewelry and, partially, the family home in Palm Beach. The settlement made it easier for Ivana to start her own successful companies.

REINVENTION

The spotlight was on Ivana after the divorce, but she had an iron will to survive and thrive. Indeed, the challenge fueled her deep-seated "I can do anything better than you" attitude. She rose to the occasion, reinventing herself[239] as an independent woman and a businessperson. Having honed her skills at Trump Organization, Ivana had sufficient business savvy to run her own two successful companies. Indeed, she was coming into her own, little by little.

Ivana built her businesses upon her strengths and core interests: being a celebrity with a unique fashion style. She also demonstrated how deeply integrated into American business fabric she was, by organizing Ivana, Inc.[240] to manage her PR and appearances, and Ivana Haute Couture[241] to markets her products. Ivana Inc. matured into a multi-million-dollar business. Ivana Haute Couture uses design in conjunction with Italian cameo sculpting firm M+M Scognamiglio. Her clothes and cosmetics may be regarded as over the top by many, but she sees them as practical. Says Ivana: "I have been working on new products and just love being involved with work. It keeps you energized, interacting with others, learning new skills. I am sure it might be good to retire, but as the wise saying goes . . . when you love the work you do, it will never be a job. And I just love the work I do, all the traveling I get to do."[242]

Ivana has continued to blossom. A sought-after speaker, she gives speeches about female athletes and about being an entrepreneur. Her motivational speech, "Women Who Dare" is about having confidence in ourselves as we balance life as a mother, wife, executive, and a woman who also needs to take care of herself. And because her talks are all based on her personal experiences, many of her speeches are about being a mother—a very important role in her life. In addition to her speaking engagements, Ivana is a successful writer. Her best-selling books include the novels *For Love Alone*[243], and *Free to Love*[244], as well as a self-help book, *The Best is*

Yet to Come: Coping with Divorce and Enjoying Life Again[245] as well as 2017 book *Raising Trump.*

A SYMBOL OF STRENGTH AND SOPHISTICATION

Being an immigrant woman is not easy even in the best of circumstances, even for those who end up becoming rich and famous. Ivana's is an extreme case of the issues plaguing all immigrant women, rich and successful included. Because of stereotyping, she was automatically under-appreciated as an executive for the Trump Organization, but carried on anyway and achieved great success. Still, the fine balance of work, family, and taking care of herself as a woman was hard to achieve—and even harder to maintain. A bold outlier, Ivana just had to do more than the average Jane, which she did, successfully integrating into the unique American culture.

Sophie Vandebroek *from Belgium*

The Life-Work Rainmaker

Sophie as judge at the first Robotics competition.

A life-work rainmaker makes no secret of how she got to the corner offices of great companies.

It was the summer of 1996. Sophie Vandebroek's three children needed attention. Her job was as demanding as ever, and tragedy had just left her a widow. The thirty-four-year-old had no choice but to move on. That meant facing the death of her husband and caring for her devastated children, all the while coping with the day-to-day drudgery and demands of her career.

Twenty-something years later, Dr. Sophie Vandebroek became Corporate Vice President, Chief Technology Officer, and President of the Xerox Innovation group, leading what are arguably the best tech industry research labs in the world. With fourteen U.S. patents to her name, Sophie has been inducted into the Women in Science and Technology International Hall of Fame.[246] Later, Sophie returned to Boston as VP Emerging Technology Partnerships, to lead key strategic initiatives at IBM.

And now the mother of six (she added three step-children to the mix), inspires, encourages, and supports other women to pursue careers in the high-tech industry by sharing the very strategies and tactics that comprise the "life-work frugal innovation" that she came up with in order to maintain a life-work balance—and her sanity.

GREAT EXPECTATIONS

Sophie grew up in Leuven, Belgium, one of four children born to an engineer father, and a poet and artist mother. Education and technology were highly prized in this family, so it wasn't surprising when, upon watching the television broadcast of the American moon landing, seven-year-old Sophie decided to become an astronaut.

Like many Belgian children, Sophie was raised with strict rules. No matter the achievement, she was encouraged to reach higher and do her absolute best. She grew to be a confident and ambitious girl whose top priority [247] was a college degree. "Academic success was believed extremely important for making it in life," Sophie said. "Getting an engineering degree and going to graduate school was valued very highly in my culture when I grew up."

Sophie exceled in her studies and earned her Bachelor and Master's degrees in electro-mechanical engineering from KU University in Leuven. Her academic excellence earned her an invitation to attend Cornell University, in pursuit of a doctorate degree in electrical engineering. Earning a Fulbright scholarship certainly helped.

SUCCESS AS PLANNED

Sophie had long been fascinated by American achievements such as the moon landing and the invention of the microchip. She was impressed with the scientific capabilities of American universities, so coming to America was like a dream come true. She and husband Bart Vandebroek, an engineering classmate also from Belgium, arrived at Cornell University with two scholarships, four suitcases, and $500 between them.[248]

The beautiful university town of Ithaca, N.Y. served as the perfect start for the couple's academic adventure; they quickly felt at home among many other international graduate students and professors in Cornell's international environment. Upon graduation, both Sophie and Bart found good jobs and decided to plant roots in the U.S. Bart started working at Electronic Navigation Industries in Rochester, also in Upstate New York.

> Sophie had long been fascinated by American achievements such as the moon landing and the invention of the microchip. She was impressed with the scientific capabilities of American universities, so coming to America was like a dream come true.

Sophie, however, went to work at IBM's research center in Yorktown Heights near New York City. This meant driving seven hours to work each Monday morning, and returning home each Friday night. After her second child was born, IBM allowed Sophie to telecommute. But she jumped ship when Xerox Corporation, headquartered in Rochester, offered her a job in their fantastic research lab. The couple bought a house, and everything was proceeding as planned.

INTEGRATION AND ACCEPTANCE

Integration was pretty easy for Sophie. The large number of international students at Cornell University helped, as did the region's diverse high-tech workforce. Her doctoral adviser, an immigrant himself, helped his students integrate into the U.S. to the extent that he would invite them for major events or special US celebrations to his home. At her first job at IBM research labs, most researchers and managers were immigrants as well, with only a couple of "token" native-born Americans—a typical environment at many high-tech companies at the time.

It was not until five years of living and working in Rochester that Sophie became aware of her Flemish accent and of being different. Although "a significant fraction of the researchers at Xerox research lab in Upstate NY are immigrants, other local employees and most of my neighbors were born in the U.S. So the differences were more obvious,"[249] recalls Sophie. But she never had an issue with being accepted, mostly because Xerox[250] has a long tradition of promoting diversity and creating an inclusive environment for all employees, regardless of race, culture, religion, gender, age, sexual orientation, gender identity, or physical capabilities. This is why, says Sophie, "I very quickly felt at home at Xerox and was always very well respected."[251]

As time went by and she traveled all over the country on business, Sophie came to appreciate how diverse America is:

> The beauty is that the US is a mixture of many different cultures. In addition, the "culture" in the US changes depending on where you are in this vast country ... Having been in the US now for almost 30 years, I now feel European as well as American," she said. "I must admit that I still enjoy checking European websites for news, and I enjoy going "home" to Belgium to visit my family.[252]

BIG CHANGES, BIG CHALLENGES

According to Sophie[253], the otherwise quiet flow of her American life was radically altered several times. The first tremendous change came about with the birth of her children far away from Belgium, with no support from extended family. That was absolutely life-altering. "My daughter was born two years after [my] immigrating to the US. My two sons were born within the next few years. Raising them away from their family was hard." But the young parents work hard at raising the kids and establishing themselves in their careers at the same time. In 1996, they were thirty-four, loved their jobs and their active lifestyle in which they spent weekends hiking, kayaking, and camping.

Then tragedy struck. Bart's sudden death from a severe asthma attack occurred during a summer trip to an isolated island in the Adirondacks, their favorite state park in Upstate New York. Bart was alive when two emergency medical technicians arrived in a rescue boat, but he died in Sophie's arms before being evacuated. The next morning, the young widow and her children aged eight, six, and three, drove back home to Rochester. One can only imagine what she was thinking during that drive. Relatives came from Belgium for the funeral, but within ten days Sophie was back to work as a manager in Xerox's inkjet printer division. Life goes on even after a tragedy, and Bart's death forced Sophie to integrate more quickly into American society, making friends and building a stronger support structure.

It would be some twelve years before this personable and intellectually attractive woman remarried. Of course, handling her steep career ascension while raising three children certainly kept her busy. Still, the analytical Sophie has another idea as to why she stayed single for so long. She says that with time, she realized that it was her heritage and culture that presented a steeper barrier for finding a new life partner[254] than her busy career ever did. This realization helped her move on, and in 2008 Sophie blended her Flemish heritage with that her new husband's Spanish descent. Her second husband, Jesus del Alamo, is an MIT professor and a longtime friend, also with an immigrant background.

LIFE WORK BALANCE

Immediately after Bart's death, Sophie's boss had suggested she trade her line job for a less-demanding staff role. But she loved her job which, she says, was "like reading a fantastic book where your brain gets so involved in a topic that you basically forget everything else."[255] She needed this intellectual challenge to keep her moving. But keeping her job meant juggling life-work challenges that seemed insurmountable at the time. Not only was Sophie's household income cut in half (Bart's life-insurance was only for a one-year salary), but she had depended on her husband to handle the daily cooking, household finances, lawn-mowing, and such. Initially, Sophie delegated cooking to a baby-sitter, mowed the back-yard herself on weekends, and started digging into financial records and obligations.

As time went by, she perfected her routine and became even more productive. Thus, at home, any time she could hire someone to do anything that gave her more free time with the children, she did it. Prior to her second marriage and moving to Boston, here's what she used to do[256]:

1. Hire smart female students who needed extra income and were (preferably) studying sciences, to be her children's sitter.

2. This 15-hour-a-week sitter would pick the children up after school and make sure they did their homework. The sitter would do the laundry and the cooking so that dinner would be ready when Sophie came home from work. Many students learned to cook at her home.

3. Sophie affixed a two-page printout of grocery items to her fridge, with a sequence corresponding to the layout at the local grocery store. During the week, she and the children would check off what they needed so that on Fridays a $10-an-hour high-school student could do all the shopping.

4. On a monthly calendar in the kitchen, Sophie and the children filled in their schedules. (She now shares a Google calendar with her second husband.) In order to keep the family from spending all weekend running from one event to another, each child agreed to participate in only one sport or after-school activity per season.

5. Sophie and kids did not watch regular television; instead, the children became avid readers, and on Friday nights the family watched one Netflix movie together. Sophie continues to enjoy her Friday night movie at home.

6. Vacations were kept simple, nothing fancy, usually skiing or camping. Sophie is a believer in the relaxing power of these outdoor activities.

7. Sophie kept her hair short to make the morning routine quicker, and she wore pantsuits and scarves to the office. Life routines were made simple too: no sending Christmas cards or thank-you notes; not too many acquaintances, only a handful of close friendships that are good for the soul. Having one best friend is critical.

8. Sophie always scheduled time to exercise thirty minutes each day. She also trained the children to not wake her up on weekend mornings, so that she could catch up with well-needed sleep. Sophie understand that taking care of herself is a top priority. She can't be a good mother, partner or a leader if she doesn't feel physically healthy and emotionally content. No one can.

9. Next to the kitchen sink, there would always hang a bunch of bananas that symbolized the rationale of her outsourced life. Some weeks the bananas were too green; others, they were too brown. If she did the shopping herself, they might be perfect. Likewise, Sophie might have done a better job than any cleaner or lawn-care provider. But it just wasn't worth her time. The bananas serve as a daily reminder of her priorities and the need to keep her life in balance.

Sophie's strategic office routine is even more disciplined.[257] Lisa Saltrelli, her amazing assistant of over a decade, limits Sophie's schedule to prevent the workday from spilling into personal time. Nothing is planned before 9 a.m. or after 5:30 p.m. In terms of travelling for business when her children were small, Sophie would avoid scheduling meetings before 10 a.m. so that she could fly out in the morning and back in the afternoon, allowing her to limit most U.S. travel to day trips. The promotion to CTO changed that, and now she can be away up to two weeks each month. These trips were especially necessary when Sophie had just taken on a new job and needed to build relationships face to face. (She later felt it was fine to maintain relationships through the phone and video conferencing.)

Sophie put one nonnegotiable condition on her career: no more relocating. She had held jobs at companies based in Rochester and Syracuse, NY; Toronto, Canada; and Stamford, CT, but she kept the family in the same house that she and Bart bought for $160,000 25 years ago. She arranged with her bosses to be in her faraway office as little as possible. For example, as chief technology officer at Carrier Corp., based in Hartford, CT, Sophie spent only one day a week at headquarters. Quite rightly, Sophie refers to relationships with neighbors, doctors, and sitters as "infrastructure" -- an investment that would take too long to rebuild if she moved. "Jobs are fairly easy to change," she says. "Relationships aren't."

Finally, another strategic piece of her life-work balance was the rejection of the so-called *life-cycle career*, a popular notion in which a rising executive tries to synchronize moves at work to the ebbs and flows of family life. To the contrary, Sophie has always taken new jobs no matter what was going on at home—and she made it a smart workable arrangement. "The more senior jobs you get, the easier it is," she says. "You get less control over how busy you are, but you get more control over decisions about when you're busy and how you're going to do things."[258] While most people equate seniority with more stress, Sophie equates it with flexibility.

Sophie has overcome tough challenges by developing successfully delegating responsibilities and keeping her own life-work balance in check. These strategies helped her carry her an enormous load with grace and precision, and to put first the people that she values most. "Although I worked very hard, never once did I doubt that my family is the most important aspect of my life. My kids always were and remain my first priority."[259]

THE PUNCHED TICKET

Sophie never thought she would be good enough to make a difference in America, especially in the competitive world of high-tech. But ambition made her set very high standards for herself: "I studied hard and worked hard to make sure I could make contributions to this top-notch high-tech industry." She credits industry, ambition, the meritocratic high-tech environment, and a lot of luck for delivering her to where she is today: "I have the privilege to lead the Xerox Innovation Group, which is one of the very best global industry research labs with locations around the globe."[260]

Sophie makes no secret of how she got to the corner office.[261]

> Thanks to having a Ph.D. in microelectronics and working at IBM TJ Watson Research Laboratories, I had my research ticket punched when I joined Xerox. As a result, I fairly easily gained the respect and established credibility with my peers and manager. My first job at Xerox was as a member of the ink-jet technology group, generating patents and working with the product teams to get the ideas into their products, which we did pretty successfully. My management recognized this, and I got promoted rather quickly.

She then described ticket-punching as situational: "You have to get your ticket punched over and over again... You have to continue to establish and reestablish your credibility every time you move into a new field or take a new job."

Sophie also believes it's important to play the "intrapreneur" role[262], that is, being i.e., an employee + entrepreneur, within a big company such as Xerox. It's not enough to know the details of the technologies, she says. Everyone needs to participate in "launching a product, delivering it to our customers, doing the fire-fighting, scaling it into manufacturing, jumping to assist with each customer request, etc." Small wonder that Xerox, led by people like Sophie, could overcome its downturn and emerge stronger than ever before.

A WORTHY ROLE MODEL

Sophie's secret of success seems to stem from her wit and wisdom that conditioned all things that made her a person she is today, particularly her get-up fighter capabilities. These strong capabilities combined led Sophie to develop a set of strategies and practices that I chose to call "life-work rainmaking" - or the accumulated know-how of beating the odds in life and succeeding big-time at work.

Of course, in Sophie, we see an immigrant woman with the most brilliant career in tech. Accordingly, as a Xerox Chief Technology Officer for over 10 years, she led the company's technology transformation from printing/copying towards digital solutions & services.

Then, in January 2017, Sophie returned to IBM to lead strategy and operations for 13 global laboratories with about 5,000 amazing researchers; their research areas include Artificial Intelligence, Quantum Computing, Cybersecurity, Semiconductors and more— my head is swimming just reading that! Furthermore, Sophie smoothly proceeded to assume responsibilities for VP Emerging Technology Partnerships and lead key strategic initiatives to scale IBM's emerging technology partnerships and ecosystems.

So, is there anything Sophie cannot do? I do not think so.

On a personal level, hers is a story of a family-oriented woman with a beautiful mind which allowed her to take good care of the life-work balance in a way that both her children and her career flourished profusely. This is why Sophie Vandebroek is a worthy role-model for every aspiring achiever-to-be.

Rosa R. de la Cruz *from Cuba*

The Philanthropic Collector

Rosa with her teenage-years boyfriend, then husband and life-long partner Carlos de la Cruz.

Rosa de la Cruz is a prominent philanthropist and collector of contemporary art who has redefined the public role of private art collector. Together with her husband, Carlos de la Cruz, she manages the 30,000 square foot *de la Cruz Collection Contemporary Art Space*[263] in Miami. This personal collection, Rosa's alter ego, is open to the public free of charge and conducts diverse educational programs with strong community outreach. Family wealth may have enabled Rosa to assemble one of the finest private art collections in the country, but she gained artistic authority and cultural influence that money can't buy. For the past thirty years, Rosa has built a reputation for being both a trendsetter and salient figure in the contemporary art world. And this was appropriately recognized by both art professionals and broader public circles when the American Federation of Arts (AFA) held its 2015 Gala & Cultural Leadership Awards, honoring

Carlos and Rosa de la Cruz as renowned Miami-based art patrons and collectors.

PROMINENCE AND UNCERTAINTY

Rosa was born in 1942 and raised in Habana, Cuba, into a family[264] of prominent intellectuals and professionals. The family had a long tradition of American education. Her grandfather Eugenio Rayneri, a famous Cuban architect, was the first graduate of architecture at the Notre Dame University. Rosa herself was sent to a boarding school in Ashville, NC, to improve her English.

Life in Habana during the Batista regime was full of uncertainties. One day, remembers Rosa, her mother got a call from an ambassador of the Dominican Republic, who informed her that Batista had requested asylum, which was news with enormous ramifications. Batista was gone and a new government was put in place. Life changed quickly under Castro. While he was an educated man and a lawyer, Castro was not respected by most Cuban professionals. Rosa's grandfather, for example, referred to Castro's regime as "theater," because he maintained that it won people's minds by cheap propaganda.

The new regime worked like a guillotine chopping off everything that disagreed with their doctrine, forcing a million Cuban professional into exile. Initially, Rosa's family hoped that Castro would confiscate money and possessions only from the rich, and that they would be spared. They waited to see what would happen. But the logic of Cuban-style socialist revolution was irreversible and hopeless, like a highway with no exit, and eventually the family had to flee. In our conversation, Rosa constantly pointed out that they were not immigrants, but exiles[265].

Life in exile was far from easy. Rosa's family never went hungry, nor did they have to rely on Welfare, nevertheless, money was in short supply. Looking at her hard-working parents, Rosa could not even think of asking for money for a salon haircut, or any other treat that a young girl might desire. She learned to be responsible with money. All the while, year after year, her grandmother hoped against hope that the family would be able to return "home," and be "in Habana next year." But that was not in the cards.

TEENAGE SWEETHEARTS

In pre-revolutionary Havana, Rosa and Carlos de la Cruz were teenage sweethearts who started dating when she was fifteen and he was sixteen. Their relationship continued abroad in 1960 when, following the ascent of Castro, they left the island to study: Carlos at the University of Pennsylvania, and Rosa at school in North Carolina. At that time, all private schools in Cuba had been closed anyway, and all who could afford it sent their children to study abroad, to escape communist indoctrination. From 1960-1962, approximately 15,000 children were reportedly sent to the US without parents.

"We wrote a letter to one another every day,"[266] said Rosa of her separation from Carlos. "People don't understand how communications have changed. Long-distance phone calls were expensive then—you would talk on the phone once a month."

Their affection for each other was strong enough to withstand the separation. Absence makes the heart grow fonder, as the saying goes. And so it was with Rosa and Carlos. The young couple demonstrated both spiritual affinity and resilience; their romance was strengthened by their exile. They married, but their wedding was hardly a time of youthful optimism, since their families had both fled Cuba to the US and the prospects for the future were uncertain.

"We got married during the trial of the Bay of Pigs," Rosa says, referring to the kangaroo courts run by the Castro regime for the captured Cuban-exile brigadiers in the wake of their failed invasion. "There was no spirit of celebration," she recalls. Many of our friends were in jail. How could we have a reception?"[267] Still, life went on, and Rosa and Carlos moved to New York City, where Carlos, with his MBA from the Wharton business school, got a good job at

Citibank Corp. They started a family, and over the years have been blessed with five children. For a while, Rosa's energy and passion was turned to raising the new generation of five young de la Cruzes! Carlos, meanwhile, distinguished himself on the job at Citi. But the couple decided to leave the U.S. and move to Madrid, Spain, where Carlos was offered an excellent job.

FINDING A HOME

Life was good in Madrid, and the family stayed there for ten years. Alas, the threat of political volatility and misgivings about the Franco regime in the mid-seventies were enough to make the couple want to leave. They wanted to escape anything similar to their Cuban experiences—especially for the sake of their five children.

The de la Cruzes returned to the U.S., settling in Miami. Rosa wanted to work and got a license—quite rare at the time—to practice as a real estate broker. She did it not just to earn an extra buck, but out of curiosity, to keep herself busy, and make new friends.

Rosa also saw that collecting art—of which she got a taste while living in Europe—was a more distinct way of expressing herself, and she made the choice to feed her passion.

The famous big collection started right there, in Miami. A 1956 Rufino Tamayo painting launched it, and hundreds of pieces followed. Carlos used the money he had earned in Spain wisely, and started his own successful business when the family settled in Florida. Having more money obviously made it easier to collect the best quality art possible. For Rosa, it was not just investment, but also a heartfelt choice, an outlet for her innate passion. Her focus of her collection started with Latin American art, which seemed a perfect choice.

In 1982, Rosa and Carlos bought a small, one-story waterfront Key Biscayne house, and over subsequent years added two large wings to house their growing collection, resulting in a gallery home of 15,000 square feet. Rosa's art collection covered the floors, walls, ceilings, and nearly every inch of her gallery home. Artists came into her house to do site-specific installations. Not only did she get to live with the likes of Sigmar Polke, Jim Hodges, Martin Kippenberger, and Felix González-Torres on canvas, but the gallery-like lifestyle seemed to her be a natural and satisfying way of life. Rosa's unusual home and collection have also been open to the public by appointment. Carlos, a true soul mate, supported her and complemented her ideas with his own creativity and business acumen.

THE MIAMI MODEL

In Miami, there is a small group of private museums/collections specializing in contemporary art: known collectively as the *Miami model.* In it, the de la Cruz Collection stood out for a number of reasons, not the least of which was the annual Art Basel Miami Beach[268] dinner parties hosted at their home. This was the fair's most coveted ticket. But one year so many guests arrived at her Key Biscayne mansion—over 1,000 party-crashers—that it became clear that the Collection had overgrown its space. This was a call for action: to find a new home for the art.

In 2009, The New York Times published an article[269] about de la Cruz art collection moving into a new three-story, 30,000-square-foot building in Miami's Design District. It noted that the de la Cruz Collection Contemporary Art Space not only follows similar endeavors owned by other local über-collectors, but that its exhibition area exceeds that of both the Miami Art Museum and North Miami's Museum of Contemporary Art (MOCA). The specially-designed modern building came with a north facing wall made entirely of windows; as different from the old one, it is open five days a week—and also for free.

"Art institutions and museums should be admission-free," says Rosa de la Cruz. "I feel that art is part of the patrimony of a nation and private collections should be accessible to the public in general."

Inside this building lies a wealth of information delivered by a vast array of contemporary artwork, a full library, and a space for frequent workshops and lectures. Access to the gallery is free of charge. "Art institutions and museums should be admission-free," says Rosa. "Charging alienates many who enjoy art but cannot afford the cost of admission, special events and workshops. I feel that art is part of the patrimony of a nation and private collections should be accessible to the public in general."[270]

Former exiles who have made a successful life in the U.S., the de la Cruz family have curated a collection influenced by their biographical experiences; many pieces explore themes of personal—and painful—dislocation.

INNOVATION

The work of Rosa and her team of five colleagues resulted in the Collection's departure not only from the local private museums' framework, but also from most national art institutions. Nobody can rival Rosa's ideas, passion, and creativity: she borrows the best features of the art institutions she likes, while adding even more ground-breaking features. Among Rosa's initiatives:

1. Not charging admission.

2. Providing every visitor with a guided tour so they can learn about each piece and its influences

3. Building a specially designed house for the Collection

4. Pressing the edge of mainstream art by acquiring and exhibiting sensational art pieces

5. Educating new young talent

6. Providing travel tours to famous collections abroad

7. Empowering budding artists with scholarship programs, etc.

8. Maintaining programs and events at the Collection site

9. Regularly rotating the art pieces

10. Inviting artists to do site-specific installation

11. Hosting residency programs, exhibitions, events, lectures, evenings of improvised music.

It's easy to see why Rosa is considered a dynamic player in the development of Miami cultural community. The de la Cruz Collection space continues to surprise initial skeptics, as busloads of students can be seen roaming the gallery, attending workshops, or sitting in the library. Indeed—unlike at most art centers in Miami—there is a constant stream of visitors.

ENERGY & INFLUENCE

The Collection is an incredibly attractive space because it reflects the energy of the curators through influential contemporary works. Moreover, it's styled with a passion infused by Rosa de la Cruz herself. She is a passionate woman who's not big on words of self-service but really big on service to the people.

GENEROSITY

Generosity, they say, begins at home. That's certainly the case with Rosa, as her own generosity is all-inclusive. Despite her many personal interests and business activities, Rosa's five children benefitted from her full attention while growing up. Rosa continued the family tradition that put a high premium on education: Spanish language for all five kids and seventeen grandkids.

Outsiders have benefitted from Rosa's generosity as well: for instance, a gift of $4,000 to a Caribbean boy who wrote a letter, explaining he wanted to join his classmates on a trip to Europe, but his mother couldn't raise the money. Rosa met the young boy years later, as a young educated man.

In the custom of a true role model, Rosa de la Cruz's generosity embraces her team of five employees with whom she shares the same no-walls room on a daily basis. She credits their expertise, skills, and ability to always keep an open mind—so necessary in the contemporary art world.

Her Collection, and her cause of promoting contemporary art, both exist due to her consistent generosity: many art works get rotated, some go to storage or to other exhibitions. Rosa is a firm believer in educating the younger generations, so art education is included in the Collection's activities. These include workshops for public schools; teaching kids the concepts of what is Form, Content, and Process in modern art; what's success or failure; what's the philosophy of modern art – and life; why people need to relate to art; how important it is to broaden one's artistic horizons overseas, etc. She is happy to fund educational activities and participate in them too (in 2013 she and Carlos took a group of Miami students on a month-long tour of Italy, one of their summer programs[271]).

ART FOR THE PEOPLE

Many wealthy people want to collect and exhibit art in their own way, without the restrictions of a board of directors or public financing—so they simply develop their own museum-like organizations. There are pluses and minuses to this approach. On a plus side, they have total control. It's their curatorial vision, their collection, their money—and entirely their own point of view ruling the seas at all times. On the down side, it's also their total risk in acquiring new art and promoting it to the public.

> Every collector needs to realize that they can't take it with them. Their collection will either go to an institution, which

might not be able to show them; to your kids, who might not want them; or to an auction house.

"Every collector needs to realize you can't take it with you," is Rosa's approach to art philanthropy. "The works will either go to an institution, which might not be able to show them; to your kids, who might not want them; or to an auction house."[272] She decided to take a different route, organize it all and show it now. She also added, "Some people enjoy going to the horse races, I love showing art to people."

A POWERFUL DYNASTY

The de la Cruz family has been recognized by *Town & Country* as one of the 50 Most Powerful Families[273], and is considered by many to be a powerful dynasty. Aware of this, Rosa wants to set the record straight: "I am not impressed by wealth. . . . Some folks are more materialistic, but we place spiritual over materialistic, we respect academia and intellectuals. Unfortunately, the US is turning into an anti-intellectual society. So, we need to take more care of educating the young and influencing their perception of life, creativity, and the world art."[274]

While Rosa is the soul and chief curator of the Collection, operational funding comes from the family business, which prospers thanks to the success of Carlos and his son Alberto. It was Rosa's initiative to develop their own philanthropic *concept of unrestricted sharing of their wealth* with the community – and do more than the others, and do it her way. It's working effectively. As a result, the couple continues to fund their Contemporary Arts Space at a very high level: a solid investment created a solid base for acquiring the most valuable art pieces they seek—and acquire.

Rosa de la Cruz believes that the U.S. is turning into an anti-intellectual society, which is why we need to take more care in educating the young and influencing their perception of life, creativity and the world art.

LIKE A MUSEUM—ONLY BETTER

Today, the de la Cruz Collection acts as a public institution in its own right. It has grown to the point of truly functioning like a museum—even better. It has formal hours, education programs, and a variety of grants for financing the work of emerging innovative artists, and the library.

Rosa de la Cruz has come up with a new kind of art philanthropy, one that works for the public-at-large. But turning her own private art collection into an institution that rivals those of many museums she has exhibited true cultural influence.

Rosa's work is unsurpassed and well recognized. Chairperson and Founder of Moore Space, an alternative venue that operated in Miami from 2001 to 2008, Rosa has long been acknowledged for supporting some of the most experimental projects in Miami. In 1988, she was a juror for the Hugo Boss Prize at the Guggenheim Museum in New York. In 1997 she was awarded the Alexis de Tocqueville Award from the United Way for community service. She received the Red Cross Chairmen's Spectrum Award in 2004, and served as Juror of the Marcel Duchamp Prix at the Centre Pompidou in Paris in 2011. Rosa and Carlos were the 1998 honorees of the Simon Wiesenthal Center, and in October 2015 were recognized as renowned Miami-based art patrons and collectors with Cultural Leadership awards by American Federation of Arts[275].

CULTIVATING COMMITMENT

Rosa's commitment to cultivating contemporary art—and the way in which she has brought art to the people on a broader scale than ever before—has not gone unnoticed. The leader of the Miami Model, she has been on the receiving end of many philanthropy and community service awards over the years. The principal reason why is obvious. She established a unique form of community service, and people appreciated it. But it's also because of her zealous efforts to mold art philanthropy into a new, more people-focused endeavor; and to provide extraordinary art education to the young generation and opportunities to emerging artists—which can be broadly consequential for shaping the future of American culture.

Hilda Ochoa Brillembourg *from Venezuela*

The Financier in the Pursuit of Alpha

Despite coming from a middle-class family, Hilda Ochoa-Brillembourg was scared of being poor. Her obsession to succeed and to support herself took root early, which is why her education, work, and passion have all been—consciously and unconsciously—directed towards her ultimate goal of being financially secure. So, at age eleven, Hilda made sewing kits from fabric scraps and multicolored threads and sold them door-to-door. While at university (and she was the first woman in her family to attend university), Hilda held a full-time job by day and studied economics at night. After graduation, she looked for new opportunities, landing a Fulbright scholarship to pursue her Master's degree at Harvard University. She doggedly worked her way up to become Chief Investment Officer of the World Bank, and to eventually establish her own firm—Strategic Investment Group.

Hilda, a role-model in strategic thinking

Hilda never stopped until she reached her goal. Having a powerful personality and intellect never hurts, of course; but it's not enough to be smart and charismatic. You have to be tenacious, and you have to do it one step at a time.

SELF-SUFFICIENCY

Growing up in Caracas, Venezuela, Hilda "felt the fear of poverty poignantly . . . Whatever it took, I wanted to get to the point where I could support myself." That fear was obviously what prompted her to study economics. In her words, "I knew nothing about it, found no flaw in it, and felt I could go anywhere in the world with it . . . Whatever it took, I wanted to get to the point where I could support myself."[276]

After graduation, Hilda took a trip to the U.S., where she fell in love with Boston, and with Harvard University in adjacent Cambridge, Mass. As would become typical for this savvy woman, Hilda surveyed the scene and made the right connections, ultimately receiving a Fulbright scholarship to pursue her Master's degree in public administration at Harvard's John F. Kennedy School of Government. She was only twenty-six. It was an excellent starting point for a career; however, she had to return to her country, to make a living, pay her student loans, and comply with Fulbright's home-residence requirement.

> Hilda Ochoa Brillembourg studied economics because she felt she could go anywhere in the world with it.

Hilda returned to Venezuela where she served as an independent consultant in the field of economics and finance, a lecturer at the Universidad Catolica Andres Bello and IESA in Venezuela, and later, a consultant to the C.A. Luz Electrica de Venezuela in Caracas. Hilda's stint in the U.S. helped her understand how Venezuela had been ravished by extraordinary mismanagement, corruption, and crime. But it also fostered her belief that she had been born in the wrong country—how could she live in a place where mediocrity trumped merit?

Hilda strategized once more and returned to America for good. Her first job in the U.S. was pre-arranged by contacts who helped her land a position as an investment analyst at the World Bank. As Hilda's job evolved with changing markets and experience, she rose to the position of chief investment officer in the Pension Investment Division of the World Bank.

Hilda first distinguished herself as part of The World Bank's executive team, and was the only woman there at the time.

Some years later, Hilda understood that she had developed a unique and valuable process for managing investment portfolios. What's more, she knew that she had the experience to implement these ideas in an independent investment firm. So, after devoting twelve years of her life to the World Bank, Hilda started her own company—Strategic Investment Group—and the World Bank became her first customer. They knew they could trust her razor-sharp brain and investment prowess.

INTEGRATING FOR SUCCESS
If cultural adaptation by newcomers is the first step towards success, integration is the second. And if success is largely determined

by how well an individual understands the rules of society and business, it can only come after sufficient cultural integration. That's certainly true for Hilda, whose success is due in no small part to wholeheartedly embracing a strong American work ethic.

And yet, it was Venezuelan culture that equipped Hilda with another important asset for an immigrant: adaptability. Adaptable from the start, she had the ability to learn from and adjust to challenges and opportunities. Hilda was analytical, which meant that she could scrutinize almost any situation and understand it in all its complexity. From there she would be able to get to the bottom of things—draw the right conclusions at the right time—and adjust her behaviors accordingly. Because she observed, analyzed, managed, and adapted, there were few challenges she couldn't navigate.

> Success is largely determined by how well an individual understands the rules of society and business, and it can only come after sufficient cultural integration.

But there were hurdles, the main one being "proving my competence and determination to succeed without losing my cultural diversity."[277] Other, more specific challenges were the direct result of her Venezuelan heritage. First, she found it hard to get used to the American propensity toward openness, and reliance on good-will. Second, and this point seems to be at odds with the last, she underestimated predatory behavior in American business. But Hilda was smart. She watched, and she learned, and as time went by, she adapted to that too.

HANDLING HARDSHIPS

The U.S. has always provided entrepreneurs with a wealth of opportunity in the form of easy access to monetary and human capital. The opportunities for personal and professional growth are almost infinite. Still, this a highly competitive country and you have to maintain your creativity, innovation, and hard work, if you want to maintain your competitive edge.[278]

"In my field," she says, "when markets turn against your strategy, it is always difficult. You overcome adversity by understanding the different outcomes that can be expected from any action and making sure you can survive the worst, while focusing on the most likely. When adversity hits you, look at the opportunity it creates."[279]

Like most immigrants, Hilda has certainly had her fair share of hard times, but she retained her compassion for others and an empathy for those who are working to transcend unfortunate circumstances. Her approach to handling hardships past and present is no-nonsense, like everything she does.

PERSONAL PURSUITS

The embodiment of success, Hilda nevertheless acknowledges that balancing family and work has been a major challenge. She knows from experience that true work-life balance allows the best focus on creativity, her existential essence. Although she married into an affluent family, Hilda "had chosen not to be a kept-woman."[280] In fact, the thought of dropping her career for "living happily ever after" never crossed her mind.

In Venezuela, Hilda had one marriage that ended in divorce. She later married Arturo E. Brillembourg, at the time a research economist with the International Monetary Fund, who went on to found AEB Capital. Hilda had sufficient insight after her failed first marriage to believe that she and Arturo could make a go of it. Their shared Venezuelan background, similar values, intellectual training, and aspirations certainly made this seem likely. Thirty years and three children later, they're still going strong. As Hilda says: "Love, respect, maturity, and resilience all [support] a focus on a sustainable partnership."[281]

> If we want to be lovers, mothers, and professional women, we need to be judicious in choosing a partner who will support us and our aspirations.

Hilda knows how important it is for women to be judicious in choosing a partner with whom they will be sharing work and family. She advises that we avoid oscillating between a "Cinderella complex" (always searching for a prince to solve all of our problems and give us a happily-ever-after that doesn't exist), and a "Superwoman complex," (a larger-than-life sense of responsibility, not to mention the belief that everyone else lacks the capacity to cope as we do.) If we want to be lovers, mothers, and professional women, we're going to need to ask for a little help along the way. We shouldn't feel guilty about retaining whatever services are necessary to meet our obligations. In fact, we should approach these processes with dedication, interest, love, and enthusiasm.

DREAMS GOING LIVE

Getting a Fulbright opened many doors for Hilda. Her springboard to the future was her goal of making it to Harvard. After that dream went live, she followed up with three others:

- Encouraging the Venezuelan government to start its own Fulbright-like program in 1974: the Fundacion Gran Marical Ayacucho, which has fostered the education of more than 100,000 young Venezuelan professionals.

- Founding her own business, Strategic Investment Group, whose aim is "to empower investors through experience, innovation, and excellence."

- Founding and sponsoring the Youth Orchestra of America, which creates intercontinental unity through music.

Hilda defined the basis of the American Dream as "freedom and resources to pursue excellence and entrepreneurship." Exactly what was needed for her American dream to go live.

PROFESSIONAL OPTIMISM

Hilda started her own business in March 1987, opening its doors for the first time just two weeks after Black Monday when the Dow Jones Industrial market dropped a dizzying 508 points. It took tremendous pluck to go into business while the U.S. economy was in a landslide and the world was on the brink of recession. But Hilda couldn't deny her entrepreneurial spirit, nor could she postpone it any longer.

She had a strong foundation:

- in-depth business knowledge

- high-end World Bank experience

- solid contacts

- sophisticated risk management models

- innovative investment practices

Was that enough? Not entirely. She added a good old-fashioned dose of gumption. "You need to persist, you need to be singularly focused on success and never give up. It's what people call 'grit.' You need to have grit."[282]

Hilda also had an unfettered optimism that was both reality-based and knowledge-based. As she explains: "we're still in a world where there is abundant liquidity which is flowing in the direction where it is needed and . . . monetary and fiscal policies are helping liquidity flow."[283] This knowledge made her a proponent of globalism, the efficient movement of money, goods, services, and people.

Her professional optimism and knowledge paid off big. Today, Hilda's business and social contributions are recognized nationally and internationally. Her firm has over $36 billion in managed assets and clients like the $210 billion California Public Employees

Retirement System, one of the largest in the U.S. Hilda retains her optimistic world view, still more sanguine than most of her valued Wall Street colleagues—and why not?

PARTICIPATORY LEADERSHIP

An eloquent achiever who leads by example—in deed, as well as word—Hilda inspires trust and motivates those around her. Yet, while she acknowledges that many forms of leadership all work in one way or another, she finds participatory leadership—what I call "inclusive leadership"— to be more nurturing, and also more sustainable than other forms of leadership. "A firm is never better than its human capital,"[284] she states in her book.

Following her own mantra, Hilda insists on true diversity of mind to make her firm adaptable: "harassment or exclusion of any kind should not be tolerated," she says. What's more, because her firm incubates managers so that they are the logical source of competitive wealth creation, the company's human capital is actually wired differently from that of its competition. Perhaps most importantly, though, is that through leading by example Hilda has encouraged colleagues to read broadly and deeply, seeking to find the dots and make new connections in evolving markets, instead of simply relying on numbers and statistics, like many competitors still do. Hilda believes that statistics are like blood tests: just the starting point.

As a result of her participatory leadership style, Hilda has pushed the frontiers of investment theory to the pursuit of the market inefficiencies. Hilda calls it "implementing portable alpha strategies,"[285] and it's how her firm added value for their clients. Financial success is no plain vanilla, period.

PASSIONATE PHILANTHROPY

Hilda has a passionate devotion to the arts[286] and is committed to many philanthropic causes. A long-term trustee and member of the Washington National Opera and the National Symphony Orchestra, she later founded—and now chairs—the YOA Orchestra of Americas, which became a world-class, multicultural orchestra, composed of 100 talented young musicians selected with stringent criteria from more than twenty countries. It has drawn participation and guidance of music celebrities like Placido Domingo and Yo-Yo Ma among others.

Now broadly regarded as a revolutionary initiative and an example of a meaningful philanthropy, this orchestra has become her very special ambition. Hilda wants it to be "a very grand metaphor for making the world work at high levels of excellence." That's why she keeps steering it to evolve into a body cultivating global leaders—musicians who are fully engaged with their communities through social enterprise and entrepreneurship.

LEADERSHIP PRINCIPLES

Hilda has advice for women seeking to rise in their chosen career:

- Life is neither easy nor predictable. The best way to succeed is by engaging as an active participant and not sitting back like a passive member of the audience or, worse, a critic. Ruminating is not useful. Judging is not useful.

- Connect with your surroundings and choose a professional and economic environment in which you can grow.

- Develop two or three different GPS routes for yourself. Identify opportunities, get the training you need, and find mentors and supporters. It's a matter of building the intellectual, emotional, and professional support systems that you need, and then maintaining an active connection to them.

- The world we live in today is governed by customs and conventions. And yet we all have the capacity to interpret those customs and conventions in creative ways, to imagine how they may be improved. Just remember that imagination must be accompanied by good judgment, adaptability, and hard work.

- Where there is enthusiasm, there is no real sacrifice. Where there is enthusiasm, there should be life, initiative, and progress.

STRATEGIC THINKER

Today, many people are aware of Hilda's sharp intellect; few know that she first displayed her brainy insights at the tender age of five. In her book, *The Pursuit of Alpha*, Hilda recalls developing her own brand of ingenuity at piñata parties in Caracas. The big thrill at these parties was to break the piñata, releasing the candy and gifts inside. The child who managed to break the papier-mâché figure was the biggest hero, but little Hilda quickly figured out that she didn't need the accolades: she wanted to collect the most goodies. She preferred results over fleeting fame. So, by standing behind the glory-seeker and watching where the goodies fell, Hilda was able to run to the spot where the goodies fell and, squatting, cover the candy with the wide reach of her organza skirt. That well-thought-out strategy yielded the most candy—enough to share with other kids. Thus, some special strategies and skills - had come into fruition, along with creative thinking and budding self-reliance of a little girl. Predisposition to choosing the strategic excellence and long-term tangible results over short-term applause will stand her a good stead in the adult career.

Since those early days in Caracas, Hilda has applied her mind to action in many high-end places: serving on the Board of Directors at General Mills, Inc. and McGraw Hill Financial; serving on the advisory committee of Harvard David Rockefeller Center for Latin American Studies; as a lifetime member of the Council on Foreign Relations[287]; as a Dean's Executive Committee member at the Harvard Kennedy School; and as a long-time member of the

World Economic Forum. Cataloging Hilda's positions is not the point here anyway—there are far too many to list—but to see *how* she managed to do it all and maintain the balance of quality work and quality personal life. Today, a former chief investment officer of the World Bank is a member of several well-known boards of directors, where her brilliant, never-resting mind continues to help people and organizations.

Hilda's innovative business concepts and vision are transferable assets that let her operate almost uncontested in lucrative markets, and she certainly benefitted from these investment opportunities. We should remember that the foundation of her financial prowess is linked to her own passion, personality, strategic thinking, cultural integration, and pursuit of excellence.

Deborah Levine *from Bermuda*

The Entrepreneur of Spirit

Many of us are afraid to admit the extent to which our accomplishments depend on luck. It's not something you can mention in the presence of self-made folks, yet Deborah Levine is an exception: she's a self-made woman who admits her luck. It's scary to think that a great deal of life is beyond our control, that as much as hard work and a clear vision are necessary to success, it can be sheer luck that opens the right door. But

Deborah, with her joy of life and spiritual intelligence, became a visible force.

Deborah wasn't easily scared. She wanted to become an entrepreneur and an influencer, like her father. That's the path she took, and she doesn't mind saying that luck was with her.

Today, this professional diversiculturist with advanced degrees in cultural anthropology, religion, and urban planning is the managing editor of the American Diversity Report[288], an award-winning author, and intercultural-interfaith coach. Her research on cultural diversity and social issues—supported by advanced degrees in cultural anthropology, religion, and urban planning—has been recognized by the National Press Association, *The Wall Street Journal*, and elsewhere. She has gained special recognition with respect to her efforts around diversity and inclusion training in the Southern states, as well as efforts to put to work the practical interface[289] of Christianity and Judaism. The victim of prejudice and discrimination as a Jewish woman, Deborah went to work for Jewish agencies, eventually becoming a writer, a diversity expert, a HuffPost blogger, and an op-ed author. Her diverse experiences and cultural anthropology training led to "marrying mentalities," not only with regard to religious beliefs, but also the cultures and mindsets of diverse ethnic-racial communities. (Something that a person with her brains and background was uniquely qualified for.) The practical interface of Christianity and Judaism brought her local, national, and international recognition. She practices a philosophy of "harmonize, not homogenize" to build the unity and cooperation of diverse proud people and to counteract prejudices for herself and for countless others.

FREEDOM AND CONFORMITY

Deborah came from a distinguished family—a Harvard-educated father and a Radcliffe-educated mother—and she credits her parents, especially her father, as being the major influences of her life.[290] The only Jewish family living and working in Bermuda for four generations, the Levines founded the first Jewish congregation and were also recognized for their entrepreneurship. Deborah's family has deep roots in Bermuda and she had a happy childhood. However, like her mother, Deborah stood out as the only Jewish girl in her school—or anywhere on the island for that matter. That's why the family moved to the US. They wanted to be part of a broader Jewish community, something that just wasn't possible in Bermuda[291].

> Young Deborah grasped the necessity of fitting in immediately upon arrival in the U.S. She jettisoned her Bermudian school uniform and begged her parents for every fashion she saw her

schoolmates wearing. Painfully, she came to understand that her British-style classical education marked her far more than her clothes ever did.

Deborah learned early what "being different" means in the US, a country with a peculiar mix of freedom and conformity. Set apart by her British-Bermudian culture, by her traditional Jewish up-bringing with its deeply ingrained ways, and—ironically—by her high IQ, Deborah grasped the necessity of fitting in immediately upon arrival. She jettisoned her Bermudian school uniform and begged her parents for every fashion she saw her schoolmates wear-ing. Painfully, she came to understand that her British-style classi-cal education marked her far more than her clothes ever did. Her British accent, diction, spelling, and vocabulary made her stand out in the East Meadow & Westbury School on Long Island. Teased at recess, misunderstood in class, and battered walking home, she went from angry to withdrawn, from proud to miserable. "When I first came to the USA as a child, both my brother and I were bullied. Never forgot it," she remembers.

Deborah felt isolated and lonely in Long Island, something she never experienced in Bermuda. She had felt accepted there, Jewishness notwithstanding. Deborah's lack of confidence led to weepy moments which, in addition to her singular style of speech, made her something of a misfit among the girls in her class. Eventually she "translated" her British English into American English, and, more or less, ironed-out other Bermudian marks, al-though they stuck as part of the identity of the former island girl.

But Deborah couldn't—and wouldn't—compromise her tra-ditional Jewish attitudes and community values. These remained dominant throughout her life, despite the pressure of American society at the time. (This was the fifties, a time of far less inclusion in the U.S.) There's something about a Jewish mentality instilled in early childhood that can make it an all-encompassing presence. In time, due to work-life circumstances, Deborah's Jewish mindset grew stronger, and she found a way to make it work for her. Her Jewish identity colored her immigrant creativity, her first marriage, and her professional pursuits.

When she arrived in the U.S. Deborah was initially placed in the second grade, but she stood out for her intelligence and was promptly put into a combination third and fourth grade class. Her mother prevented her being promoted even further ahead so that she wouldn't be a total oddity among her peers. Deborah's class studied mathematical set theory from a text book so experimental that it didn't have a cover. Her math elective included some matrix algebra and basic computer programming. Not that Deborah particularly liked math; she was drawn to history, culture, and languages. But math came easily to her, and she excelled. When high school counselors informed Deborah that her IQ was higher than Einstein's, she hid that fact from her schoolmates for as long as possible because she knew that the reaction was more likely to be hostility, rather than admiration—a response that could be summed up as, "Funny, you don't look a genius."

THE ECCENTRIC AMERICAN
Deborah longed to fit in and was willing to re-invent herself to do so. She "had to work hard to become American," although she still speaks and writes in what feels like a formal British style (especially when tired) and prefers the BBC to CNN. And yet, while Deborah may think of herself as "a Bermuda island girl at heart," she realizes that as a member of the only Jewish family in Bermuda she didn't entirely fit in there, either.

Research shows that feelings of cultural ambivalence often make people unique and more creative: they can see the world multiple perspectives or "live in two worlds." Immigrants naturally bring this bicultural vision into their creative pursuits because they can see things through several filters and find multiple, or even opposing, connotations in the same event. And not to forget, experience in a different educational system (emphasizing not only different specific knowledge but also the underlying logic and thinking process) results in different thinking and decision-making styles: holistic, analytical, or emotive-synthetic, vs. US pragmatic.   Still, multicultural people have a broader need of a deeper integration which facilitates success in America. Their trials and tribulations in a new land make them try ever harder to integrate, and habitual perseverance leads to persisting in "crazy" creative ideas, bringing them to fruition. And this is exactly what happened to Deborah. It was her instinct that there was a "proper" way to integrate, and she worked on that.

> Almost all immigrants have to decide for themselves whether to accept and conform by *going with the flow,* or take the more difficult action and *swim upstream.*

Deborah's cultural make-up evolved, shifting to the quintessential American culture but never fully dissolving its roots. The result is what she calls an "eccentric American," natural for those who experienced living in different regions or cities in the USA where one's personal core culture adds to the rich mix of America's diversity.

There's another aspect of integration that is often overlooked: almost all immigrants have to decide for themselves whether to *go with the flow* (accept and conform) or *swim upstream* (take a more difficult action), both in terms of integration and career choice, as these are often interwoven. The decision seems to depend not just on how resolved the immigrant is to succeed, but also on her personal psychological predisposition. "I go with the flow until I can't stand it," said Deborah. While she says that she's always been that way, she does say that age has made her more willing to go against conventional attitudes and take the consequences. "I believe this is part of the growing awareness that my efforts to go with the flow never quite got it right,"[292] she says.

COMPARING CULTURES

As a cultural anthropologist, Deborah has a unique insight into American culture. She's particularly attuned to the limitations she herself faced because of her British colonial ways. Among the cultural restraints that delayed her success in America, Deborah cites the fact that "Brits tend not to promote themselves. It's bad form. Americans do it [self-promotion] in their sleep and expect successful leaders to do the same. It's been a struggle to market myself American-style."[293] Ingrained modesty is a common trait among British women, drilled down since childhood; but it's a drawback for their success in the U.S. where humility and modesty are not considered prominent traits of successful leaders, while confidence and can-do attitudes are.

> The British consider it bad form to promote themselves. Americans do it naturally and expect others to do the same.

That said, America has much to offer, and Deborah has found many American features particularly attractive, which today she embraces with pride. These include a future-oriented orientation, personal ambition, and the Southern manners of Tennessee, where she eventually settled.

When asked about the strategies that helped her to "discover herself in America," Deborah didn't hesitate for a moment. Two things above all led to her success: the value placed on education in the Jewish community, and the role models she found in her parents and grandparents. They had managed amazing things no matter what, and they remind her every day when to be kind and when to be bold. That said, Deborah adds that she did give up on of her cultural values in America. "I learned to swear, forbidden in Bermuda. It has helped a lot"[294]

SUCCESS AND SETBACKS INTERTWINED

It took Deborah less than three months to land her first job, that of a file clerk for *Sport Illustrated Magazine* during summer at college, earning $400 a month. Later, she would change jobs and careers more than once. "I follow the money," she explained, "but when my health fails, I follow the passion."[295] Fair enough.

Her worst setbacks were health issues which required that she took more time off than she ever desired or imagined. It was devastating both to Deborah and to her family. Her professional advancement and income suffered, but so what? "You learn to scramble, fight and persevere early on," said Deborah. Her inborn entrepreneurial spirit never stopped looking for something. That's when she started writing, which turned out to be a true gift that she now relies on.

THREE DIFFERENT AMERICAS

Deborah has benefitted from a strong intellectual capacity, excellent education, and solid family values. Most everything required for a successful career. But a little luck doesn't hurt either. Opportunity led Deborah to live and work in three distinctly different American regions that could be considered three different Americas: the New York area; the Mid-West; and Chattanooga, Tennessee, where she settled. Chattanooga is unique among U.S. cities. A culturally diverse population with a flair for entrepreneurship, it has an ecosystem tailored to the unique human capital of the city and supported by various business-friendly stakeholders. As a free spirit who found herself in the right place in the right time—that quality of luck again—Deborah explored the area and felt inspired to share her ideas and skills.

It was in Chattanooga that Deborah's own entrepreneurial spirit grew into a flame. A late bloomer like her father, she accumulated a wealth of experience along diverse career paths, digesting them, and coming up with a transformational concept of "marrying mindsets" or bringing them to a common denominator so they could coexist in peace living and working to each other's benefit. Her work with expatriates, immigrants, and the native-born Americans who moved to the economically booming city of Chattanooga enabled

Deborah to see first-hand how diverse cultures impact each other. This multicultural frame of mind helped her to tailor her ideas of intercultural and interfaith actions to assist Chattanooga's manufacturing sector. In fact, the Chattanooga business climate supported Debora's breakthrough from her Jewish-centered work to broader all-inclusive cultural activities. The city asked for it and Deborah delivered[296], building a Jewish Cultural Center in 2000.

It wasn't easy for the introverted Deborah to become a much-in-demand consultant and leader, but she did so by teaching others cross-cultural communication, designing inclusion-oriented community projects, and engaging diverse women in pilot projects. This ultimately led to her self-discovery as diversity professional and an award-winning author.

"My efforts [in Chattanooga] re-invigorated the Jewish community, providing it with a pre-school, an art gallery, community gathering place and an identity. I went on to create the women's council on diversity, the American Diversity Report, the Global Leadership Class and the Cross-Cultural School of the South."[297]

COMING INTO HER OWN

"Entrepreneur of spirit" is the phrase I use to describe a leader who combines a rich spiritual life with intellectual capabilities, creativity, and business acumen. Since many of Deborah's accomplishments stem from her being Jewish, it's certainly appropriate in her case.

"In my early days in NYC, I was offered a job at an employment agency with the stipulation that I change my name. I believe it was too Jewish for them," Deborah says. "As for discrimination for being a woman, I couldn't find a job out of college as a manager, and finally went to secretarial school to support myself. I ended up as a Gal Friday in the NYC garment district."[298]

After studying at Harvard and NYU, Deborah was no longer identified as an immigrant, but "people did identify me as Jewish and I believe that some jobs were closed to me because of it. That's one reason I went to work for Jewish agencies. I didn't run into the problem [of denial] there, however, the Jewish agencies beyond the local level that were run by women were few and far between."[299] Deborah became one of the first women running such organizations, an accomplishment that stems, in part, from her frustration in trying to get ahead in the secular world.

Even so, the soft-spoken Deborah frequently ended up as an anonymous administrator, all the while aware that her greater capabilities and talents were going to waste. So, she made a difficult decision to use her knowledge of the Jewish world, her unusual education mix, and her family contacts to create a career that would make a difference to others while being personally satisfying.

Although non-profits didn't pay much, she felt personally rewarded. " As I increasingly own my Jewish heritage, things are changing," she said: "For the first time, I agreed to be on the local Holocaust Remembrance Committee, to publish my parents' letters from WW II, and talk about my father being a liberator of the Nordhausen work camp."[300] This work also helped her to discover herself.

> My joy has come from creating beautiful projects, alternate universes, out of virtually nothing. I am an artist, inventor, teacher, anthropologist, and Jewish leader - a combination that my husband suggests has no name. His love and that of our daughters [from their prior marriages] fills and entertains me in good times [and] sustains and energizes me in dark times. When there is another crash and burn of my immune system, I turn to them and to Judaism's mystical elements. I create through my writing, restoring my soul. I am amazed, honored, and grateful to Ha Shem (Literally "The Name", meaning G-d) for this extraordinary life and the faith that the best is yet to come.[301]

AN INCLUSIVE LEADER—AND A BUSY ONE

Deborah Levine loves to stay busy and be needed: "I always have at least one new major initiative underway and it's truly hell.

But I know of no other way to live." An inclusive leader in the local community and in the blogosphere, she is also an influencer and author of best-selling books such as *Teaching Curious Christians about Judaism*[302], which was recently presented to Pope Francis. She consults for international clients such as Volkswagen, Nissan, International Paper, and Kimberly Clark, and is a member of the Tennessee Advisory Committee of the US Global Leadership Coalition and an advisor to the International Council of Birmingham. Quite an impressive roster for the girl who felt marked for being different.

But of course, it was feeling different—that is, Jewish—that led Deborah to move beyond mainstream-American organizations and find gratifying work with Jewish non-profits. And it was that work, in turn, that led her to "marry mentalities" by writing and acting towards interfacing religious beliefs, cultural values, and practices—which, in turn, brought her success as diversity and inclusion consultant.

Today, Deborah's entertaining and instructive seminars, workshops and stories help facilitate dialogue on such difficult subjects as bullying, race, identity, and discrimination. Looking at her manifold activities of an award-winning author of thirteen books; speaker and coach; founder/editor of American Diversity Report for over seventeen years; and op-ed columnist of Chattanooga Times Free Press – we can safely say that Deborah specializes in creativity, innovation, and collaboration.

She knows that the "energy, passion, dedication, and perseverance of immigrants are unparalleled in any other element of the population,"[303] and works to ease the acculturation process for those newly arrived in the South and in America-at-large. Deborah's input into contemporary interfaith and intercultural concerns makes her a valuable role model for those seeking success in the underexplored terrain of spiritual entrepreneurship—wherein the future is surely found.

Edwina Sandys *from England*

The Intuitive Artist

Edwina near her sculpture *Eve's Apple,* at Ann Norton Sculpture Gardens, West Palm Beach, FL

A Londoner by birth and a New Yorker by choice, Edwina Sandys (pronounced "sands") is a renowned sculptor, artist, and writer. A recipient of many prestigious accolades, including the 1997 United Nations Society of Writers & Artists Award,[304] she is also the granddaughter of Sir Winston Churchill.

Edwina's art combines the lighthearted and the profound, the sacred and the secular. And she loves to provoke. Edwina works in various media and has made her most distinctive marks in sculpture, painting, collage, and works on paper. Early in her career, she created three pieces for the United Nations' Year of the Child (1979), which are now installed in the UN centers in New York, Geneva, and Vienna. Her sculpture *Breakthrough*, comprised of twelve dismantled sections of the Berlin Wall, is now permanently sited at Westminster College in Fulton, Missouri, the very place where Churchill gave his historic "Iron Curtain" speech. The piece was dedicated by former President Ronald Reagan, and later—in a highly symbolic move—celebrated by former General Secretary of the Soviet Union Mikhail Gorbachev.

BREAKING THE MOLD

An outstanding artist by any measure, and a descendant of a renowned aristocratic family, Edwina grew up surrounded by the influential figures of the time, such as Field Marshal Montgomery. Her famous grandfather was at home with his family after the war, and young Edwina would watch him paint. (A wonderful artist with a fabulous sense of color—bold, not wishy-washy—he influenced his granddaughter in her painting patterns. Edwina's art may be unearthly compared with Winston Churchill's soundly representational paintings, but she too is often monumental in scale.)

Edwina was well educated at boarding school, but as was the *habit of women in her day,*[305] *she didn't go to college. Edwina married on her twenty-second birthday.* Bitten by the political bug after the birth of her two sons, she became a town councilor and thought of standing for Parliament. Alas, her husband wanted that role, and as a traditional wife and mother, it fell to Edwina to help with his campaign. Blocked in her own path for a political career, energetic Edwina turned to literature, writing the novel *Truth Lies Somewhere in Between,* which would eventually lead her to write a weekly lifestyle column in the *Sunday Telegraph* in London. The woman who wanted to be something more than just a wife and a mother had found an outlet for her energy and ambition.

It was around this time that she started painting. Edwina may have grown up watching her grandfather paint, but with no formal training she had to rely on her own intuition and sense of beauty. To her surprise, she actually found painting more enjoyable than writing. "It seemed to be much more spontaneous," she said. And she sketched everybody who came her way. "My artistic career," said Edwina, "started in 1970 with felt pen colored drawings on paper. I had a show in London and sold them all and got commissions to do portraits of ambassadors and diplomats. Hitherto I had only drawn people as characters, not as likenesses."[306]

> Edwina Sandys grew up watching her famous grandfather paint, but with no formal training she had to rely on her own intuition and sense of beauty.

As life went on, Edwina and her husband grew apart, eventually divorcing. The divorce was a turning point for the artist, who began painting in all seriousness, branching out into sculpture, modeling in clay which was then cast in bronze. Her first big show[307] was at the Crane Kalman Gallery in London, and many critics, including *Daily Telegraph,* wrote that Edwina's lines recalled those of Matisse.[308] Art became her overriding passion, and she *forged boldly ahead.*

AMERICAN BEGINNINGS

Edwina was still living in London when she first got to know some Americans, many of whom were diplomats and men of letters. "I started liking Americans before coming here, from the beginning, from the first meetings," she said, and "this liking intensified."[309] The bonds of friendship have always been central to Edwina's life, and she was quick to appreciate the fact that Americans are open, that you don't have to wait for months before becoming friends. "Making friends and connecting them with each other," she says "has never lost its thrill."[310]

> "People always think I came here to get away from the constraints of England, but I didn't. I came here to get something *extra.*"[311]

Edwina reverted to her maiden name after her divorce. And it was in search of "fresh fields and pastures new" that she made a step forward to America when her exhibition at Hammer Galleries was arranged by her Gallery in London. New York has a profound effect on everyone, it seems, even those who grew up in a metropolis such as London. For Edwina, the sheer scale and physical excitement of New York was a tremendous draw. "Things are smaller in England," she said. "People always think I came here to get away from the constraints of England, but I didn't. I came here to get something *extra*. I came to add another string to my bow."[312] Indeed, after her divorce, reverting to her maiden name, and living in her own right without the necessary validation of the man to whom she was attached by marriage provided a new sense of freedom for Edwina. She thrived.

At first, Edwina traveled often between London and New York. She soon realized, however, that New Yorkers are quick not just to appreciate, but to invest in art. That was appealing to the young artist, and further attracted her to the city. With her sons in boarding school in England, Edwina decided to spend more of her time in New York, so she rented an apartment near the East River with a view of the UN. And when it became increasingly difficult to live in two countries, she made the choice to slide into living and working in New York full time: "It was a gradual, smooth transition, not an overnight decision. Marrying Richard [her second husband, the architect Richard D. Kaplan, a native New Yorker who passed away in 2016, F.C.] made me want it even more: he wouldn't move to London while I was already based here."[313] So, it was her second husband who solidified the deal—and Edwina became a New Yorker.

CHALLENGES IN AMERICA

Analytical by nature, Edwina is objective in comparing the UK and the US. She's complimentary when speaking of American culture, and cites openness, friendliness, and enthusiasm as her reasons for liking it. She admires the way people can get things done quickly here, and appreciates the way that Europeans become more accessible in America than they are in Europe.

But she's candid when talking about the hurdles she has faced:

It's a challenge to get into the right galleries, and I haven't been totally successful with this; part of the reason is that I have a hang-up from old-fashioned times when a woman needs to wait to be invited. Being a woman, you have to play on two sides: you are meant to back up your man in his career; you need to be charming—I've been brought up this way and have hesitated to be too strident, still having a feeling to be 'womanly.' So, it's probably my fault.[314]

Not all of Edwina's hurdles were the product of her upbringing. Some came about simply because she was ignorant of the realities of working here, including the way in which American labor unions operate. In her early years in New York, for example, Edwina had a marble sculpture shipped from Italy, her first piece for the UN. Advised to use a certain shipping company, Edwina thought that shipper too expensive, so found one at a third of the price. The sculpture had been delivered on time, but Edwina's shippers lacked the necessary credentials and were not allowed to take the sculpture to the Plaza. Edwina remembers it as if it were yesterday: "I was a babe in the woods knowing nothing about a mafia, and just watched how for three days my shipper arrived with my sculpture and then took it back. Then some kind person from a forwarding insurance agency helped me: he found a trouble-fixer who went to Brooklyn and talked to mafia, saying 'Let that lady go!' And the issue was resolved."[315] Now having lived in New York for half of her life, Edwina looks back at the incident with her characteristic humor, for she can look with humor at almost everything.

Edwina Sandys cites openness, friendliness, and enthusiasm among the most positive of American qualities.

Edwina speaks with a natural humility when assessing career opportunities lost and found: "I haven't done as well as I should have. Some opportunities—like work for UN or the Berlin Wall—wouldn't have happened to me in Europe. On the other hand, some jokes I put in my art may be more appreciated in Britain, as humorous art is more in the English tradition"[316] Edwina explains it as a by-product of being brought up in a culture where people are generally praised for originality, as the British like to be unique. "I like things [that are] serious as well as frivolous, and I believe there's no reason for a woman to be only one thing and not another."[317] In a Foreword to "Edwina Sandys Art," Anthony Haden-Guest presented her as a remarkable oddity,[318] but I believe it's more accurate to speak of Edwina's individuality (as different from individualism) and her penchant for all things different, authentic, and thought-provoking.

Edwina is proud of her work, which has reached wide audiences and been subject to international acclaim. "I'm ambitious," she admits, "and I want my work to be enjoyable and inspiring to people."

FEMINIST VALUES AT WORK

An outstanding artist and sculptress by any measure, Edwina distinguished herself by her profound ideas. Addressing numerous political and women's issues came naturally to her, and her embedded creativity led her to express her own perception of the world's critical issues in a provocative way that makes people think.

Edwina grew to be a feminist by watching her grandfather. Winston Churchill was not afraid to be emotional. He'd even recite poetry to the point of bringing tears to his eyes. He was a multi-talented man, and people appreciated that. And he also married the right woman who, in Edwina's words, "was very strong, very beautiful, very wise."[319] Edwina saw first-hand in her own family how important it was for a woman to be strong in order to be an adequate partner for a strong man. Only then could the world benefit from their combined strengths.

> Edwina Sandys' feminist focus is not cerebral or purely intellectual, but originates from her sense that the "essence of a woman" is everywhere we turn.

Much of Edwina's later work is about women and their place in society—and her focus on those issues has resulted in strong, distinctly feminist ideas and interpretations. She started by depicting things that were going on in her life: relationship, separation, divorce, and hence, a conflict between a man and a woman. Her books put these respective conflicts into words and drawings, while her art delivers the lingering effect of visual feminist statements.

In addition to her monumental sculptures, Edwina's other major work is her series *The States of Woman*, a collection begun in the early nineties which focused on the social status of women in our time. The collection, which was made in a variety of media, includes the works: *Marriage Bed, Biological Clock, Target of Abuse, Glass Ceiling, Gilded Cage, Erotic Woman, Maternal Woman* and *Ancestor Woman*. Of particular interest is *The Marriage Bed,* which is in the permanent collection of the Brooklyn Museum of Art. A full-sized metal bed divided with nails and big red roses, it exemplifies the idea that marriage is a bed of nails and roses. Today, Edwina's feminist-related works are mainly large-scale metal sculptures, including her iconic *Eve's Apple* and her *Sunflower Woman*, commissioned by Henry Buhl for his celebrated Sunflower Collection.

Somewhat apart, is her piece *Christa*[320]—a female on-the-cross Christ figure—which is probably the most notable of all her bronzes. Created in 1975 and displayed in numerous churches, *Christa,* which portrays a women's perspective on suffering, was finally installed at Easter 1984 in New York's Cathedral of St. John the Divine. The media coverage created a worldwide commotion, and Edwina experienced the double-edged sword of public debate, as both applause and critique flooded in.

Edwina has invested a lot of artistic energy in drawing attention to women—she has referred to them as "second-class citizens"[321]—and elevating their status in this world. Unlike some other feminist artists, Edwina's focus is not cerebral or purely intellectual, but originates from her intuition that the "essence of a woman" is everywhere we turn: love, children, relationship, flowers, and life at large. Accordingly, Edwina's feminism is an expression of her childhood belief about the importance of each individual woman, as well as the meaningful power of collective womanhood.

CONTRIBUTIONS TO AMERICAN CULTURE

Over the last thirty-five years Edwina has created art of international acclaim and her work has reached wide audiences. "I'm ambitious and I want my work to be enjoyable and inspiring to people,"[322] she said.

Edwina has contributed to American culture by creating major works of art in the U.S. and exhibiting them in museums and galleries across the country. She has directed the public's attention to political and humanitarian issues, and to feminist-related issues as well. What's more, she has also helped to bring together American and British cultures. In 1983 she organized many events in the "Britain Salutes New York Festival" in which British museums loaned their treasures to American institutions. And she even brought her grandfather Winston Churchill's paintings to be exhibited at the New York Academy of Arts and to the Smithsonian. When asked to create a city-wide program showcasing the Royal Oak Foundation, she did that too. Edwina's role was—as she modestly acknowledges—to identify opportunities and ask, "Would you like to do something for "Britain Salutes New York?" And they did.

TOPICS OF IMPACT

Edwina's art deserves worldwide recognition for its lingering imprint of a deep-rooted democracy, and for the way in which it promotes women's relevance in a free world by capturing not just their transcending beauty, but their suffering as well. Consider the iconic "Woman Free" sculpture she made for the United Nations in Vienna. Using positive and negative shapes, each as important as the other, Edwina cut a woman out of rough marble block, a figure that stands free and clear, ready to reach her full potential. It's a powerful image and a powerful message.

"I want my work to have an immediate, instant impact," she says. "You look at it first because it catches your eye. And you want to look at it again. Then you realize it's something different than what you originally thought."[323]

Many critics say that her sculptures play with the line between literal representation and alternative reality and that her paintings recall Matisse, with a hint of the playful surrealism of Magritte. Edwina calls works like *Breakthrough*—one of her most iconic sculptures—yin and yang. She would cut something out and then show the reverse. "You've got to read the space, she said, and "the idea was how to portray an abstract idea like freedom. To portray freedom, you need to portray non-freedom. The wall represents a barrier, and the man and woman breaking through the wall was the push for freedom."[324]

Life of an artist is never stopping for Edwina, with her new project commissioned by Cornerstone Schools in Detroit. This new piece will be crafted out of one of her favorite mediums, steel, designed to inspire the students and staff, as well as foster the neighborhood redevelopment. The idea of an arch - the hands of friendship, caring and loving – would make her grandfather Sir Winston Churchill who loved and cared for America feel proud for Edwina.

Edwina refuses to be restricted. "I like men and women, she said, I like flowers very much. I like situations and juxtaposing opposites to tweak people's minds. I like the puzzle and challenge that a commission gives you—not just working on your own but sometimes being forced to consider things from another's point of view."[325] And every time she rises to the challenge.

PART TWO

Seven Success Values

Introduction

The success values exemplified by the women in this book are intangible must-haves—those imperatives that guide us like a built-in GPS, helping us to make the right decisions, no matter what the goal. These values form the fundamentals of who we are, and are inextricably linked to both our principles and our passions.

A success value is different from a rule or commandment, the focus of many leadership books today. Rules are typically focused on ingredients-plus-process, and they are also tied intimately to outcome. Do *this*, says the rule, and your result will be *that*. Rules can be helpful, of course, but when it comes to pursuing something bigger—those meaningful achievements and relationships that make a life worthwhile, we need to consider the very foundation of success. That's where values come in.

The Seven Success Values in this book are a common denominator pad to all prominent achievers, and were collected/abstracted from interviews, questionnaires, books, and other supporting materials. The values are organized under the headings of: Character Building; the American Mindset; Emotional Intelligence; Communication Skills and Creativity; Strategic Thinking; Inclusive Leadership; and Perseverance. Each section is further organized to present the qualities that support each value, followed by a "How do we . . ." segment that provides an illustrative "case study." So, for example, the fifth value—STRATEGIC THINKING—is supported by the quality of adaptability, the capacity to adjust to new conditions. That quality is exemplified by the examples of Irmgard Lafrentz, who developed adaptability by building a bridge between two cultures, and also by Alfa Demmellash, who fostered a future-oriented outlook.

Think of each of these values not as a goal, but as a process, that is, something to be cultivated. Building a value set of our own is a dynamic thing. When we cultivate a value, we're teaching ourselves to foster the growth of something important to us. Values come from our principles and beliefs. They require us to adapt our awareness and our actions to get closer to what we care about. Strong values and the willingness to act on them are vital to success; nevertheless, they are not goals that we can cross off one list so that we can move onto the next. Our value set is our internal engine—like software that makes our hardware (brains and talents) work.

Over the years, I've given a lot of thought to the notion of values. Like so many people, my values were formed by my family, and I'm grateful to have had two strong role models in my mother and father. I remember when my father was dying of cancer for three long months. He had been placed in the best hospital in town, not because he was a well-deserving veteran who had fought fascism in the second world war, but because my brother Simon was a famous doctor and head of that hospital's department, a small detail of life in Ukraine at the time.

My father was in agony, with ever-increasing pain, so the family took turns sitting by his bed. Someone was with him day and night. My shift was during the day; I could dedicate long hours since I was on creative leave from the university, for finalizing my doctoral thesis. It was hard. My father was aware of his diagnosis, but we never discussed it. In moments of relief, he would tell me his wartime stories, most of which I had known since childhood. A former captain in the Chemical Division of the Army, he would recollect how he and his lieutenant pried into the enemies' frontline to see if they were preparing chemical nerve-gas weapons for attack. They drove a horse and cart, as a local peasant would, passing through a village taken by the enemy and turning back just before the trenches, quickly whirling back. They were almost out of trouble when the shooting began. He smiled at this memory: it felt good to be alive.

He would also reminisce about happier moments: day trips to the woods, sleeping in a tent and cooking food over the fire; treating the family to Black Sea vacations. A chemical engineer by training, my father also recollected some innovations he introduced at his jobs. Indeed, inventing and changing things were his favorite occupations, passions that were passed down to my brother and me. We're both kind of restless and seeking something new all the time.

My father would also share with me his wisdom of how to love well, how to care about the family and such. These conversations were casual, with no mention that he would soon be gone. Once he asked me what I would be doing that evening, and I said I would be sewing a new dress. Quick as an arrow, he asked, "What color?" and was visibly relieved to hear, "Red."

"Black," of course, would signal preparations for his funeral.

On the last day I saw him alive, my father took my hand and said, "I'm so happy you'll be a doctor, but it's not the doctor I need: your doctorate is about suffixes-prefixes." (That's how he referred to linguistics). I said, "Papa, my suffixes-prefixes are really complicated and I'm not even sure I can pull them out!" He looked me straight in the eyes and replied, "Never doubt it! You are *my* daughter. Just think of what *I* did in my time and *how* I did it. Remember, there's no elevator to success, you have to take the stairs."

Something turned in me; a lump formed in my throat. This was his good-bye, his blessing. And for many years now, I've been doing just that: climbing the stairs—yes, sometimes with my teeth clenched—trying to be worthy of my father. When I think of the big questions of my life, I always consider my father: What would *he* have done? Would *he* approve? Have I been good enough? Asking these questions over the years has helped me to measuring my success against his values. And those values helped me build myself from the ground up.

The First Value

Character Building

*Character—the willingness to accept responsibility for one's
own life—is the source from which self-respect springs.*
Joan Didion

If you want to be successful, you have to start from within. You need
to make a constant effort to build your own character, and you need
to persist. Follow your instinct. Cultivate the drive and determination to do things your own way. And remember that almost nothing
good happens overnight.

Self-coaching is a serious approach to character-building, to
sustaining who you are and what you want to be. You need to
build your success from within, however slowly it takes. So, build
your character and earn respect for your strength and integrity.
Starting now.

BREAKING THE MOLD
The women leaders I interviewed for this book have all demonstrated the inherent ability to break the mold, showing the true
pioneer spirit in everything they do. And by "breaking the mold"
I mean exhibiting strong character in pursuing their goals and in-
sisting on their right to do things their own way.

How can we break the mold?

- By moving out of our comfort zone.

- By demonstrating grit.

Moving Out of Our Comfort Zone

Consider Edwina Sandys. It isn't easy to break the mold if you're born into the English aristocracy—a hierarchal society where tradition takes precedence. Edwina was expected to do certain things a certain way. But she had a bold personality, and while she may have started along the traditional path of wife, mother, and society maven, she always wanted more. Edwina understood that to break the mold she would have to break out of her comfort zone. That meant getting out of the conservative aristocratic mentality—and out of Britain.

In England, Edwina had been discouraged from pursuing her own political career; hers was to be a supporting role. But the young wife and mother needed an outlet for her creative energies, so she took first to writing, and then to painting. Edwina had no formal training, but she had tremendous insight and instinct. Novelty was a magnet to Edwina, and she traveled to New York City in search of a place to satisfy her desire to create something radically new, something "extra." It was this drive, combined with a sense of beauty and a desire for social justice, that set her on the road to becoming a renowned artist and sculptor. Edwina persisted in breaking the mold and forging profound new paths which left her mark in art and sculpture. Conveying her leadership in artistic ideas took character and spirit. But Edwina has always had the guts to insist on her artistic vision and her right to do it her way.

Demonstrating Grit

You can only break out of the mold if you're willing to learn new things. That means there's always a first, always a new situation in which you'll be expected to hit the ground running without having the requisite knowledge or skill set in place. Ivana Trump found that out when husband Donald put her in charge of several massive projects in the Trump Organization. A former model who wanted to be more than just a titular head of projects, Ivana had to learn on the go. That meant relying on her inner grit, studying relentlessly, and picking up speed daily. Sure, this was an opportunity to show her natural talent for interior decorating, but there was much more to the job than that. Ivana had to learn how to manage a business and its people, the toughest charge of all. Eventually, she was managing 4,000 employees with a payroll of $1.2 million a week. She did it by demonstrating her grit and learning on the go:

- by using her unmistakable taste for all things beautiful;

- by drawing on her instinct to motivate the people she managed; and

- by being tough and getting down-to-business.

Ivana proved her mettle by working day-in and day-out: signing every check, training and retraining personnel, and re-designing the interiors in her own inimitable, and luxurious way.

STAYING STRONG AND POSITIVE

If there's one thing leaders have in common, it's a positive attitude, the belief that with hard work, ingenuity, and perhaps a little luck, things will turn out okay. Sure, there will be setbacks, even failures. But if you believe in yourself, if you maintain a strong vision and an optimistic outlook, you can weather the storm.

How can we stay strong and positive?

- By developing self-confidence.

- By succeeding in a can-do nation.

Developing Self-Confidence

Confidence is key. Success isn't possible without it. Raegan Moya-Jones's had only her killer instinct—that is to say, a confidence in herself and a certainty in her product—to rely upon in the early years of her company. She had pride, too, and she never allowed anybody to see the blood, sweat and tears behind the energetic façade of a self-made businesswoman. Likewise, Hilda Ochoa Brillembourg, who started her financial company at the time of financial distress, in 1987, would never have succeeded had she not had faith in her sophisticated risk management model and solid contacts.

Weili Dai had confidence in spades, not to mention an excess of energy and a positive attitude that she inherited from her mother, whom she chose as a role model. But it was moving to the U.S., and being faced with the realities of the competitive American market-place that pushed her further. Pursuing a career while nurturing her family, Weili knew that she had to stay positive. "I believe in myself (in my in-built engine) and can focus and observe discipline—and I do believe that upbringing is core for success."

Playing competitive sports gave Weili a lot of confidence, and it also showed her the supportive power of teamwork. She has no problem delegating tasks or in being involved in many events simultaneously. She knows how to distribute her personal resources evenly along the way. Weili's endless energy may have prompted comparisons to the "Energizer Bunny," but it's her optimism and positive attitude, fortified by her competitive spirit and skills as a team player that have made her success possible.

Succeeding in a Can-Do Nation

Rohini Anand learned that succeeding in America, with its can-do culture, takes a very strong character. In a country where "Yes We Can" could fire up the whole nation, there's no place for doubt or delay. So, Rohini has worked-out to become strong. Over the years she has conscientiously fine-tuned her own character to cultivate a can-do attitude. For Rohini, that means, being:

- **Optimistic:** Seeing the glass as half-full, not half-empty.

- **Strategic:** Looking forward, not backwards.

- **Self-Reliant:** Being grounded. Knowing who she is and what she stands for.

- **Authentic:** Being herself, with no pretense. Ever.

- **Resilient:** Remembering her strengths and keeping things in perspective. And never taking anything personally.

A constant learner, Rohini absorbed the lessons that experience provided. She became a pragmatic risk-taker (not something that came naturally to her), and constantly sought out new experiences. This was especially true of her decision to return from India to the U.S., which she did to restart her career and raise her daughters with American values. Rohini pushed herself to succeed in a can-do nation—and she made it.

SAFEGUARDING THE SELF

All too often, immigrants and minorities are undermined and scapegoated for petty political gains. What's more, the moment an immigrant crosses a border, she loses social status. The good news, however, is that while immigrants suffer a decrease in their social standing, they still retain their values, their identity, and, perhaps most important of all, their pride. Indeed, numerous studies[326] show that most immigrants are proud individuals, as non-verbal expression of pride generalizes across cultures. (Darwin was right when he said that, "Of all the complex emotions . . . pride, perhaps, is the most plainly expressed.[327]")

It's important to know how to safeguard yourself, not to mention your self-esteem, when making the transition from one country to another. While it's important to adapt to your new circumstances, it's equally important to stand tall, to remember who you are and where you came from. Pride can help with that. Pride, virtuous pride—which is built on an innate sense of value and personal identity rather than fleeting standards such as wealth or status —is an important part of an immigrant's character. Sometimes it can seem like an immigrant's guardian angel. Virtuous pride supports self-confidence and fosters strength, as well as perseverance. What's more, pride can even alleviate the burden of prejudice: the more prejudice you face, the more pride you need to offset it.

How do we safeguard the self?

- By counteracting prejudice with pride

- By doing good, being proud.

Counteracting Prejudice with Pride
Deborah Levine's goal of integrating into mainstream American culture was initially hampered by her visibly Jewish looks and deeply rooted Jewish upbringing. Yet on the other hand, many of her accomplishments stemmed from her pride in being Jewish. Working for Jewish agencies, Deborah eventually became a writer, a diversity expert, and a Huffington Post blogger. Her now famous "marrying mentalities" approach included tackling not just religious beliefs, but the cultures and mindsets of diverse ethnic-racial communities, something she was uniquely qualified to do. This approach stemmed from pride in her identity as a safety net for integration pains, and is now broadly used to counteract prejudices.

Doing Good, Being Proud
If Deborah Levine's strong character was forged while opposing the lingering prejudice against the Jewish people, it was her personal integrity and cultural pride that motivated her to stand up, speak

up, and contribute to America's well-being. Capable and educated, Deborah at first found her professional efforts frustrated by discrimination. She didn't stop at being a victim of bias, though; she found work with various Jewish agencies, eventually becoming an expert on diversity.

Over time, it became clear that many of Deborah's major accomplishments stemmed from her pride in being Jewish. And when she found that her compassionate actions could also affect others who, like herself, had been subjected to injustice, she dedicated her life to "marrying cultures and mentalities," bringing together not just religious groups, but diverse ethnic-racial communities as well.

Deborah Levine is a natural do-gooder and compassionate woman who has forged a career—and a life—out of pride, compassion, and inclusivity.

BREAKING THE GLASS CEILING

It's been forty years since Marilyn Loden coined the phrase "glass ceiling"[328] to describe the invisible barriers that prevent women from reaching top leadership positions. While the glass ceiling still exists, many breakthroughs have been made. As the women in this study demonstrate, it can be done.

How can we break the glass ceiling?

- By proving our worth in insider circles.

- By developing leadership capabilities.

- By punching our tickets.

Proving Our Worth in Insider Circles

Ying McGuire is a self-made woman, a leader in a male-dominated industry where the glass ceiling is especially hard to break. A young single mother of two; an immigrant with an accent; a fresh MBA grad—she started at Dell with a lot of ground to cover. But she was extremely ambitious and had a contained fire that was just waiting for the right time to ignite.

Ying worked hard and was well qualified to do the job at hand. Still, she left nothing to chance. Most of her colleagues were men, and she knew how important it was for them to consider her as one of them, "not an outlier." So, in addition to building relationships on the job, she joined them for happy hour and other social events, such as dove shooting. "I was able to join a group of twenty-five male colleagues as the only woman to shoot doves in San Antonio one year. I practiced, shooting clay birds beforehand. On the day of the event, I shot more doves than many men in the group. As a result, I gained more respect from them at work."

Ying understood that the office environment has its limits. She felt that casual off-campus occasions provided an opportunity to network, to get to know her team members in a more relaxed way—and let them get to know her. By taking action to "lean in" in a subtle way, she was able to reframe the perception of some of her male colleagues who respected women, but—in that not-only-Texan tradition—did not always seem ready to accept them as equals on the job. Ying knew that it wasn't enough to be excellent. She had to change perception to be accepted in insider circles.

Developing Leadership Capabilities
Sophie Vandebroek learned to be a self-directed leader. Here's how:

- **Cultivate a Good Reputation:** Make sure you have a good name, and that you are known for inspiring optimism, loyalty, reliability, and commitment.

- **Build Relationships:** As a single mother of three kids and no family in the U.S., Sophie realized the critical importance of relationships with neighbors, kids' teachers, kids' friend's parents, babysitters, cleaning ladies—all the people who are part of the personal infrastructure that helps life run smoothly. Don't take relationships for granted, she advises. Jobs are easy to change; relationships are not.

- **Be Roughly Right:** Don't strive for perfection. It's impossible to achieve. Nobody can have the perfect home or the perfect body. Your kids won't have perfect grades. It may be fun to try, but the amount of extra effort required will only give you incremental results . . . and a lot more stress.

- **Don't Be Afraid of Change:** Each crisis brings opportunity. Tragic events bring new friends, new relationships, new beginnings. Major life changes can be hard to deal with, but they create openings for personal growth, for asking and for giving help to others.

- **Have Fun:** Life is too precious not to enjoy what you do each day at work and at home.

Punching Our Ticket

Sophie Vandebroek has brought a lot to the American experience. Her strict upbringing, passion for high-tech, ambition, and work ethic combined to get her into the corner office of Xerox Innovation Group, the best industry research lab worldwide. Her passion for innovating—and cultivating innovation company-wide—is innate. She compares her job to "reading a fantastic book where your brain gets so involved in the topic that you basically forget everything else."

Sophie shared her personal passion and her methodology of sustained success in high-tech using the metaphor of the "punched ticket," which means gaining respect and credibility from colleagues, planning your career, and making sure your achievements are acknowledged each step of the way. The secret is to "get your ticket punched over and over again," she says. That is, you have to keep innovating with the same non-stop passion, because every time you move to a new field or take a new responsibility you need to reestablish your professional credibility. So, keep punching.

The Second Value

The American Mindset

If you don't get out of the box you've been raised in,
you won't understand how much bigger the world is.
Angelina Jolie

Each of the women profiled in this book has spoken of the adaptations she has made in an effort to feel at home in her new country—the cultural assimilation that requires all sorts of adjustments. We all understand how language influences perception (certainly a language barrier seems like the first large hurdle to overcome); and yet, when it comes to acclimating to a new country, cultural adaptation is actually more important than language proficiency.

Cultural assimilation—the process of adopting an American mindset—comes from understanding the realities that shape behavior, in all their many forms. Cultural assimilation prompts us to accept the new ways of doing things, to consider the outlook of those we want to connect with, and to do what we can to ensure that our message is received as intended. Context is important for the new immigrant. And culture is king.

REALIZING THE AMERICAN DREAM

The American Dream is sometimes denounced for being a shallow, economic cliché—the shiny engine of our consumer society. Nothing could be further from the truth. Consider the four facets that Ted Ownby identifies in his book, *American Dreams in Mississippi*: abundance, democracy, freedom of choice, and the dream of novelty and unhampered innovation. It's these qualities that hold this diverse nation together. Moreover, it's these same qualities, and the dream they represent, that attracts newcomers in the hope that a country that emphasizes personal freedom can help them realize their own unique potential.

How can we realize the American dream?

• By accepting positive American traits.

• By counting our blessings.

Accepting Positive American Traits

Josie Natori loves the U.S. for the way in which it enables people who have come from nothing to aspire to something. There are more opportunities here than in any other country in the world. Her favorite American traits: can-do attitudes; sense of freedom; friendliness; mobility, including social mobility; diversity; developed philanthropy; personal anonymity; and punctuality. They inspired her to stay in the US and aspire higher.

Josie appreciates the freedoms available to her in the U.S. (Philippine society is more rigid and structured.) She enjoys her personal anonymity and appreciates American punctuality. (Philippine culture is more informal.) And she has come to love the American custom of helping the less fortunate. Josie's success has made it possible to engage in big philanthropic efforts. She feels tremendous satisfaction in caring for people. Overall, Josie's grateful for everything America has to offer, culturally and otherwise—and she's well-integrated for continued success.

Counting Our Blessings

Ani Palacios McBride feels tremendous gratitude for the blessings of her new home country. She is particularly grateful for the American abundance mentality that slowly outplaced her Latino immigrant scarcity mentality. Growing up in Peru, Ani felt that opportunities were few, that there would never be enough for everyone to go around, and that her choices for the future were limited. After immigrating to the U.S., Ani felt a shift, and was able to gradually open up to the possibilities that lay ahead. She acknowledges that her achievements—indeed, her whole family's achievements—would become possible only in the States. And she is very grateful.

ADAPTING TO MAINSTREAM CULTURE

Emigrating is not for the faint-hearted. Not only does it mean major adjustments to your daily routine (how to catch a bus; how to order a meal), it requires you to look anew at the way in which you navigate the world. Adapting to a new mainstream culture means learning a whole new set of customs, traditions, and values—and it can seem insurmountable. But it can be done.

How can we adapt to mainstream culture?

- By blending cultures.

- By working for inclusive companies.

- By articulating our experiences to help others.

Blending Cultures

Bridging the cultural differences between China and America could seem like an insurmountable challenge. Not for Ying McGuire. She had a tremendous drive to succeed in her new country, and understood that such a goal could only be achieved by blending cultures and becoming a part of mainstream American society. It wasn't easy, but eventually, she was able to bridge the culture gap.

I think [of] myself as a Chinese-American. In this case, Chinese is an adjective but American is the noun. I am blessed to have the opportunity to be an American while being able to take the essence from both cultures and heritages and weave them into the fabric of my life and my children's lives. [For instance], I love food and love to cook. My cooking is a perfect reflection of "east meets west." I take my favorite ingredients and materials from both worlds and make unforgettable "fusion meals."

Ingrained cultural traits do not fade away readily. A fact that Ying knows. The once rebellious girl who often did the opposite of what she was told, used to be shy in expressing herself. Ying knew that her reticence was hurting her career, so she made a huge effort to overcome her shyness, going against the grain of her upbringing. It took determination and courage, but eventually Ying started speaking up and communicating confidently as Americans do. As a result, she developed a brand for herself as a driver, a leader, and a confident public speaker. Eager to bridge the cultural gap, Ying took to heart communication techniques that native-born folks also use, mastering them and outperforming many.

Working for Inclusive Companies

After earning her doctorate from Cornell, Sophie Vandebroek started working at IBM research labs where most of the researchers and managers were born overseas, with only a couple of "token" U.S. born colleagues. Working in this high-tech environment helped her feel at home almost immediately. But five years after immigrating, having moved to Rochester, N.Y. to work at Xerox research labs, Sophie suddenly became aware of being different.

Although a significant percentage of the researchers at Xerox were also immigrants, other local employees, and most of her neighbors, were American born. The differences were now obvious.

Luckily for Sophie, she never had an issue with being accepted—because Xerox is a company with a long tradition of valuing diversity; where management continually works on creating an inclusive environment. Says Sophie: "No matter your race, culture, religion, gender, age, sexual orientation or gender identify, at Xerox we want to make sure everyone can truly be themselves."

Sophie has pointed out that the high-tech industry presents the best opportunities to work with amazing people from all around the globe—and allows the ability for an individual to adapt swiftly and comfortably. She's also mentioned that out of their closest neighbors in Boston, MA, only one is a non-immigrant family; the others came from South Africa, Scotland, France, and Romania. As with many big American cities, Boston is a diverse environment where newcomers quickly feel at home, free to absorb American culture at their own pace.

Articulating Our Experiences

Ani Palacios McBride used her hard-won American experiences to "build a better self," and she generously shared her adaptive knowledge in the book "Living in a Double World." According to Ani, adaptation is facilitated by:

- Keeping in touch with those left behind.

- Talking about feelings, either with family, support groups, or communities of co-nationals.

- Volunteering to become immersed in the lives of the local community.

- Trying out different venues for networking—churches, playgrounds, grocery stores, school events, festivals, etc.—which can help to develop a sense of belonging.

- Retaining a sense of humor.

Converting her experiences into advice allowed Ani to step back and see a bigger picture of her own adaptation process—and adapt even further.

OVERCOMING IDENTITY ISSUES

Uprooting yourself and moving to a new country can be exciting, a time for novelty and exploration. But it can also lead to feelings of displacement and uncertainty for immigrants who are grappling with their new lives without the support of friends and family—of all that is familiar to them. These identity issues can feel overwhelming . . . but they don't have to be.

How can we overcome identity issues?

- By contemplating matters of identity.

- By realizing our true potential.

- By growing a second heart.

Contemplating Matters of Identity

Elena Gorokhova was fortunate: "a steady teaching job, a Doctorate in education, and a daughter" helped her to integrate. Not to mention a loving husband who provided a daily support system that was instrumental in easing her into the process of adaptation. Nevertheless, her original cultural make-up was stubborn. It just wouldn't dissolve. As time went by, Elena came to terms with the fact that she'd always have a hyphenated Russian-American identity. "The Russian part never goes away, but the American part does become stronger," she says. It really helps to be open about it.

Realizing Our True Potential

Rohini Anand came to America for graduate school, married an Indian, moved back-and-forth from the U.S. to India—and decided to stay in India. After three years, however, the family realized that

India was not for them and returned to the U.S for good. Rohini came to love American culture, with its integrity, hard work, can-do attitudes, and a strong volunteer mentality. Most importantly, her values changed: "I realized that I changed tremendously in America . . . and what I valued most was the possibility to make an impact for what I did in the workplace . . . I came into my own in the US." Now she feels confident that "the US is home, not India." Her cultural heritage helps her to stay on course, navigating Sodexo's diversity and inclusion as a global business imperative.

Of course, she loves India, but—and this is a big BUT—she's absorbed enough of the American mindset to realize that she "fits in" in India no more. Bottom line: In the struggle of the Indian and U.S. identities, the American identity prevailed when Rohini realized her true potential with a job she loved.

Growing a Second Heart

Ani Palacios McBride's adaptation process started by living in the two worlds; however, as time went by and she grew to understand Americans and American culture, she grew a second heart, with which to love her new home country. She still loves Peru and honors its traditions, but she is very clear about her mission: becoming a cultural ambassador and raising the level of mutual understanding and cooperation. Her mission is at the heart of her new identity blossoming in the States.

MAXIMIZING CULTURAL HERITAGE

It may help to think of cultural heritage as our legacy, those attributes we grow up with that make us who we are. Our cultural heritage comes from our families and the communities of our native countries, and it forms, among other things, our manners, work ethics, and social attitudes. We carry this heritage wherever we go. So, how best to make it work for us?

How can you we use cultural heritage to our advantage?

- By adapting native products and workmanship

- By recognizing how original culture can help—or hurt

- By using our immigrant identities to forge a new career

Adapting Native Products and Workmanship

Raegan Moya Jones was born with an entrepreneurial spirit, and longed to prove herself in business. But it was the fact that she was an Australian that enabled her to identify a niche in the American market and to come up with a fresh business idea. While expecting her first child, Raegan went looking for a lightweight muslin swaddle, which is the must-have for all Australian babies—but they weren't sold anywhere in America. So, it was that having her first baby lead to a breakthrough business idea: "I would never have started aden + anais if I hadn't been raised in Australia and moved to the USA. It was the marriage of the two cultures that ultimately led to my success."

Likewise, Josie Natori internalized the entrepreneurial spirit, self-help practices, and matriarchal culture of her native Philippines—just what she needed to assert herself as a strong woman and free spirit in the U.S. Most importantly, perhaps, is the way in which she built her business on Asian-style embroidery, designs, colors, and detail-oriented workmanship. And it all came about when a buyer at Bloomingdales loved her Philippine-embroidered blouse, and suggested she sell it as a nightshirt. Just one suggestion, and Josie built a business around it.

Recognizing How Culture Can Help—Or Hurt

Rohini Anand believes that the enablers of her success are rooted in her heritage. She cites an emphasis on academic achievement; drive and ambition; a high level of empathy to people of different backgrounds; relationship-building; and flexibility as being ingrained in the Indian culture. Not only did these elements of her native heritage help her to become prominent on the job; they were essential to her own immigrant experience.

Irmgard Lafrentz knows that Germans have a reputation for being blunt and hard working. And she has tried to use that to her advantage. "Maybe showing that as a German I am direct, no-nonsense, and get-the-job-done person made people understand and accept me, and some actually loved me for it." But sometimes her directness and honesty have backfired, as it did when she articulated in a Rotary Club survey the cliquish nature of the members. Management asked her why she thought so—but even after clarification, Irmgard was ignored at the club for a long time. Cultural heritage, it seems, can be a double-edge sword.

Using Our Immigrant Identities to Forge a New Career

Feeling culturally isolated, Ani Palacios McBride built her whole career on the fact that she was an immigrant willing to help other immigrants find shortcuts to integration and success. She did it through applying her journalistic skills to writing books and articles, as well as starting her publishing company and "Contacto Latino" media outlet. Sharing her immigrant learnings made her influential among Hispanics, and interesting to the general public as an effective connector to the Latino market.

BEING GENEROUS FOR A GOOD REASON

The U.S. is the richest country in the world and American affluence fosters more generosity than any other nation. By-and-large, Americans are great philanthropists: "helping those less fortunate" and "giving back" seems to be part of the country's cultural DNA.

How can we be generous for a good reason?

- By giving as true feminists do.

- By engaging in philanthropy close to the heart.

- By giving to education as a source of all progress.

Giving as True Feminists Do

Isabel Allende's words reflect her feminist convictions, but her helping hand to women goes beyond her inspiring books. Every year, Isabel earmarks a substantial part of the income from her book sales to benefit *The Isabel Allende Foundation*[329]. She started this Foundation in 1996 to pay homage to her daughter, Paula Frias, whose untimely death at age twenty-eight broke Isabel's heart. Paula worked as a volunteer in poor communities in Venezuela and Spain, dedicating her time and skills as an educator and psychologist. Whenever she doubted her mission, she would ask herself the same question: 'What is the most generous thing to do?'

Isabel's foundation—based on her late daughter's ideals of service and compassion—was created to continue this work.

Isabel took to heart her daughter's motto, "You have only what you give" implementing it so that it became central to her own sense of fulfillment. "It is a wonderful truth that the things we want most in life—a sense of purpose, happiness and hope—are most easily attained by giving them to others. "The Allende Foundation's mission is to help women in need from societies where they are oppressed, and it maintains clinics for women and schools for girls in remote villages in Asia and Latin America. Isabel is generous to women in need, in the name of her late daughter who, too, cared deeply for others.

Engaging in Philanthropy Close to the Heart

Meaningful philanthropy is central to Raegan Moya Jones's work and life. When starting her own company, she made herself a promise that if aden + anais became successful, she would find a way to give back. The first big step in this direction was to establish the Swaddle Love Foundation in 2010, to support orphaned infants, with a core mission to "eliminate touch deprivation." Raegan also champions raising awareness of SIDS (Sudden Infant Death Syndrome) and other infant safety issues, as well as supporting the

CJ Foundation, a national non-profit devoted to eliminating the tragedy of sudden unexpected infant and early childhood deaths.

Giving to Education as the Source of All Progress

Weili Dai knows that education is the source of all progress, the best route for development, and the surest way to benefit the next generation. That's why she has promoted partnership with and gives to the *One Laptop Per Child* program,[330] an initiative which aims to provide children in the developing world with a "a rugged, low-cost, low-power, connected laptop."[331] She further contributes to Sutardja Dai Hall at her alma mater, the University of California at Berkeley, which is now home to the *Center for Information Technology Research in the Interest of Society*[332].

Rosa de la Cruz also engages in this type of progressive philanthropy, by supporting modern art and educating the young. As an initiative to support the local art scene, Rosa regularly invites Miami artists to do site-specific installations exhibited at her famous Collection. To serve local schools, she established a series of workshops and art classes in collaboration with Dade County Public Schools for both teachers and students. And in 2009, the de la Cruz Collection initiated scholarship and travel programs designed to enrich the education of the local art students.

The Third Value

Emotional Intelligence

*I've learned from experience that the greater part of our happiness
or misery depends on our dispositions
and not on our circumstances.*
Martha Washington

Some people just get along with others. They connect with other
people and respond sensibly even when challenged. They tend to
be balanced, caring, proactive, and have great insight into themselves and others. All these traits come from a set of skills called
emotional intelligence.

Emotional intelligence can be learned. And like so many practical skills, it is best learned by doing, either through experience,
or—if you want to be proactive—by experiential learning, perhaps
by taking a mentor, or following in the footsteps of a role model.
Emotional intelligence helps tremendously with acculturation.
What's more, it's tied to success, more so than technical skills or
conventional know-how.[333] So, emotional intelligence can lead to
accomplishment, and it can be learned. No wonder it's a success
value for prominent immigrant women in their personal, social,
and business relationships.

ACHIEVING A STRONG INTERCULTURAL MARRIAGE

Stable relationships and strong families can contribute to the emotional foundations of success. Of course, "marrying well" means different things to different people, but in my opinion (and I've been happily married for forty years), it means forging a life with your most loyal friend and partner. And yet, while it's true that every marriage has its ups and downs, it can seem like the challenges of the intercultural marriage are greater. Couples have to negotiate different expectations, different communication styles, and even accept new traditions. But a good intercultural marriage is possible. It just takes a shared family vision, and a good deal of give and take.

How can we achieve a good intercultural marriage?

- By thinking of good marriage in terms of give and take

- By exercising emotional intelligence

Thinking of Marriage as Give and Take

Adults who marry later in life have to pay the typical costs of re-adjusting their routines. When that marriage is intercultural, a whole new layer of challenge is added. That's what Isabel Allende found out when she tried to integrate into a new marriage and a new culture. Isabel's marriage was a success, not just because of her great love for her new husband, but because of her readiness to change herself in the name of love. "I could invent a fresh version of myself only for him," she said.

Maintaining a positive attitude is easier said than done, but Isabel indeed made numerous personal adjustments. What's more, she put her accumulated savvy in relationships and foreign-culture integration to use.

> I sent him by express mail a two-column contract: one outlying my demands and the other listing what I had prepared to offer in a relationship. The first was longer than the second

and included several key points—such as fidelity, because ex-perience had taught me that unfaithfulness is destructive and tiring—and other less essential requirements, such as reserv-ing the rights to decorate our house to my taste. The contract was based on good faith.[334]

William Gordon, her husband-to-be, was so amused that he signed it—which saved them some conflicts later on.

When two adults from different cultures come together, both need to anticipate problems and agree to make sacrifices, as Allende example makes clear. Here is this wise woman, speaking from the heart:

> To make my life in the United States with Willie, I left behind nearly everything I had, and adjusted however I could to the disarray of his existence. But he had to make his own conces-sions and changes in order for us to be together. From the be-ginning, he adopted my family and respected my work; he has accompanied me in every way he could; he has backed me up and protected me even from myself; he never criticized me; he gently laughs at my manias…and even in the fights we've had, he acts with honor; without him I wouldn't be able to write as much and as calmly as I do…[335]

As a result of these mutual concessions—this give and take—their relationship grew richer, becoming a model for both intercultural and single-culture couples.

Exercising Emotional Intelligence

Hilda Ochoa-Brillembourg maintains that family can be an empow-ering factor for career woman in America, insofar as it can provide a base for emotional health, forming a strong support system. Indeed, Hilda herself married a respectful, intelligent man who shared her values, someone who has her back. As to the ideal of marrying for love, Hilda maintains that "you need to marry for strength," meaning that you need to find the person who gives you strength. This insight—that a great marriage is based on equality and true partnership—is emotional intelligence at work.

KNOWING HOW TO BE HAPPY

Happiness may be the most subjective feeling in the world. In fact, nothing tells us more about a person than what makes them happy. That said, happy people do share some attributes, such as a tendency toward gratitude, a glass half-full attitude, not to mention the ability to absorb set-backs and savor a sense of accomplishment. Above all, as the women in this book make clear, happy people make better achievers.

How can we be happy?

- By appreciating progress made rather than ultimate success

- By savoring a sense of accomplishment

Appreciating Progress Made

Josie Natori has a no-boundaries approach to goal-setting. And she enjoys life as it comes. Talking about what makes her happy, she says that she doesn't associate happiness with success, but with progress. For example:

- I was happy when I finished schooling and got my first job within two weeks.

- I was happy when I became a VP at Merrill Lynch.

- I was happy when I started a business and it went well.

- I was happy when, at fifty, I gave a piano concert for 2,500 people at Carnegie Hall.

Whatever it is that makes us happy—our underlying inclinations or our aspirations fulfilled—we need to take them seriously, because a happy being is critical for our continuing success.

Savoring a Sense of Accomplishment

Weili's sense of accomplishment derives from her passion, perhaps the most important application of which comes out in her conviction that technology's great purpose is to create products that regular people can afford to change their lives for the better. And so, it is that, among her multiple successes, Weili Dai cherishes the day that *Time* magazine named her company's Chromecast dongle as Gadget of the Year. She recognizes this as one of those "mission accomplished" moments because it relates directly to her personal passion, as well as to the mission of her company *Marvell*.

Rohini Anand also takes time to appreciate her accomplishments, as doing so helps her sustain her priorities and remind her of what makes her truly happy. As to what that is? Again, it's about accomplishment, such as finishing her Ph.D., sustaining a happy marriage, and seeing her daughters grow-up into accomplished young women. Of course, Rohini can't talk about accomplishments without mentioning her career: she finds the greatest pleasure in working for a value-driven company that has empowered her to change its very culture. Knowing that she makes a positive impact gives her a tremendous sense of satisfaction and accomplishment.

FOSTERING WORK-LIFE BALANCE

Work-life balance is a big concept in women's studies, indeed in women's daily lives. A concept that focuses on prioritizing work, family, and lifestyle, work-life balance seems illusive to many. But not to the women in this book; they have opted to "have it all" by balancing careers, families, and community obligations—and mixing in some fun along the way.

How can we keep life-work balance?

- By delegating + simplifying + leveraging IT

- By shifting the emphasis from children to work to balance

Delegating + Simplifying + Leveraging IT

After the death of her husband, Sophie Vandebroek raised three kids on a reduced income, with no hands-on help from her family who lived over 3,000 miles away in Belgium. A seemingly insurmountable challenge, this life-altering event prompted lifestyle creativity on Sophie's part. Nevertheless, she moved on heroically without compromising her job or her family. Sophie may hold fourteen U.S. patents, but perhaps her most important invention is the life-work balance solution that enabled her to be both a rainmaker in high-tech and a devoted mother.

Sophie generously shared the principles of "maintaining fun" in her famous speech to the women at Xerox, in which she emphasized three principles: delegate, simplify, and leverage IT. And they're all connected. "Simplifying my life also allowed me to find funds to delegate more," she says. "And between delegating and simplifying you will be surprised how much quality time you have—for your kids and for yourself."

It comes as no surprise that someone with Sophie's background would be first to make tech work for her. "I've had high-speed cable at home since 1990. It allowed me to work from home when the kids were little," she says. Few of us can live without our smart phones now, but Sophie was only the second employee at Xerox to have a Blackberry when they first came out. "It saved me at least one hour work each night not having to catch up with tons of email. It allowed me to be in touch with the kids and other people I care about all the time while working hard."

A WORK-LIFE BALANCE SOLUTION

Delegate: Delegate almost everything, except quality time with your kids. Delegate laundry, errands, cooking, yard work, taxes, etc. Bear in mind that when you delegate, you have to be willing to compromise and live with a "roughly right" outcome.

Simplify: Don't buy a home that's larger than you need. Don't buy expensive items that will only require a lot of time to maintain. Don't organize complex vacations or sign your kids up for more than one sport. Don't maintain a circle of fifty friends . . . a handful of close friends may give you more satisfaction.

Leverage IT: Technology can save time—a lot of it. From working at home to being connected on the road, technology is the closest thing to being in two places at once. Learn how to make it work for you.

Sophie Vandebroek

Shifting Emphasis from Children to Work to Balance

Ying McGuire holds that balance doesn't mean less work or more play. She defines it as being able to make an impact in her job, in her community, and in the world at large—while leaving room in her busy schedule for family, friends, and personal indulgences.

While having a young family can be a limiting factor for professional women, those limitations are only temporary. That's how Ying coped: "I put my career on hold and stayed at home as a full-time mother for a few years when my children were young. Once they started school, I was able to continue higher education and restart my career. I had to work extra hard to . . . make up for my lost time." Focusing on children first, and then on work, paid off in both family and career. By shifting emphasis in this way Ying was able to provide her family with a solid foundation for a better life.

The Fourth Value

Communication Skills and Creativity

The most effective way to do it, is to do it.
Amelia Earhart

Creativity, professionalism, and drive are qualities valued world-wide. But how does the newcomer communicate these assets? Communication is culture-bound and that can present difficulties for foreign nationals who immigrate to the U.S. Americans tend to have terrific creativity and communication skills, and for a simple reason: they start training these muscles early in school, continue through college, and into the workplace. Americans have communication and creative thinking courses at their disposal. Decent books and dedicated coaches, too. That's why immigrants need to upgrade the cultural component of communication. Only then will they reap the benefits of their tremendous creativity, passion, and drive.

OVERCOMING THE LANGUAGE BARRIER

Learning the native language of a new country is a must. No matter how slow the learning process, it's important to advance language skills every single day: delay in breaking down the language barrier will only delay success. While most adults find it hard to learn a new language, perseverance and constant practice will be rewarded. It takes hard work, but language proficiency can be achieved.

How can we overcome a language barrier?

- By speaking up, whatever the accent.

- By finding work that requires communication.

- By repeating a mantra and persevering.

- By writing in a second language.

Speaking Up

Alfa Demmellash had a seemingly insurmountable language barrier when she arrived in the U.S.; she had to learn English from scratch. It took four months of total immersion classes in American English, but Alfa finally reached an understanding of what was going on around her. A few years later, she became Valedictorian of her 8th grade class, and went on to attend one of the best schools in Boston.

But Alfa's stubborn accent stayed with her: "I have a love-hate relationship with my accent," she said. After twenty-one years in the U.S. she still has difficulty mixing certain vowels. She can hear it herself. But when there's so much going on—so much to say and so fast—who has the time to worry about an accent? Alfa has learned to accept her language goofs. What's more, she has developed a way of using proverbs to make her point come through. "I would like to think people have a way of remembering better when they hear it in a new way," she says. Her self-consciousness and humor certainly help her to stay confident, whether she speaks English with an accent or not.

Finding Work That Requires Communication

Ani Palacios McBride never considered any kind of work to be beneath her. She spoke limited English when she followed her husband to the U.S., but it was her first job, as a cashier, that helped her improve her English considerably. Working behind a counter forced Ani to communicate with customers all day: face-to-face interactions with real people, in real situations. It was the first step in her journey to near-native proficiency today, and it wiped away her fear of communicating in English.

Repeating a Mantra and Persevering

Ivana Trump knows that English is a difficult language, with "so many nuances, and words that mean different things." She advises newcomers "to stick with it." What's more, she says, "if you really don't understand—smile a lot. [It] makes you look very wise and happy."

Veronica Montes learned her first English words at eighteen, which made it hard for her to overcome her language barrier simply by attending English as a Second Language classes. Coming from a disadvantaged background, with nobody to practice English with, she was tempted to quit multiple times. She would have, too, had she not repeated to herself, like a mantra: "I can do it . . . I can do it!"

Veronica kept her goal of higher-education in mind, and kept working at it until she made it through. Today, she feels more confident in her English, in her accent, and in being a Latina of color. Overcoming the language barrier enabled Veronica to become an American in her own right, and to go on to teach sociology at the college level.

Writing in A Second Language

More than half of the women profiled here have authored books in America. It comes as no surprise: the immigrant experience provides a unique perspective on American opportunities, evolving values, leadership-in-the-making, and most importantly, cultural integration as a prerequisite of success. Elena Gorokhova worked on her English relentlessly.

When I arrived here, for several years I read nothing in Russian, writing down snippets of good American writing in a special notebook I kept on my desk. Now I read in both languages, but I only write in one [English]. If feels as if there were two brains in my head, a Russian one and an English one, and they function independently. There is no crossover. There is no translation going on between them.

Elena's first memoir, *A Mountain of Crumbs*, was so successful that *Simon & Schuster* followed it up with a second, *Russian Tattoo*. As an author, she takes readers to a new understanding of the guts of immigration, and she does it by writing in her second language.

ADAPTING COMMUNICATION STYLES
Successful people know that while we each have our own unique communication style, it's often necessary to adapt according to different circumstances. To be an effective communicator, you have to understand not just how to communicate, but what's expected of you. That can be tough for people from other countries who, having grown up with one set of expectations, now have to learn what's expected—and accepted—in a whole new culture.

How can we adapt our communication style?

- By recognizing a liability, and working to improve it.

Recognizing A Liability
Ying McGuire was very much aware that her native culture, however dear to her heart, was both an asset and a liability. She still thinks of it primarily as an asset, because her Chinese upbringing equipped her with a strong work ethic, discipline, and a drive for excellence. All good-for-business values that helped her career. What didn't help, however, was her excessive modesty.

Ying's humility, a highly-regarded trait in China, made her downplay her achievements. As a result, managers saw her in a supporting-role rather than a results-oriented driver. Delayed promotions were the inevitable result.

Ying made a huge effort to Americanize, to overcome her intense modesty along with her poor communication style. Attending a seminar at Dell and reading the book "Brag! The Art of Tooting Your Own Horn without Blowing It," by Peggy Klaus was an eye-opener. In fact, the book became something of a success manual for her. Not only did it help her to communicate better, it helped her to understand that, in America, eloquence is valued as a special talent.

Ying put her heart into absorbing American communication strategies and techniques. She forced herself to express her opinion and to speak up at corporate meetings, while developing as a leader and confident public speaker. In time, Ying's new communication style complemented her professional skills, becoming part of her arsenal for success.

NURTURING CREATIVITY AND INNOVATION
We achieve better results when we follow our passions. In order to do that, we have to identify the passion that drives us, and the talents that fuel that drive. But this isn't a one-of task. The dynamic world in which we live demands creativity, and that can mean invention and reinvention. We have to be bold. Sometimes this means forging full-speed ahead, while at other times it means stepping back, looking at our best experiences, understanding our innate talents, and building on them.

How can we encourage creativity?

- By recognizing our natural talents.

- By reinventing ourselves.

- By fostering innovation on a shoestring.

Recognizing Our Natural Talents

Ivana Trump has taken on a wide array of roles in her life, all of which demonstrate an assortment of natural talents: skier, model, wife, mother, businesswoman, and celebrity in her own right. Ivana is known for her glamorous sense of style and her ability to express it in a winning, if somewhat "over-the-top" way. PR, marketing, and self-promotion came naturally to her, but it wasn't until her "Trump years" that she understood the full range of her natural creativity and was able to further hone her instincts. Working within the Trump organization, Ivana took advantage of every opportunity to customize her skills and amplify her talents. Business proficiencies honed during this time stood her in good stead after her divorce, when she developed a clothing line, fashion jewelry, and beauty products. She has gone on to write several bestselling books, and found her own successful companies which have matured into a multi-million-dollar business.

Reinventing Ourselves

Irmgard Lafrentz consciously identifies with immigrants, not native-born Americans. But that hasn't stopped her from reinventing herself in her new country. She transitioned from an employee with a stable paycheck in Germany to an entrepreneur with all the attendant financial insecurities. She revised her personal values, including her attitude toward money, becoming more generous as she grew to appreciate the American charitable tradition of showing compassion to others. And the once traditional Irmgard has become more liberal since moving to the U.S. She credits her son with this, as well as the influence of the Silicon Valley culture.

Fostering Innovation on a Shoestring

Don't think that a big investment is needed to encourage employee creativity and innovation. Consider Maya Strelar-Migotti—she did it on a shoestring.

Here's the story: in May 2013, speaking to a gathering of entrepreneurs at TiEcon, a popular annual tech and networking fest, Maya acknowledged that her innovations were born out of culture shock. When she first arrived in the U.S. Maya was dazed by Silicon Valley's unique innovation culture, especially when she learned how some companies were giving their employees one free day a week just to think about innovation. Maya aspired to be competitive as well, but without a lot of money at her disposal, she was forced to come up with a different way of stimulating innovation. So, she set aside one percent of her company's budget to create an innovation culture, much like the venture capital model. She gave inventive team members (those with qualifying ideas), one week of free-wheeling experimentation, along with $500 to buy books and software. She emphasized learning and encouraged her employees to reframe the notion of failure. She provided internal motivation rewards for "best manager," "best idea," "best facilitator," even "best failure!" And because Maya wanted her managers to get together with the "idea people," she encouraged collaboration.

Innovation on a Shoestring

Legitimize frugal innovation: Set aside a modest portion of your annual budget to create a culture of innovation that rewards invention and encourages promising ideas.

Emphasize learning: Innovation doesn't fear failure, so spread the word that failure is OK, as long as you don't give up when results are less than expected.

Appeal to internal motivation: Provide recognition to employees who foster innovation.

Encourage collaboration: Make it possible for managers to connect with "idea people," thereby fostering inclusive leadership for mass-scale creativity.

Anticipate customer needs: The best way to stay ahead of the market.

Maya Strelar-Migotti

The Fifth Value

Strategic Thinking

Dreaming, after all, is a form of planning.
Gloria Steinem

Strategic thinking takes on a special meaning for aspiring achievers, particularly when they are immigrant women. In addition to facing the glass ceiling, immigrant women experience language and cultural issues which may include breaking with traditions that emphasize subservience. This is in addition to the more generalized stress of reestablishing themselves in a highly competitive country.

Immigrant women need to think strategically, matching their course of action to their long-term goals. That can be hard when just meeting the demands of the day can push them towards operational thinking with the aim of, "just get it done." It takes great resolve to look at your goals and figure out the strategy that will take you there. But it can—and must—be done.

DEVELOPING ADAPTABILITY
Moving to a new country—in many cases, a whole new world—means facing a future of uncertainty, often without the support structures of family and community. Immigrants have to learn

things the hard way and fine-tune their decisions on the go. Which is why adaptability, that quality of being able to adjust to new conditions, is vital. And yet, to become a high achiever, it's not enough just to adapt. You have to be strategic in your adaptation process, which means learning how to move between your original and new cultures, just as you learn how to move between past and present, while keeping your eyes fixed firmly on the future.

How do we develop adaptability?

- By building a bridge between cultures

- By being future oriented

Building a Bridge Between Cultures

Irmgard Lafrentz takes cultural integration and issues of belonging seriously. Despite her vague nostalgia for Germany, she trained her eyes forward and didn't look back, even after a painful divorce when many would have returned home. Irmgard knew that she had to look to the future, in both her professional and personal lives; ironically, she found that one of the best ways to do that was to make use of her nostalgia for Germany, in effect building a bridge between two cultures. While Irmgard adopted many of the practices of her new country, she also imported a number of cultural traditions from Germany to help her feel at home here. And she never missed a chance to travel to Germany to keep in touch with her original German culture, thus alleviating—and making use of—her natural nostalgia.

Being Future Oriented

Alfa Demmellash has achieved her own American Dream. The social entrepreneur who helps hundreds of people a year, knows from experience that overcoming adversity means looking to the future. Here's how she did it:

1. Uplifted herself with education

2. Formulated a unique business idea

3. Achieved an excellent idea-to-implementation track-record

4. Attained cultural integration in both her business and personal life

Alfa conceived a great idea. She found a way to give the American economy a respectable makeover while empowering small and micro-business people, with a special focus on women. And now she looks to the future with a sense of purpose.

LAUNCHING A SUCCESSFUL COMPANY

A number of the women profiled here have stepped outside the boundaries of their existing roles to start their own companies. It's not for everyone. Starting a business requires hard work and determination, not to mention the willingness to take on a high level of risk. As for where to start, well, you have to have your own strategic twist.

How can we launch a successful company?

*   By starting with a hunch.

*   By starting small.

Starting with a Hunch

Raegan Moya Jones's business model started with a hunch along the lines of, "I bet other women would value a breathable muslin baby swaddle as much as I do." She turned a hunch into a successful company by:

*   identifying a niche in the American market;

- researching the market, developing a plan, and finding a manufacturer;

- raising seed money;

- making use of her own professional sales skills; and

- educating herself in supply chain and finance.

Four years after launching her company, Raegan received the first round of private equity funding; the second round of investment followed promptly. Today, she is CEO of a global brand that started on a hunch and survived due to sheer persistence.

Starting Small

Weili Dai and her husband—a duo of hands-on geeks—had great ambitions, nevertheless, they started small. The couple funded their business with their own savings and those of extended family. They adopted a no-frills approach and started their company with second-hand computers and furniture. Weili even cooked stir-fries to keep their engineers happy and well-fed. But the scrimping paid off. In approximately three years Marvell became profitable, and in five, the company went public.

SUSTAINING A SUCCESSFUL BUSINESS

Starting a small business is one thing; sustaining it through good times and bad is another. That requires grit and determination, a sense of purpose, and above all, a big picture vision of who you are and what you want to achieve.

How can we sustain a successful business?

- By strategizing 24/7.

- By being flexible.

Strategizing 24/7

Presiding over a company with approximately 7,000 employees worldwide, Weili Dai felt a tremendous responsibility to sustain a successful business. Her thoughtful strategy included four key elements, all based on win-win human interactions:

- Forge close relationships with customers by ensuring that product leadership, personal strategic thinking, business acumen, and passionate networking all work in sync.

- Strike strategic partnerships to enable Marvell technology penetrates the diverse markets.

- Make use of her Chinese connections to become the ambassador of opportunity between the U.S. and China, especially when it comes to promote green technologies and high-tech education.

- Advocate worldwide for better use of technology to improve the human condition, further increasing her personal and corporate authority, brand recognition, and of course, market share.

It also helped that Weili and her husband—who headed all technology developments at Marvell—couldn't stop themselves from strategizing at home setting. Business is still on their minds literally 24/7. They make it work for them.

Being Flexible

Alfa Demmellash knows that flexibility and strategy go hand in hand. She also knows that flexibility can be one of the most challenging skill sets to develop. While some might view being flexible as flip-flopping, Alfa sees it as putting yourself in a "listening mode." If, for example, success continues to elude you despite your best efforts, you've got to modify both your behavior and your priorities to come up with a new plan. She explains: "You have to hear to better understand what the best patterns of behavior are for you and how you can change aspects of your approach and your priorities without compromising what is ultimately important." That is flexibility at its best.

BECOMING AN INTRAPRENEUR

Intrapreneurs are highly valued team members and executives who apply the principles of entrepreneurship to their existing roles. Intrapreneurs are passionate, open minded individuals. Future oriented and results driven, they may not have an ownership stake in the companies they serve, nevertheless they fulfil strong leadership roles within their organizations—hence the label, "intrapreneur."

How can we become an intrapreneur and enhance our success on the job?

- By demonstrating a stake-holder's attitude

Demonstrating a Stake-Holder's Attitude

Sophie Vandebroek's success was fostered by her attitude of ownership, and by taking responsibility for her team's results. She poured her passion into everything she applied herself to, and on each and every job. Sophie knew that being an intrapreneur was more than just an attitude, so the engineer immersed herself in her company's practices and production procedures, in effect, applying passion to process. That's leadership. Sophie found that adopting the stance of an owner and encouraging commitment and passion in others showed in the results for her whole team. And now, in her presentations and mentoring sessions at Xerox, she recommends that every employee develop the attitude of an owner.

GETTING USED TO RISK

Cultural anthropologists tell us that European and Asian attitudes tend to be risk-averse. Mainstream American culture, on the other hand, can trace its roots back to the risk-prone spirit of the pioneers. (Just think of the risks the first settlers faced.) That's why many newcomers to the U.S. find it hard to integrate into the risk-inclined American business culture. This said, immigrants tend to take significant risks in moving from one country to another in pursuit of a better life. Which is why, as a group, they present a curious mix of resolve, risk, and caution. Still, coming to America makes them – to a different degree – move their "risk buttons" even further on the risk scale.

How can we get used to risk?

- By merging cautiously into American risk culture.

Merging Cautiously into the Risk Culture

Risk was initially a significant cultural challenge for Ying McGuire. Brought up to be non-confrontational, she regarded any form of conflict as risk, taboo in her culture. Even today, though she has learned to accept risk, she speaks her mind "with a certain level of diplomacy."

Understanding now that life "is about taking risks and conquering unknowns," Ying has learned to systematically take calculated risks. She has even worked out a *special technique for it:* "I write down a list of pros and cons, speak to my mentors or people I trust prior to making major decisions. I even thoroughly analyze all the possible colors before I would pick a color to paint my house." She developed her calculated risk technique out of necessity, because at the beginning of her years in America she used only her gut feeling and made several wrong moves that cost her dearly—so now she knows better how to take risks if need be: carefully calculating pros and cons.

The Sixth Value

Inclusive Leadership

If you have knowledge, let others light their candles in it.
Margaret Fuller

Inclusive leadership is a process that considers both leaders and those who follow them. Inclusive leadership places human relationships front and center, and recognizes that the purpose of an organization extends beyond purely financial goals. Inclusive leadership is a mindset. It encourages respectful service above self-interest; advocates reasonable restraints in the use of power; and shows concern for both the sustainable development of employees and the cohesiveness of the organization as a whole. Inclusive leadership considers strong human connections to be the prerequisite of true success, and acknowledges that no positive change can be accomplished without involving the broad circles of human capital. In essence, inclusive leadership accepts that, as Arianna Huffington once remarked,[336] "democracy is not a spectator sport."

BECOMING AN INCLUSIVE LEADER

Inclusive leaders set themselves as models based on their own self-awareness. They lead or manage with a mindfulness that makes room for differences. Since inclusion and leadership attitudes, skills, and behaviors are learned — not inborn — developing inclusive leaders is fundamental to the transformational diversity[337] initiatives that foster fairness in life and work.

How can we become inclusive leaders?

- By acting on a leadership fitness formula

- By bringing global inclusive practices into the workplace.

- By exploring issues we're passionate about.

- By exercising inclusive leadership on a daily basis.

Acting on a Leadership Fitness Formula

A prototype of the inclusive leader, Rohini Anand used her own immigrant experience to inform her relationships. Rohini understands how important it is to put respectful service above self-interest, and why it's essential to level the playing field so that diverse talent is presented with an opportunity to succeed. She led her company's initiative to make its culture truly inclusive, especially for women and underrepresented groups. And she did it by implementing the same formula she applied to her own career: considerate + authentic + resolute + optimistic = Inclusive Leader

Rohini had to be serious about her own character-building in order to take advantage of the career opportunities her abilities and education prepared her for. She had to show great personal resolve when settling in the U.S. for good, and she did this by applying an authentic and optimistic outlook which made it possible for her to be "comfortable with all shades of grey areas."

Rohini's strategic thinking involves "a vision and an ability to connect." Good thing too, because her ability to influence people requires her to put her vision into practice—that is, to lead the way. Indeed, if it were not for her ability to combine vision and strategy with execution, she would not have been able to spearhead cultural change at her company. Rohini created a general vision, broke the larger goal into smaller manageable pieces, and inspired people to implement it—one step at a time.

Bringing Global Inclusive Practices into the Workplace

Maya Strelar-Migotti's tolerance and inclusiveness were forged in her youth and enhanced by her four-country expat experiences. She knows that inclusiveness is good for business, and works hard to advance inclusive practices and encourage teamwork and creativity in high-tech cultures. Maya brought the world's best practices to her workplace at Ericsson, which resulted in increased innovation and improved business results worldwide. Here's what it took:

- A willingness to go against the grain. It took all her personal courage and propensity to realize positive change, especially with executives who were set in their ways.

- The ability to unite globally dispersed operations, ensuring cooperation with respect and inclusivity.

- Directing her managerial talents to global assignments, where she created new leadership and enhanced overall performance by emphasizing motivation, quality, and customer satisfaction.

"I did reinvent the ways of working," said Maya, simply, "by putting employees in prime focus, taking care of them, creating culture of support and risk taking, where mistakes are taken as a great learning and not a subject for retaliation." That's what Inclusive Leaders do.

Exploring Issues We're Passionate About

Alfa Demmellash made the most of her Harvard scholarship. Naturally curious about the workings of governments in third-world countries, she raised money to conduct a field study in Rwanda, where she saw first-hand how poverty and fear are the biggest obstacles to elevating countries to democratic and fair conditions. A gifted student herself, Alfa knew that only through education could people be uplifted from poverty. One thing led to another, and upon graduation from Harvard, Alfa and her husband implemented a concept of business leadership known as "social entrepreneurship."

Their company—Rising Tide Capital—set about training people how to think about business, structure business plans, and access markets. The approach attempts to initiate sweeping changes in the U.S. economy in the hopes of sustaining economic growth at the grassroots level. And it took an immigrant with a fresh outlook and creative thinking to lay down the foundation.

Exercising Inclusive Leadership on a Daily Basis

After having experienced repeated humiliations at her corporate job, Raegan Moya-Jones makes a point to exercise respect and inclusiveness towards all employees. She believes that a truly inclusive company climate ensures its sustained success. Here's how she does it:

- Puts inclusiveness at the top of her leadership priorities.

- Respects the rights of young mothers to take all the time they need for maternity leave.

- Appoints women to leadership positions.

- Displays leadership within her family circle. (Raegan and her husband share household responsibilities equally, setting a good example for their four daughters with their fair family culture.)

BECOMING A MODERN FEMINIST LEADER

It is a big question of how the leadership styles of men and women differ. Another big question is how our society can better prepare women for leadership roles through mentoring and advancement. Indeed, how can we create cultures in which companies promote women into upper management *on merit*, not because of subsidized diversity policies? Looking at the women's equality issues from various angles and reading about women leaders who stand up for other women, in #MeeToo and other movements, we can clearly see that modern feminism is no longer a "dirty word." Quite the contrary. Many of today's worthy men proudly call themselves feminists.

How can we become modern feminist leaders?

- By learning to stand up and speak up – following the proven role models of today.

Due to various circumstances, our book subjects have absorbed different feminist flavors—which conditioned their specific leadership styles. Going back to their respective profiles, you can see how each feminist flavor came about. Now, take a look at these brief cases.

The Case of Isabel Allende: Forever Feminist

Born and raised in an intelligent Chilean family, Isabel has expressed her feminist ideas early on, when writing a column for a feminist magazine in Santiago and also when scripting feminist plays. Becoming an internationally renowned writer saved her feminist spirit from despising self for her boring life in Caracas, Venezuela: it felt like a humiliation to sink into a typical bourgeois woman's collaboration with the rules of the macho society.

Isabel's writing talent and her feminist learnings got a second start after she began to write professionally. To put it in a nutshell, Isabel's feminist thought leadership has been rooted in watching her mother's embarrassments after her husband left the family; also, the positioning of women as always-sub-servient in Chilean traditional macho culture inspired her rebellious essence.

Here's the wealth of feminist flavors:

Rohini Anand, start-at-home feminist, believes that feminism, like charity, should start at home. This is in sync with Gloria Steinem saying that "women are not going to be equal outside the home until men are equal in it." Six points in Rohini's Portrait elaborate that.

Deborah Levine, vocal feminist, maintains that women need to get rid of false modesty, their typical self-protection tool. She is calling women to "lean in" in her local Chattanooga community, and promoting women in STEM in her web-based American Diversity Report and the Huffington Post blogosphere.

Maya Strelar-Migotti, executive feminist, came to the US from a country more advanced in terms of women's equality – and was more than willing to promote it. She created the *Women in Leadership* initiative at Ericsson in order to empower women. She also encourages male managers to lean-in to women.

Sophie Vandebroek, can-do feminist, has her personal diversity points of pride on promoting women in high-tech. Out of 104 engineers she hired at Xerox R&D, 34 are women, a high score for her industry. Her personal get-up-fighter qualities and stellar work-life balancing act certainly make a mark in modern feminism.

Hilda Ochoa-Brillembourg, formidable feminist, is a living proof that gender equity is good for both men and women – and in her public speeches she shared innovative insights for women's career-building in competitive professions.

Edwina Sandys, artistic feminist, stands out with her bold feminism as part of her leadership achievement in sculpture. Her artistic focus on women resulted in strong, distinctly feminist works such as "Christa," "Marriage Bed," "Eve's Apple," and the United Nations and the world recognized that.

Weili Dai, fusion, or soft feminist, who is a modern maven and mother, never shies away from pointing out her feminine looks and love of cooking and decorating—or sticking to her long-held belief that "women are caretakers." At the same time this executive leader is passionately promoting women in engineering and technology, because "women are the future of the tech."

Alfa Demmellash, firm feminist, has figured out how to help those women who are trying to reach their economic stability/independence. Her company actions are precious for those starting from scratch. The pieces of advice she provided to women and girls in Ethiopia deserve a special mention.

Irmgard Lafrentz, undercover feminist, was craving for independence and recognition, if only to prove herself to her mother. Although she never expressed her pro-feminist views distinctly, her actions charting her own independent course in a heavily male-dominated industry make her a good role model.

Raegan Moya-Jones, missionary feminist, has been suffering from sexism during her corporate career in America. She set out to prove that it's "sexism" that should be a dirty word, not "feminism." In her Portrait, you can find nine reasons to explain what makes Raegan a missionary feminist.

Veronica Montes, a grass-root feminist, is a free thinker. Her doctorate thesis about women of two transnational Mexican communities in the US proved, through rich sampling and analysis, their vital role in the Mexican family and community—which counteracts current stereotyping, and is a new win for feminism-at-large.

Looking at these inspiring feminist women who help so many others to become true leaders, it is my feeling that the time has come—despite some political setbacks and rise of sponsored misogyny—for modern feminists of foreign descent to be universally recognized for their remarkable contributions to America national well-being and culture. The richly deserve it!

So, grow your influencing skills, for inclusive leadership and influencing go hand in hand—and inclusive leadership capabilities will make a difference in whatever you do!

The Seventh Value

Perseverance

*When you get into a tight place and everything goes against you,
till it seems you could not hang on a minute
longer, never give up then,
for that is just the place and time that the tide will turn."*
Harriet Beecher Stowe

The mindset to do whatever it takes to be successful is typical among immigrants. But sometimes that's not enough. Sometimes we stumble. Sometimes we fall. That's why the capacity to persevere, that quality of not just surviving, but overcoming, is considered by many to be the one true test of personal leadership. Everyone is faced with ups and downs. No one is immune. That's why, when we come across adversity—the minor disappointments and major tragedies that comprise a life—it helps to have a set of skills to see us through. Because in the end, it's all about perseverance.

BUILDING A STRONG EMOTIONAL BASE
We can't be prepared for every situation. Not every challenge can be anticipated. Still, building fortitude and a strong emotional base can help us counteract setbacks and move on.

How can we build a strong emotional base?

- By not taking things personally.

- By drawing on emotional support factors.

Don't Take It Personally

Raegan Moya Jones experienced repeated setbacks when launching her own business while working full-time at *The Economist*. Especially humiliating were the remarks of her high-brow colleagues who said that she lacked entrepreneurial abilities. But Raegan had worked in sales for most of her professional career, where she heard the word "no" every day. She knew better than to take things personally. "I have a very thick skin," she said. "I allow myself an hour of "wallowing," then I shake it off and get on with it."

Drawing on Emotional Support Factors

On top of the usual stresses of being a working mother, Ani Palacios experienced what she calls the "emotional pressure-cooker" of being an immigrant. Here's what helped fuel her success, as well as soften the blows of life's ups and downs:

- **Virtuous Pride:** knowing that she belongs to a tough breed of immigrants who can make it without complaining.

- **Clear Vision:** knowing what she wanted from the immigration experience.

- **A Solid Marriage:** knowing that her husband supported her unconditionally and that he encouraged her ambitions.

- **Family Obligations:** knowing that she was responsible for the future of her three children.

EMBRACING CULTURE TO PREVENT SETBACKS

The best defense is a good offense—or so the saying goes. And sometimes the best way to counteract setbacks is to prevent them.

Wholeheartedly embracing a new culture can help newcomers feel they belong and are working towards a new life. That in itself can help you to persevere.

How can we embrace culture to prevent setbacks?

- By identifying with other immigrants.

- By engaging with those around us.

Identifying with Other Immigrants

Ironically, sometimes embracing a new culture means identifying with other immigrants who have had experiences similar to ours. Emigration is predictably hard. Qualifying for entry to the U.S. can mean jumping through hoops—again, and again, and again—with no guarantee of success. In Ying McGuire's case, it meant resigning from her government job simply to apply for an American visa. Experiences like these can leave their mark; but they can also form the basis of friendship. Birds of a feather, and all that. When you've got so much shared experience with others, you'll do wise to draw on their emotional support.

Ying has found common ground with immigrants who had to make their own sacrifices, who, like her, had to leave behind family and friends in order to establish themselves in an unfamiliar land. She's met many like-minded people through her community service—her favorite after-work occupation—and learned to find her element among people like herself, born and raised abroad.

Engaging with Those Around Us

Alfa Demmellash found that engaging with others and learning from them helped provide a broad base for preventing setbacks. She showed an interest in those around her by asking questions about their backgrounds and professional histories, which helped her find common ground. From her American friends, Alfa has learned to appreciate spending time in nature. She took up hiking and found it a great way to experience nature, clear her head, and attain greater spiritual connectedness. Alfa has also learned the value of another American characteristic: openness. That means saying sorry and asking for forgiveness. She finds the American habit of inviting openness by acknowledging mistakes a two-sided approach to building healthier relationships at both individual and national levels. Not to mention that it's easier to move on from setbacks when we're open about them.

COUNTERACTING SETBACKS

Hard-work, determination, and an open-heart can get us far. But they won't protect us from setbacks. They happen to everyone, no matter what our character or circumstances. So how do you pick yourself up and move on?

How can we counteract setbacks?

- By being tough.

Being Tough

If you want to nurture personal and social success, you've got be tough. "It's the only way to reach your goals," says Hilda Ochoa Brillembourg, adding that "sometimes you have to crawl on all fours to get there." And she should know. The first woman in her family to attend Harvard, she worked her way up the ladder to a top position in the world of finance. And now, after more than thirty years in business, and after standing at the helm of her own extremely successful financial firm, Hilda acknowledges that she's met her primary goal: "I do feel financially independent," she says. "I feel I have achieved what I wanted to, which was to manage my life."

Hilda's take on her past struggles has acquired a philosophical hue, "Setbacks make you stronger . . . unless they weaken you." Now she speaks quietly about the human spirit, and the extraordinary ability we all have to transcend even the most terrible circumstances.

Like most immigrants, Hilda certainly had her fair share of hard times, but she's retained her compassion for others and empathy for those who try to overcome unfortunate conditions. Her approach to handling hardships past and present is no-nonsense, like everything she does.

But being tough isn't just one thing. Of course, it's about hard work and perseverance, and above all, the ability to endure setbacks. But what makes this toughness possible? For Hilda, it's making sure that all your actions match your values. It's about building the foundation for all your personal endeavors.

A Recipe for Counteracting Setbacks

Be Flexible: When you see a dead end, change direction—or even professions—and acquire new skills. Change will set you free.

Set Goals: Having an end goal in mind will help you to look beyond current obstacles.

Work Hard: Know what your deficiencies are and work hard to overcome them.

Continue to Learn: And learn from the best.

Persevere: Suffering a downfall? Get up, wipe your tears, and focus on your mission.

Establish Yourself: Become integrated. Have a voice in your local community. Create a rewarding and progressive career, a loving family, and a network of good friends.

Ying McGuire

The Achiever's Handbook

Advice is what we ask for when we already
know the answer but wish we didn't.
Erica Jong

There are no shortcuts to success. The journey to becoming a high-end achiever doesn't happen overnight, and it certainly isn't a Cinderella-like transformation. Realizing your own unique potential requires vision, hard-work, and tenacity. And yet, while everyone has their own individual goals, not to mention inimitable talents, it can help to follow in the footsteps of achievers who have made similar journeys and broken down their own barriers. That's why we should borrow liberally from those who have gone before us, and apply their lessons to our lives, our way. After all, who better to give us advice than those who have walked their own long road?

Success Takeaways

Passion is energy.
Feel the power that comes from focusing on what excites you.
Oprah Winfrey

As a professional educator, I cherish that moment of "knowledge implementation," when I speak to my audience about what they've learned, and hear how they hope to apply the day's lessons in real life situations. It's always gratifying to find out how they intend to adapt their newly acquired knowledge for their own personal, professional, and organizational success. It's one of the reasons I love what I do.

The pages that follow provide advice from an array of accomplished women who earned their stripes the hard way. They changed the face of American success, giving it a feminine edge and an international outlook. A diverse group of achievers reflecting our diverse nation, these women are happy to advise those who came after them. They are brave, sensitive, and talented trailblazers—and they have much to offer.

One

Start by Mapping Out
Your Opportunities

Nothing is more important than taking an active role in shaping your own future. And to do that you need to know want you want and how to get there. Industry groups, as well as professional and networking associations, offer a slew of resources dedicated to teaching people how to break into a particular field, get trained, and successfully launch a business or career. Begin with a simple Google search. You may want to try "Getting a job in . . ." or "Launching a business in . . ." for starters.

Exploration is the first step toward your better future, so discover what's out there. Make a commitment to investigate all sorts of new and exciting possibilities. Take advantage of every opportunity to meet new people, attend events, sit in on webinars, sign up for newsletters, join organizations or fan pages, and immerse yourself in the worlds that your passions can open up to you. Keep exploring until you get there.

Two

Be Open-Minded and Creative

Don't get stuck on landing a specific job, or starting a particular business. There are lots of opportunities in between that can help turn your talent and passion into your work. Seek out what speaks to you. You may, for instance, have trouble getting a job doing XYZ. But what about taking on a project or a consulting opportunity? An internship can help you get one step closer to your goal, as can temporary and volunteer work.

There's a world of opportunity out there, so try breaking away from the get-a-job mindset. Keep your mind and your options open. Get creative and design your own future. There are lots of ways to make money doing just about anything . . . if you have the imagination.

Three

Tap into Your Passion

Everybody is passionate about something, even if it doesn't strike you as worthy of a career. Think about all of the things that get you fired-up and eager to act, and write them down. Ask those near-and-dear to you for input—they could have ideas that you may have overlooked. Study your list for a few days. Add notes, details, and illustrations. Fill the page with things you love and are good at. Those are the best clues you're going to get. Then challenge yourself to translate what's on that page to real life experience. Find ways of channeling your abilities and your passions towards some form of work.

It's far too easy to feel defeated or depressed when things get difficult. Be positive and be your own biggest cheerleader. But listen to your gut. If it's telling you to get out of what you're currently doing, or away from the path that you're on now, pay attention. Look closely to recognize new opportunities presented by your challenges. They're always in there.

Opportunity lies in every setback. Own this concept.

Four

Turn Your Biggest Differences Into Your Greatest Assets

You don't necessarily need to be an expert in your area of passion. You don't need years of experience under your belt either. That will come. Know yourself and your strengths, and know what it is that makes you different. Being like everyone else is boring. Take whatever it is that makes you different, unique, special, interesting, quirky, or uncommon and turn that into a fascinating story of why you're pursuing XYZ. Share it with everyone you can. Having an interesting story about how you ended up in your new venture will make people curious about you. Then back up your pursuit with a fierce passion and the commitment to take it forward. Other people will respond to that: people always respond to passion. If you're learning on the go, share what you discover along the way. Build a fan base, a following, gain exposure, and soon enough, opportunities will start to present themselves. Stay as different as you are.

Five

Find Others With Shared Values

Find something you're passionate about. And then find people who share that passion. There are always others who love the things you do, who share your values and ideals. Find them. Online, offline, it doesn't matter. Spend as much time as you can in these circles to fire you up, and to learn. Shake up your environment and influences from friends and contacts. If you've ever traveled internationally, you know that exposure to different cultures changes your perspective, often profoundly. Shake up your routines, influences, and contacts locally and expose yourself to new influences. If more drastic changes are in the books—say, to a new company or geographical location—think of them as you would adapt to a different country or culture. Do the research. Talk to others who've been there, get expert advice, read what people say online, etc. and apply it to the new area or industry you're contemplating. Find your sweet spot.

Six

Define Your Options

Never tell yourself you're stuck. You're not. You always have more options than you could ever dream of. In fact, you could spend your whole life researching opportunities and you still wouldn't uncover everything that's possible. Your passion is your asset and there's always a way to support it. Challenge yourself to uncover five to seven new opportunities this week, then another five to seven the week after. If you're really feeling inspired, brainstorm ten or twenty of these opportunities with your friends or family. It's an amazing exercise to do with a group. View the road ahead of you as an open one. Get excited about having so many options. That energy will fuel your drive tremendously as you set out to pursue the ones that rise to the top of your list. You need to define your options on a daily basis, regardless of whether you are doing well with them or not. And remember: you are not stuck.

Seven

Expand Your Leadership Opportunities

Competition can be daunting, which is why it's important to break free from the pack. Whether you're trying to find a job in a field where everyone seems to be looking, or fully employed and vying for leadership opportunities, there's a wonderful concept you should know about. It's called Blue Ocean strategy[338] and it's based on a book by the same name. The concept is simple. Most people tend to stick to a confined area where they fight like mad to compete for the same pool of opportunities and resources. The result: a blood red ocean of rivals fighting over a shrinking profit pool. But the ocean is vast and abundant. You just have to start fishing further from the shore, in the beautiful blue waters where few others have ventured. You will thrive as a leader there like a fish thrives in water—provided you learn the rules of this ocean: leadership fitness, inclusiveness, and openness.

Self-Assessment &
The American Success Scale

Real confidence requires self-knowledge,
which includes recognizing one's shortcomings
as well as one's strengths.
Virginia Postrel

All success requires a measure of self-assessment, something to help us check-in with ourselves to determine where we are today—and where we want to go from here. But success is both a subtle and profound experience that doesn't lend itself easily to measurement. Not to mention that for many of us it's not just about the destination, but the very journey that takes us there. But I've heard it said that "what gets measured gets done," and I think there's a lot of truth in that statement. That's why I came up with own American Success Scale, and it's a simple question: "Where, *to your mind*, do you stand in life and career today?" Here's this scale.

1-------2------3-------4-------5-------6-------7------8-------9-------10

1   a minimal achievement

2   a low achievement, in your opinion

3   basically satisfactory, all things considered

4   a very good-level achievement, despite all odds

5   your achievements match your original goals

6   you have achieved more than initially planned

7   your achievements have exceeded all original expectations

8   you are nationally recognized because of your achievements (or pure luck)

9   you have achieved international fame

10   stands here as an abstract construct meaning that've have reached heaven on earth

I encourage you all to measure yourselves on The American Success Scale. Self-assess yourself realistically for today's situation, and plan to do it again yearly.

Here's how some of our achievers measured up at the time I asked them this question:

Alfa Demmellash: Self-assessed at 10. "I am deeply humbled and grateful. . . . I am surrounded by people I love and do what I love. I have achieved national and international recognition by hard work and luck, and not really by intentional design. I meet people who inspire me every day and even the problems and challenges I face are invigorating. I have the opportunity to shape my life experiences in such a way as to make sure I don't burn out. Even though I do not have the level of material wealth to match my philanthropic and social entrepreneurial aspirations, I believe I have been provided with the tools, resources and people I need to help [me] continue to push for my vision in a sustainable, love-centered way. . . . Even motherhood is providing me with lots more windows of opportunity for learning, empathy and inspiration. Maybe I am just an incurable optimist?"

Hilda Ochoa Brillembourg: Hilda self-scored at 9 which registered the fact she has achieved international fame. With respect to a score of 10 being an abstract construct meaning that she has reached "heaven on earth," Hilda, characteristically, noted that "Heaven on earth is possible, but not sustainable."

Elena Gorokhova: "Success in the U.S. includes financial stability but does not end there. Success involves making a unique contribution to this country: its culture, technology, science, or economics." When coming to the U.S. as a young wife at the age of twenty-four, Elena had no particular goals. But after thirty years in this country, she has become nationally recognized after publishing her two memoirs, so it is safe for her to say she's achieved a score of 8.

Weili Dai: "I think 10, overall. My results speak for themselves; you know my ingredients. I am happy, I believe. I make other people smile too."

Rohini Anand: self-scored 8 to 9, which means that not only did she achieve her original goals when she came to the U.S. as a student, but that her goals have continued to evolve. In fact, she sets new goals for herself all the time—as an established achiever should.

Josie Natori: It only took Josie a minute to self-score an 8, adding, "It is 8 – and going!"

Maya Strelar-Migotti: Raised to be modest rather than over-confident, as befits a girl from Europe, Maya considered her goals "accomplished to some extent." She self-scored at 7 while noting that there's only one secret to success: "Very-very hard work and perseverance."

Raegan Moya-Jones, a self-made businesswoman, was overly modest when assessing herself at a 7, meaning her achievement has exceeded all original expectations. I personally believe that she's on the right track to get to 8, meaning that she's nationally recognized.

Verónica Montes: "I cannot say that teaching at a private university was like making my dream come true, as I never thought that something like that could happen to me. . . . I never dreamed of becoming a college professor, therefore I can only say that my achievement *has exceeded* all original expectations." She self-scored at 7.

Ani Palacios McBride: The author, publisher, and editor was the first to write about immigration issues facing Latinos in the US, helping them to understand and overcome the challenges of American culture. Starting low and rising to the top, Ani estimates her success score at 7, while acknowledging that her pre-immigration plans pale in comparison to reality—all because she pushed herself harder in the U.S. in order to show her family and friends that she could make it in America.

Advice from the Heart

Teachers open the door, but you enter by yourself.
—Anonymous

I'm proud of the information and insights presented in this book, and the women who shared it. And as much as the prominent achievers featured here have offered the stories of their own unique paths to success, they didn't hesitate when asked to answer one last question: "what advice would you give to the immigrant women who come after you on how to accelerate their success in the United States?" Advice from the heart . . . that's what this is. Workable tips and guidance from each woman profiled, and not just for immigrants, but for all aspiring achievers.

Josie Natori, American fashion designer, founder and CEO of The Natori Company

- Being an immigrant was essential to my entrepreneurial success. Of course, the education, genes, savvy—it all counts.

- I consider my heritage to be a fundamental asset, a cornerstone of my success; I inherited the design aesthetics from my native land and used my heritage to succeed.

- Look for the angle that differentiates you from the crowd. Look for the point of differentiation in your career.

- Whatever your success is, be humble.

- A special note to immigrant entrepreneurs: there's no better place in the world for an immigrant to succeed than in the U.S.

Raegan Moya-Jones, founder and former CEO at aden & anais, Inc.

- Be a calculated risk taker; have an idea, then find a way to go for it.

- Make sure you have a support network in place. Have a partner who will step up for you.

- Listen to what other people say, but go with your gut in the end.

- Stay authentically you. You don't need to change who you are to be successful in America.

- Be your feminine self. You don't need to act like a man to be successful.

- Find your passion, follow your dream and never ever, ever give up.

- Forge your own path; don't follow mine.

Irmgard Lafrenz, founder and former President of Globalpress Connection

- **Build Relationships:** Never forget that business is conducted by people who like and respect each other.

- **Develop Emotional Intelligence:** If you can't read your prospects, you will never connect with them.

- **Be Flexible:** You have to adjust to changing market conditions, and be prepared to modify your living situation to accommodate setbacks as well as success.

- **Focus:** Make a plan, then focus. Define your results in terms of dollar value, number of prospects, and deals.

- **Invest in Yourself:** When starting a new venture, try to prepare for twelve months without income. Otherwise the financial pressure can become so great that you'll give up.

- **Persevere:** Understand that the only option is to carry on, no matter what the circumstances.

Isabel Allende, bestselling Chilean-American writer

- Never forget that immigrant women enrich this country with biculturalism and bilingualism. The U.S. is richer because of it.

- Take the best this country has to offer and combine it with the best of what you brought with you. And don't look back.

Edwina Sandys, renowned British-American sculptor and artist

- Be respectful to your new country.

- Learn the language.

- Don't be somebody you're not.

- Remember that double standards exist everywhere.

Elena Gorokhova, educator and critically acclaimed author

- Re-create yourself. Be whatever—and whoever—you want to be.

- Preserve your own culture: that's what makes you unique.

- Use the skills you learned in your native country to help overcome hardships.

- Learn to speak and write in English.

Veronica Montes, Ph. D., Assistant Professor of Sociology, Bryn Mawr College

- Understand that, while the U.S. may be full of opportunities, life here is not easy, particularly for women of color.

- Refuse to be held back by stereotypes and racial prejudices.

- Make alliances with other women, both immigrant and non-immigrant. Solidarity is key.

Ivana Trump, business woman and socialite

- Believe in yourself and all you can do.

- Be open to deals and know they will come to you.

- Be confident and understand that in business you need to have a certain ego.

- Set goals. Achievement isn't possible without them.

- Remember: life is meant for living.

Alfa Demmellash, co-founder and CEO of Rising Tide Capital

- Know that there is an inherent value in being different.

- Invest your resources in your goals.

- Figure out how you can add value and contribute, with all of your differences.

Ani Palacios McBride, writer, journalist, publisher, and founder of Contacto Latino

- Make sure you insert yourself into society-at-large.

- Give yourself an equal opportunity by learning English, making American friends, and exploring American customs.

- Take the opportunity to rid yourself of those customs you never cared for. Add new customs from your new country.

- Immigrating is a second chance at life. Make sure your sacrifices are not lost in the shuffle; make sure you get what you want.

Hilda Ochoa Brillembourg, founder and former CEO of Strategic Investment Partners

- Don't assume anything about anyone. Ask questions— many questions—before placing someone in context.

- Nurture your entrepreneurial spirit.

- Rely on training, imagination, teamwork, and perseverance.

Plus,

HOW TO LAY THE FOUNDATION FOR SUCCESS

Pursue Education: A must. There is no substitute.

Develop Street Smarts: Know what's going on around you. Lean to think fast and act fast.

Cultivate Charisma: Nothing is more important than the ability to communicate with an open mind and connect with an open heart. A sense of humor doesn't hurt.

Build Professional Acumen: Become highly trained in your field and stay abreast of advances.

Accept Support from Family and Friends: These are the people who will bring joy and balance to your life. Keep them close.

Stay Curious: Be inquisitive. Try new things. Don't let preconceived notions stand in your way.

Hilda Ochoa Brillembourg

Maya Strelar-Migotti, former vice president, Head of Development Unit IP & Broadband, Head of Ericsson Silicon Valley; CEO and Investor at 4PIA, Inc.

- Understand that your success is built on relationship-building.

- Spend time creating and becoming part of a network.

- Advancement for women depends on company culture, so look before you leap.

- Develop emotional intelligence.

- Prepare for setbacks, but never give up.

- Focus! Persevere!

Epilogue

All too often it seems as if we're drowning in information yet starved for knowledge. I hope that this book has provided you with both information and knowledge, and that it encourages you to see your own possibilities in the stories of the successful women profiled in these pages.

The immigrant achievers featured in this book were often estranged in their new country. At times they felt as if they didn't understand the rules of the game, that they were saying the wrong things and making every possible mistake. Indeed, many of them experienced the fear and distress that comes from having to depend on people who didn't always mean well or act in their best interests. There was nothing they could to do about it—except persevere. And persevere they did.

These stories of success[339] are as diverse as could be. Our immigrant achievers come from all over the world—from Peru to Germany, from Mexico to Ethiopia—and from all walks of life. All of the women have graciously shared their immigration stories, and described the often-confusing terrain in which they started their new lives. They are writers and artists, business women and philanthropists, and they have forged their own professional paths while caring for their families, contributing to their communities, and making a difference in any number of ways.

The native creativity in each of these women was enhanced by their immigration experience. The feeling of living in two worlds, as difficult as that can be, often encourages a dual perspective that brings about new ideas, creative new organizations, innovations, and opportunities. While these stories may be different in pitch and timbre, each is a case study in tenacity and hard work. Each makes clear that the United States is a country of opportunity. But never forget that these opportunities are reserved for the talented, the determined, and the prepared.

Our achievers' combined know-how is now yours—so use it. After reading the Profiles and perusing the Seven Success Values, I hope you will take the opportunity to go through The Achiever's Handbook, to learn from The Success-Takeaways and Advice From the Heart, and finally, to do your own Self-Assessment on the American Success Scale. I believe that the lives of these extraordinary women will benefit you in many ways. Because we are all stronger together.

Afterword

Fiona Citkin has made this book "work" in spite of some inherent challenges. For starters, it's hard to pin down. Is it a series of inspirational sketches of impressive women? Is it a study of the challenges of being a female immigrant in America? Is it a self-help book for women?

In the end, it is all three, but the elements are presented in a sequence that builds and delivers a real payoff in the final section. The 18 profiles which comprise more than half the book are fascinating and—against *all* odds—not repetitive. Citkin has chosen her subjects wisely; each is so different you don't feel you're hearing the same story from 18 different people. If you read this book only for their stories, you will not be disappointed. Two of my favorite moments (out of many) are the Croatian Maya Strellar-Migotti's observation that "You plan—and God laughs." And the story of how Ivana Trump's father, for fear that her privileged background might rob her of any ambition, sent her to work on the assembly line of a shoe factory.

After the sketches, Citkin goes back and distils the essence of the women's achievements into the seven success values of the subtitle. This section could easily have been preachy, but the author brings the 18 subjects back for encore appearances, always keeping the women the focus of the book. That's a very smart choice because people are inherently more interesting than abstract values and rules for success; our keen interest in the women makes it easy to absorb the lessons their stories have to teach.

Part Three is the self-help component of the book, and it's an almost seamless transition from what has gone before. This section could easily have fallen flat, especially for readers who are just not that interested in helping themselves, thanks anyway. But again Citkin brings the women back to do one final bit of inspiring, and because you like these women, you pay attention.

In the end *They Made It in America* works because Citkin trusts the voices of her subjects. And are these women ever interesting!

Craig Storti,
author of *Why Travel Matters: A Guide to the Life-Changing Effects of Travel.*

Notes

Introduction

1   **special skills for a woman:** Joanna Barsh, *How Remarkable Women Lead: The Breakthrough Model for Work and Life* (New York: Crown Business Publishing; December 27, 2011)

2   Ted Ownby: *American Dreams in Mississippi*:

3   **Center for American Progress:** "The Facts on Immigration Today," accessed 2/16/16 https://www.americanprogress.org/issues/immigration/report/2014/10/23/59040/the-facts-on-immigration-today-3/

4   **Booker T. Washington:** *Brainy Quotes*, accessed 2/16/2016 http://www.brainyquote.com/quotes/quotes/b/bookertwa107996.html

5   **Economic Census's Survey:** Survey of Business Owners (SBO), 2007, accessed 2/29/16, https://www.census.gov/econ/sbo/07menu.html

6   **Susan C. Pearce:** Susan C. Pearce, Elizabeth J. Clifford, and Reena Tandon, *Immigration and Women: Understanding the American Experience* (New York: New York University Press, 2011)

The Achievers

7   **"Descendant of a robust Basque sailor":** Isabel Allende, *Paula: A Memoir* (New York: Harper Perennial, 2013), 3.

8   **In her own words:** Ibid, 6.

9   **"I want to be like my grandfather, and protect my mother":** *Paula*, 37.

10   **"This was not only stupidity on my part; it was misdirected energy and excessive love":** *Paula*, 145.

11   **"until men are equal in it":** Marianne Schnall, "Interview with Gloria Steinem on Equality, Her New Memoir, and More," accessed 2/16/1016, http://www.feminist.com/resources/artspeech/interviews/gloriasteineminterview.html

12   **"The impact of arrival was that of having fallen onto another planet":** Ibid, 238.

13   "I slumped to the anonymity and daily humiliation of a person looking for work": Ibid, 243.

14   "...but when I finally succeeded, I felt freed of the back-bowing burdens I had carried in my own country": Ibid, 239.

15   *The Sum of Our Days*; Isabel Allende, *The Sum of our Days* (New York: HarperCollins Publishers, 2008).

16   "as if I had a lighted flame inside me": Ibid, 275.

17   "And had a tattoo on his left hand": Paula, 299.

18   "Essence of our union": Paula, 76.

19   *Paula:* Isabel Allende, *Paula: A Memoir.*

20   *The Sum of Our Days*: Isabel Allende, *The Sum of Our Days* (New York: HarperCollins Publishers, 2008).

21   "I could invent a fresh version of myself only for him": Paula, 302.

22   "The inevitable problems of children in a family artificially glued together": Ibid, 113.

23   "I like sleeping with him": Ibid, 95.

24   "I have been an embarrassment for the family": *Paula*, 15.

25   "Perhaps, it isn't only in my case": *The Sum of Our Days*, 198.

26   Being a workaholic in Venezuela: Interview

27   "I am a writer": Interview

28   "That is unforgivable": Quoted in Wikipedia, accessed 2/12/16, http://en.wikipedia.org/wiki/Isabel_Allende

29   Awards: Wikipedia, accessed 2/12/16, http://en.wikipedia.org/wiki/Isabel_Allende

30   Dorothy and Lillian Gish Prize: ibid

31   "catapulted into fame": *The Sum of Our Days*, 85.

32   "I had to lean on Willie": *Paula*, 331.

33   "One day I will also go to college": Ibid

34   "Thanks mom for teaching me by example": Interview

35   "My life is already settled here in the U.S.": Ibid

36   accept this fact and adapt to it: Ibid

37   accept this fact and adapt to it: Ibid

38   "sow the seeds of pursuing the higher education, especially in my family": Ibid

39   "I re-invented myself by adapting to a new culture": Ibid

40   "In order to survive, you need to re-invent your own world: Ibid

41   "passive, submissive, dependent and uneducated": Ibid

42   **"based on my accent"**: Interview and students' ratings of Verónica Montes,   http://www.ratemyprofessors.com/ShowRatings. jsp?tid=1861537

43   **"very culture-sensitive to others"**: Interview

44   **unique study with manifold implications**: - Montes, Verónica. *The Role of Emotions in the Construction of Masculinity: Guatemalan Migrant Men, Transnational Migration and Family Relations.* "Gender & Society, Sage publications," Jan 2013 http://gas.sagepub.com/content/early/2013/01/17/0891243212470491

45   **"this passion for winning"**: Interview with Weili Dai, March 3, 2015

46   **one of the most successful**: Russell Flannery, "25 Notable Chinese-Americans", *Forbes*, 08.09.10, accessed 2/18/16, http://www.committee100.org/media/articles/Forbes-notable-chinese.pdf

47   **the only female co-founder**: Weili Dai, "Women! Embrace Your Inner Geek," CNN, 20 March 2012, accessed 11/12/12 and 2/28/16, http://edition.cnn.com/2012/03/07/business/weili-dai-women-geeks/index.html

48   **A driving force**: "150 Women Who Shake the World," *The Daily Beast.* 04/17/12, accessed 2/28/16, http://www.thedailybeast.com/features/150-women-who-shake-the-world.html

49   **"The first victory, the happy memories"**: Ibid

50   **Market share**: Suzanne Herel, "Meet the Boss: Weili Dai, Marvell Technology Group," *SFGate*, June 6, 2011, http://www.sfgate.com/business/article/Meet-the-Boss-Weili-Dai-Marvell-Technology-Group-2369284.php

51   **has had annual revenues in excess of US $3 billion**: Marvell website, http://investor.marvell.com/phoenix.zhtml?c=120802&p=irol-newsArticle&ID=2018406

52   **"values, creativity, and educational environment"**: Ibid

53   **"Naïve"**: Ibid

54   **never "graduate" from your family"**: Ibid

55   **American Dream**: Ibid

56   **AD foundation**: Ibid

57   **"you accomplished something"**: Interview

58   **Confucius**: - http://www.1000advices.com/guru/people_skills_relationship_confucius.html

59   **Article**: Lydia Dishman, "Innovation Agents: Marvell Technology Group's Weili Dai, Semiconductor Pioneer," *Fast Company*, accessed

5/2/12, http://www.fastcompany.com/1834893/innovation-agent
s-marvell-technology-groups-weili-dai-semiconductor-pioneer

60   **co-founder of Lark Technologies, Inc.:** Ibid and http://www.web.lark. com/#top

61   **more women engineers:** Christina Warren, "Women in Tech: How One Entrepreneur Blazed a Trail," *Mashable*, accessed 2/16/16, http:// mashable.com/2012/03/21/weili-dai-women-tech-entrepreneurs/ #t6gJoaml6uq7

62   **"the social aspects of our lives":** Danielle Kucera, "Technology Industry's Gender Gap Seen Hampering Competitiveness," *Bloomberg BusinessWeek*, accessed 5/2/12, http://www.bloomberg.com/

63   **care-and-fair life philosophy:** Herel, Suzanne, "Meet the Boss: Weili Dai, Marvell Technology Group," *San Francisco Chronicle*, June 6, 2011, accessed 2/28/16, http://www.sfgate.com/business/article/Mee t-the-Boss-Weili-Dai-Marvell-Technology-Group-2369284.php

64   **new Chromecast video adapter**: https://gigaom.com/2013/07/24/wh y-chromecast-is-such-a-big-deal-for-google-and-a-threat-to-apple/

65   **TIME Magazine:** http://techland.time.com/2013/12/04/technology/ slide/top-10-gadgets/

66   **One Laptop per Child program**: https://en.wikipedia.org/wiki/ One_Laptop_per_Child

67   **Give2Asia:** http://www.give2asia.org/

68   **Committee of 100**: http://www.committee100.org/

69   **C200:** https://www.c200.org/

70   **TechNet:** http://www.technet.org/

71   **Center for Information Technology Research in the Interest of Society:** https://en.wikipedia.org/wiki/Center_for_Information_Technology_ Research_in_the_Interest_of_Society

72   **Bullying on the playground:** Ibid

73   **what it means to be an American**: Ibid

74   **"What does it mean to love well today?":** Ibid

75   **founded the *Rising Tide Capital*:** Steve Mariotti, "Her Own Rising Tide: Alfa's Story," *The Huffington Post*, February 11, 2014. http:// www.huffingtonpost.com/steve-mariotti/her-own-rising-tide- alfas_b_4762392.html

76   **Community Business Academy:** Alfa Demmellash, "Building Communities, Building the Economy," *The Huffington Post*, October

12, 2012, http://www.huffingtonpost.com/alfa-demmellash/building-communities_b_1959579.html.

77   **intensive business academy:** Dalila Wilson-Scott, "Innovative Rising Stars: Building Communities," *Forbes.com* - June 11, 2013, http://www.forbes.com/pictures/elli45gghl/alfa-demmellash-co-founder-chief-executive-officer-rising-tide-capital/

78   **invited to the White House:** President Obama recognizes CNN Hero and Rising Tide Capital CEO Alfa Demmellash - June 30, 2009, http://www.cnn.com/2009/LIVING/worklife/06/30/cnnheroes.demmellash.obama/index.html?_s=PM:LIVING

79   **not been negatively impacted:** Ibid

80   **Developing affection for America:** Ibid

81   **"ready for something new":** Ibid

82   **"had the *common sense* to see what was obvious":** Ibid

83   **"had the *common sense* to see what was obvious":** Ibid

84   **something so new and unique:** Take 5 with Warren Interview with Irmgard Lafrentz, Video, accessed 2/18/2016, https://www.youtube.com/watch?v=SSFLSIdnF4s

85   **"Fear made me snap out and be accountable again":** Interview

86   **"lucky to be living in the 'new world' of America":** accessed 2/18/2016

87   **German immigrants in America:** Library of Congress European Reading Room, http://www.loc.gov/rr/european/imde/germchro.html

88   **Described:** "The Silent Minority," *The Economist*, http://economist.com/news/united-states/21642222-americas-largest-ethnic-group-has-assimilated-so-well-people-barely-notice-it

89   **anti-German:** "Internment of German-Americans," Wikipedia, https://en.wikipedia.org/wiki/Internment_of_German_Americans

90   **"rooted neither here nor in Germany":** accessed 2/18/2016

91   **"debt is part of life and considered normal":** Ibid

92   **"system's different here":** Interview

93   **"I am more generous now":** Ibid

94   **"less-direct way of communication":** Ibid

95   **"Maybe I am a natural leader":** Ibid

96   **"helped launch hundreds of companies":** The Global Matchmaker, video about Irmgard Lafrentz and Globalpress Connection, https://www.youtube.com/watch?v=VGpkFCFI-HU

97 **achieved a lot in the 10 years here:** Debbie Brannigan, "Women of the World: Irmgard Lafrentz," 2008, in http://capitalistchicks. com/?q=node/482

98 **putting her failures behind:** Interview

99 **"Accidental immigrants":** Ibid

100 **"most of it was up to me":** Ibid

101 **"give it all up for the opportunity of being here":** Ibid

102 **"Know who your friends are":** Ibid

103 **"Many come out of it stronger":** Ibid

104 **"people without an accent":** Ibid

105 **"My entire career was built on the fact that I'm an immigrant":** Ibid

106 **"Many come out of it stronger":** Ibid

107 **"living in a double world":** Ibid

108 **end up being hybrids:** Ibid

109 **"if you work hard enough":** Ibid

110 **"Even faster not to behave as friends:** Ibid

111 **"if you work hard enough":** Ibid

112 **"to have more, to give back more":** Ibid

113 **"the emotional pressure cooker":** Ibid

114 **Contacto-Latino:** http://www.contacto-latino.com/

115 double cultural ambassador: **Ana Maria Quevedo, "Having it all without losing yourself,"** *Latino Arts for Humanity,* **May 22, 2012, accessed 2/28/16, http://latinoartsforhumanity.blogspot. com/2012/05/having-it-all-without-losing-yourself.html**

116 **aden + anais:** Cara Waters, "How Raegan Moya-Jones Scored Prince George as Her Number One Customer for aden + anais," *The Smart Company,* accessed 2/14/16, http://www.smartcompany.com.au/leader-ship/profiles/41564-how-raegan-moya-jones-scored-prince-george-as-her-number-one-customer-for-aden-anais.html

117 **products are now carried:** Elena Donovan Mauer, "Inspiring Mompreneur: Raegan Moya-Jones, Co-Founder and CEO of aden + Anais", *The Bump from the Knot,* last accessed 2/18/16 http://blog. thebump.com/2013/08/09/inspiring-mompreneur-raegan-moya-jones-co-founder-and-ceo-of-aden-anais/

118 **"been discriminated against":** Ibid

119 **for over 10 years:** Interview with Raegan Moya-Jones, September 11, 2014

120 **"born with an entrepreneurial spirit"**: Questionnaire by Raegan Moya-Jones

121 **"never an option to me to not "keep on going"**: Ibid

122 **"Have I bitten off more than I can chew?"**: Ibid

123 **"given what they have gone through"**: Ibid

124 **"Australians tend to be much more direct"**:

125 **"I find New Yorkers really friendly"**: Ibid

126 **"Australia formed me"**: Ibid

127 **"My children will be culturally richer"**: Ibid

128 **"if I had not persevered"**: Questionnaire

129 **prioritizing like this**: Ibid

130 **"Women can have it all"**: Questionnaire

131 **"contributed to my personal success"**: Ibid

132 **Josie Natori**: "The 130 Most Inspiring Asian Americans Of All Time. Josie Natori," *American Media Group,* http://goldsea.com/Personalities/Inspiring/natori.html

133 **her grandmother saying**: Interviews with Josie Natori, 9/10/14

134 **"this special energy of New York City"**: Ibid

135 **"accepted a strong woman as his wife"**: Ibid

136 **aspects of her native culture**: Ibid

137 **"It's easy to take for granted the amount of work"**: Ibid

138 **secret of her big success**: Ibid

139 **"where life meets art"**: Ibid

140 **business went international**: Andrea N. Browne, "7 Self-Made Immigrant Millionaires," *Kiplinger,* Nov 9, 2012, accessed 12/18/14, http://finance.yahoo.com/news/7-self-made-immigrant-millionaires.html

141 **"Internet is a game changer"**: Interviews

142 **"when old Senator Aquino was assassinated"**: Ibid

143 **"a cycle of life"**: Ibid

144 **"had to reinvent the product"**: Ibid

145 **"I never understood feminism"**: Ibid

146 **"Women are more equal and less subdued"**: Ibid

147 **"lift other women around the world"**: Ibid

148 **"We, the immigrant women, need to help each other"**: Ibid

149 (https://www.census.gov/prod/cen2010/briefs/c2010br-11.pdf),

150 **"success in fashion is not enough"**: Josie Natori Story, http://www.natori.com/Content/Natori%20Story

151 Billy Collins, per the author's website.

152 **"image of my motherland: overbearing, protective, and difficult to leave":** Elena Gorokhova, *A Mountain of Crumbs* (New York: Simon & Schuster Paperbacks, 2011), 1.

153 **influenced Elena:** Alden Mudge, "From Russia, with Love, Interview with Elena Gorokhova," *BookPage* January 2010, http://bookpage.com/print-edition/34-january-2010

154 **she didn't have much choice**: Interview

155 **private scandal in her family kitchen:** Interview with Elena Gorokhova, October 18, 2014

156 **"I felt like a 3-year-old":** Elena Gorokhova, *Russian Tattoo* (New York: Simon & Schuster, 2015), 111.

157 **"I was an alien, and I felt like one":** Ibid

158 **"in Texas, which involved a double culture shock.":** Interview

159 **"people - most of the time and at least on the coasts - are not judged by their accents":** Ibid

160 **"What I don't know is whether I write with an accent":** Ibid

161 **the cultural differences she observed:** Ibid

162 **"his brain has always been the master of his heart":** *Russian Tattoo,* 77.

163 **"The U.S. is a country that lives by its laws, unlike today's Russia":** Interview

164 **"To lose my Russian connection would be like losing my soul":** Ibid

165 **"The 'Russian me' is for my mother and my sister and my daughter, my blood":** *Russian Tattoo,* 226.

166 **"a wound, the inner divide of exile":** Ibid, 226.

167 **"Russia, like a virus, has settled in my blood":** Ibid, 219.

168 **"where I belong:** Rusian Tattoo, 166.

169 **"I never arrive home":** Tara Bahrampour, Review: "Russian Tattoo," by Elena Gorokhova, *The Washington Post,* January 9, 2015

170 **"the *me* I would like to be":** *Russian Tattoo,* 98.

171 **"Stop wishing for another hand":** *Russian Tattoo,* 204.

172 **"a constant witness to every moment of my less than perfect, tattooed life":** *Russian Tattoo,* 286.

173 **"took me a few years to learn the English rhetoric how to become a writer":** – Interview

174 **"I simply had to write":** – ibid

175 **how to create company culture that spurs innovation:** Mike Cassidy, "Ericsson Silicon Valley's Maya Strelar-Migotti's Six ways to fire up

innovation in big enterprises," Silicon Beat, May 19, 2013, accessed 2/23/16, http://www.siliconbeat.com/2013/05/19/ericsson-silicon-valleys-maya-strelar-migottis-six-ways-to-fire-up-innovation-in-big-enterprises/

176 **took adjustments to her original plans philosophically:** Interview with Maya Strelar-Migotti, February 28, 2014

177 **"I did re-invent myself, and culture, and the ways of working":** Ibid

178 **"I feel great here":** Ibid

179 **an advisor to a smaller company:** Ibid

180 **"The US is more gender-traditional than Europe, especially Sweden":** Interview

181 **some surveys:** Diversity & Inclusion: Unlocking Global Potential Global Diversity Rankings by Country, Sector and Occupation, accessed 2/23/16, http://images.forbes.com/forbesinsights/StudyPDFs/global_diversity_rankings_2012.pdf

182 **"We immigrants belong to "OTHERS," and that makes us bond somehow:** Ibid

183 **"integration is great – you create diversity of thoughts":** Ibid

184 **"Here people are pulling off so much by themselves":** Ibid

185 **"the characteristically American traits":** Ibid

186 **It took time to get accepted and change the culture:** Ibid

187 **"failures are always a possibility":** Ibid

188 **"I keep the learning and forget the failure":** Ibid

189 **what Inclusive Leaders do:** Interview

190 **leadership skills develop:** Ibid

191 **promoting women's equality:** Angela Swartz, "Maya Strelar-Migotti: Speak out, Step up, Listen to Pink," *Social Capital*, Apr 3, 2015, accessed 2/23/16, http://www.bizjournals.com/sanjose/print-edition/2015/04/03/maya-strelar-migotti-speak-out-step-up-listen-to.html?surround=etf&ana=e_article&u=16731966574f7dc7c7c126a1284bfd&t=1428089672

192 **2014 Global Gender Gap Report:** World Economic Forum Ranking, accessed 2/23/16, http://reports.weforum.org/global-gender-gap-report-2014/rankings/

193 **parents reinforced the message:** Interview with Rohini Anand, February 12, 2015

194 **molded her into a different, better person:** Ibid

195 **"it was not an arranged marriage":** Ibid

196 **the US felt like HOME:** Interview

197 **"I came into my own in the US":** Interview

198 "Have the minority identity shaped for them at a very early age: Ibid
199 the negative stereotyping: Ibid
200 "the US is home, not India": Ibid
201 "It was not for the financial reasons": Ibid
202 Comparing cultures: Ibid
203 "I have no issue with my accent": Ibid
204 "I work with Asian women": Ibid
205 "If I were not an immigrant": Ibid
206 On CEO, Michel Landel: Interview
207 Sodexo awards: Enrico Dinges, "Sodexo Executive Dr. Rohini Anand Honored with Mosaic Woman Leadership Award," *3BL Media*, December 1, 2011, http://3blmedia.com/theCSRfeed/Sodexo-Executive-Dr-Rohini-Anand-Honored-Mosaic-Woman-Leadership-Award
208 Sodexo's goal is to move women-in-top-management: "Profile of Rohini Anand, Ph.D., Senior Vice President and Global Chief Diversity Officer, Sodexo," *The Working Mother*, April 14, 2011, accessed 2/21/16, http://www.workingmother.com/profile/rohini-anand-phd
209 her parents' high regard for education: Interview with Ying McGuire, June 11, 2014
210 "my early dream": Ibid
211 waitressing in the US: Ibid
212 "Divorce was not in our vocabulary": Ibid
213 make America a great place to live: Ibid
214 could not understand American slang: Ibid
215 accent was not a limitation but just a unique signature: Ibid
216 deal with setbacks: Ibid
217 was offered four jobs: Ibid
218 "I almost fell off my chair": Ibid
219 original culture helpful in a new setting: Ibid
220 Humility is a well-regarded virtue in the Chinese culture: Ibid
221 fellow Asian immigrants: Ibid
222 "becoming an American is beyond passing the citizenship exam": Ibid
223 "I have Americanized": Ibid
224 made four points: Ibid
225 "I joined the ski circuit: Interview with Ivana Trump, 4/24/14
226 Obtained a foreign passport: Norma King, 34.
227 "I began modeling for Audrey Morris": Interview

228   **gave her an obvious edge**: Norma King, 66

229   **she was a mirror image of him:** Norma King, 71

230   **"We were married in 1979"**: Interview

231   **her thick accent aside:** Inteview

232   **"While married to Donald"**: Interview

233   **"My biggest challenge was to motivate"**: Norma King, 132.

234   **"You can't be a pussycat"**: Ibid, 133.

235   **named Hotelier of the Year in 1990:** https://en.wikipedia.org/wiki/Ivana_Trump

236   **"this is my upbringing"**: Norma King, 170.

237   **"I give her a dollar a year and all the clothes she can buy"**: Norma King, 137.

238   **"Everything that has engines, I am good at"**: Norma King, 167.

239   **She reinvented herself:** Interview

240   *Ivana, Inc.*: http://www.ivanatrump.com/

241   *Ivana Haute Couture:* http://www.ivanatrump.com/

242   **"I just love the work I do"**: Interview

243   *For Love Alone*: Ivana Trump, *For Love Alone* (New York: Pocket Books, 1992) 532 pages

244   *Free to Love*: Ivana Trump, *Free to Love* (New York: Pocket Books; Pocket Books edition, 1993) 504 p.

245   *The Best is Yet to Come: Ivana Trump, The Best is Yet to Come: Coping with Divorce and Enjoying Life Again,* (New York: Pocket Books, 1995) 269 pages

246   **her personal achievements:** LinkedIn profile, accessed 2/22/16, www.linkedin.com/in/sophievandebroek/

247   **One of her top priorities:** Interview with Sophie Vandebroek, July 12, 2013

248   **two scholarships, four suitcases, and $500 between them:** Ibid

249   **the differences [cultural] were more obvious:** Ibid

250   Xerox: David Zax, "How Xerox Evolved from Copier Company to Creative Powerhouse," The Fast Company Magazine, December 11, 2013, accessed 2/24/16, HTTP://WWW.FASTCOMPANY.COM/3023240/MOST-CREATIVE-PEOPLE/DREAMING-TOGETHER-HOW-XEROX-KEEPS-BIG-IDEAS-FLOWING

251   **quickly felt at home at Xerox:** Interview

252   **"The beauty is that the US is a mixture of many different cultures"**: Ibid

253 **According to Sophie:** Ibid

254 **"culture … presented a *steeper barrier* for finding a new life partner":** Ibid

255 **she loved her job because:** Ibid

256 **here's what she used to do:** Daniel McGinn, "How She Does It," *Fast Company Magazine,* April 1, 2006, accessed 2/24/16, http://www.fastcompany.com/55888/how-she-does-it

257 **routine is even more disciplined:** ibid

258 **"you get more control over decisions about when you're busy and how":** Interview

259 **her culture places value on family over everything else:** Interview

260 **"I have the privilege to lead":** Ibid

261 **the metaphor of "punched ticket" example:** Sophie V. Vandebroek, Xerox CTO and President Xerox Innovation Group, "Innovation, People and Culture" – a meeting address, January 17, 2006: materials provided by Sophie Vandebroek to author.

262 **how to play the "intrapreneur" role:** Ibid

263 **de la Cruz Collection Contemporary Art Space:** accessed 2/28/16, http://www.delacruzcollection.org/

264 **Family:** Interview with Rosa R. de la Cruz, May 18, 2015

265 **Exiles:** Ibid

266 **"a letter to one another every day":** Ibid

267 **Rosa recalls:** Ibid

268 **annual Art Basel Miami Beach:** accessed 2/28/16, https://www.artbasel.com/

269 **an article:** Brett Sokol, "Rehousing a Miami Collection," *The New York Times,* Nov 25 2009, http://www.nytimes.com/2009/11/29/travel/29headsup.html?_r=0

270 **"Free art":** Edwin Heathcote, "Money Meets Art: the Rise of the Private Galleries," *Financial Times,* March 24, 2011, http://www.ft.com/cms/s/0/fa365518-4e59-11e0-98eb-00144feab49a.html#axzz34Xbjt46O

271 **Educational summer programs:** Anne Tschida, "Going Public," *Biscayne Times,* December 2011, accessed 2/28/16, http://www.biscaynetimes.com/index.php?option=com_content&id=1025:going-public

272 **"You cannot take it with you":** Interview

273 **one of the 50 Most Powerful Families:** Ben Shaul, "50 Most Powerful Families," *Town & Country,* April 2014, http://www.

townandcountrymag.com/society/tradition/g644/most-powerfu
l-influential-families/?slide=31

274 **"US is turning into an anti-intellectual society":** Interview

275 **Cultural Leadership Awards:** American Federation of Arts, accessed 12/12/15, http://www.afaweb.org/prog_events/Gala-past.php

276 **"I studied economics":** Sandra McElwaine, *Fearless Leadership,* "Hispanic Enterprise Magazine," April/May 2008.

277 **"without losing my cultural diversity":** Ibid

278 **"if you want to maintain your competitive edge":** Ibid

279 **"When adversity hits you, look at the opportunity it creates":** Ibid

280 **"had chosen not to be a kept-woman":** Ibid

281 **focus on a sustainable partnership:** Ibid

282 **"You need to have grit":** - Jan Turner, *You Have to Have Grit: A Free-Range Conversation with Hilda Ochoa-Brillenbourg,* "Womenetics," June 11, 2013.

283 **helping liquidity flow:** materials provided by Hilda Ochoa Brillembourg

284 **"A firm is never better than its human capital":** *The Pursuit of Alpha,* 47.

285 **Implementing portable alpha strategies:** Interview

286 **passionate devotion to arts:** Philip Glass and Brian Anderson, "Between Love and Lust There Can Be Music—and Other Arts," *The Huffington Post,* March 22, 2010, Updated May 25, 2011, accessed 3/1/16, http://www.huffingtonpost.com/brian-henderson/

287 **Council on Foreign Relations:** accessed 2/16/16, http://www.cfr.org/about/membership/roster.html?letter=O

288 **Editor:** American Diversity Report, http://americandiversityreport.com/

289 **Practical interfaith:** Deborah Levine, "Interfaith or Bust," *American Diversity Report,"* Oct. 23, 2012, accessed 2/14/16, http://americandiversityreport.com/2012/10/23/interfaith-or-bust---an-advocates-guide-by-deborah-levine.aspx

290 **the major influences of her life:** Interview with Deborah Levine, February 15, 2015

291 **than was possible in Bermuda:** Donald H. Harrison, "Under the Surface, a Troubled Past for Jews in Bermuda," *Judah in Bermuda,* S. D. Jewish Press-Heritage, Oct 29, 1999, http://www.jewishsightseeing.com/bermuda/sd10-29_bermuda.htm

292 **"I go with the flow":** Ibid

293 **"It's been a struggle to market myself American-style":** Ibid

294 **"I learned to swear":** Ibid

295 **follow the passion:** Ibid

296 **Deborah delivered:** Sean Phipps, "C-SPAN coverage of Chattanooga to include local author Deborah Levine," Nooga.com. January 6 2014, http://nooga.com/164878/c-span-coverage-of-chattanooga-to-include-local-author-deborah-levine/

297 **has influenced the locals:** Ibid

298 **Discrimination:** Interview

299 **"some jobs were closed to me":** Ibid

300 **"I increasingly own my Jewish heritage":** Ibid

301 **"My joy has come from":** Interview.

302 **Book:** Deborah Levine, *Teaching Curious Christians about Judaism,* (CreateSpace Independent Publishing Platform, June 29, 2014), accessed 2/22/16, http://www.amazon.com/Teaching-Curious-Christians-About-Judaism/dp/149958752X, 76 pages

303 **"and perseverance of immigrants are unparalleled":** Ibid

304 **1997 United Nations Society of Writers & Artists Award:** "Chartwell Bulletin in Conversation with Edwina Sandys," *The Churchill Center,* Nov 2011, accessed 2/16/2016, http://www.winstonchurchill.org/support/the-churchill-centre/publications/chartwell-bulletin/2011/41-nov/1318-chartwell-bulletin-in-conversation-with-edwina-sandys -

305 **Never went to college:** Interview with Edwina Sandys, November 15, 2014

306 **"drawn people as characters, not as likenesses":** Interview

307 **first big show:** Interview

308 **"recalls Matisse":** *Edwina Sandys Art, 39.*

309 **"this liking intensified.":** Interview

310 **"making friends and connecting them with each other has never lost its thrill":** Edwina Sandys, *Social Intercourse* (New York, 2012), ISBN 978-0-615-80556-6, 7.

311 **"another string to my bow":** Interview

312 **"another string to my bow":** Interview

313 **"I was already based here":** Ibid

314 **"So it's probably my fault":** Ibid

315 **"And the issue was resolved":** Ibid

316 **"humorous art is more in the English tradition":** Ibid

317 **"the whole gamut of emotions":** Ibid

318 **Remarkable oddity:** Anthony Haden, "Foreword," *Edwina Sandys Art* (New York: Glitterati, 2011), 6.

319 **"They need a partnership":** Interview.

320 **Somewhat apart, is her piece *Christa*:** Sian Ballen, *Interview with Edwina Sandys*, "New York Social Diary," November 18, 2011, http://www.newyorksocialdiary.com/node/1907604

321 **"Women were second-class citizens...":** Interview

322 **"inspiring to people":** Ibid

323 **"it's something different than what you originally thought":** Interview

324 **"man and woman breaking through the wall was the push for freedom":** Ibid

325 **"I like the puzzle and challenge":** Ibid

326 **Studies show:** J.L. Tracy and R.W. Robins, "The nonverbal expression of pride: evidence for cross-cultural recognition," *Journal of Personality and Social Psychology.* 2008 Mar; 94(3):516-30. doi: 10.1037/0022-3514.94.3.516, accessed 2/29/16, http://www.ncbi.nlm.nih.gov/pubmed/18284295

327 Darwin, *The Expression of the Emotions in Man and Animals*

328 http://www.loden.com/Site/Site/Articles%20-%20Videos%20-%20Survey/C615CFE8-A70C-4E3A-9F81-8EACB0E087D0.html

329 **The Isabel Allende Foundation:** accessed 2/24/16, http://www.isabelallendefoundation.org/

330 **One Laptop Per Child program:** Wikipedia, accessed 2/29/16, https://en.wikipedia.org/wiki/One_Laptop_per_Child

331 Onelaptop.org

332 **Center for Information Technology Research in the Interest of Society:** Wikipedia, accessed 2/29/16, https://en.wikipedia.org/wiki/Center_for_Information_Technology_Research_in_the_Interest_of_Society

333 **factors that distinguish star performers were tied to EQ:** Stéphane Côté and Christopher T. H. Miners, "Emotional Intelligence, Cognitive Intelligence, and Job Performance, " *Sage Journals*, accessed 2/29/16, http://asq.sagepub.com/content/51/1/1.short

334 **"The contract was based on good faith":** Ibid, 305.

335 **"Without him I wouldn't be able to write as much and as calmly as I do":** *The Sum of Our Days*, 113.

336 **as Arianna Huffington remarked:** Paul Bedard, "Arianna Huffington Explains Why Obama Disappoints," *US News and World Report*, Aug. 23, 2010, accessed 2/23/16, http://www.usnews.com/news/blogs/washington-whispers/2010/08/23/arianna-huffington-explains-why-obama-disappoints

337 **Transformational Diversity initiatives:** Ibid

338 **Blue Ocean strategy:** W. Chan Kim, W. Chan Kim, and Renée Mauborgne, Blue Ocean Strategy, Expanded Edition: How to Create Uncontested Market Space and Make the Competition Irrelevant (Boston: Harvard Business Review Press, January 20, 2015)

339 **stories of success:** Malcolm Gladwell, *Outliers: The Story of Success* (New York: Back Bay Books; Reprint edition, June 7, 2011)

About the Author

Born and raised in Ukraine, Dr. Fiona Citkin came to the U.S. as a Fulbright Scholar studying languages and cultures at Kent State University, OH. A professional educator, author, and internationally renowned intercultural consultant, she has two doctorate degrees and speaks three languages.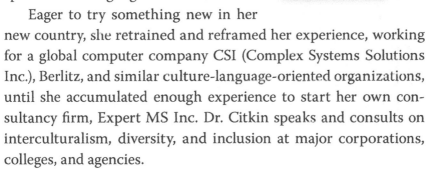

Eager to try something new in her new country, she retrained and reframed her experience, working for a global computer company CSI (Complex Systems Solutions Inc.), Berlitz, and similar culture-language-oriented organizations, until she accumulated enough experience to start her own consultancy firm, Expert MS Inc. Dr. Citkin speaks and consults on interculturalism, diversity, and inclusion at major corporations, colleges, and agencies.

Dr. Citkin's first book written in America was rooted in her consulting practice: TRANSFORMATIONAL DIVERSITY: WHY AND HOW INTERCULTURAL COMPETENCIES CAN HELP ORGANIZATIONS TO SURVIVE AND THRIVE (SHRM Publishing, 2011). That book, which marries intercultural studies with diversity and inclusion, has been widely used by human resources departments, consultants, and college instructors.

At the request of the Diversity and Inclusion Division of SHRM, Dr. Citkin has designed and facilitated the innovative course, *Global Cultural Competence for Business Leaders*, which has become a staple for leadership education in our multicultural world. For *Transformational Diversity* book and her consulting combined, she was also awarded a prestigious *2012 Top Champion of Diversity* title by DiversityBusiness.com, a think-tank.

An evangelist about diversity and the resilience of women, Fiona Citkin will partner with her readers in their efforts to make it in America.

You may contact the author visiting her website http://fionac-itkin.com/, reading her new blogs at http://fionacitkin.com/blog/ and even contributing to the topic yourself at http://fionacitkin.com/guest/.